**TEACH**

CW00515813

Choosing a PC

Alan Clark

Hodder & Stoughton

A MEMBER OF THE HODDER HEADLINE GROUP

For Michelle and Gary

British Library Cataloguing in Publication Data

A catalogue record for this book is available from the British Library

ISBN 0 340 61110 3

First published 1995

Impression number	10	9	8	7	6	5	4	3	2	1
Year		1999		1998		1997		1996		1995

Produced by GreenGate Publishing Services, Tonbridge, Kent
Printed in Great Britain for the educational division of Hodder Headline Plc,
338 Euston Road, London NW1 3BH by Cox & Wyman Ltd., Reading, Berkshire

———— CONTENTS ————

── INTRODUCTION ──

· Ways in which you can use this book ·

If you are on the point of buying your first computer, this is the book for you. If you bought a computer five years ago, and are thinking of replacing it, this is the book for you, too.

This book is intended to give you some ideas about what to look for, and what questions you need to ask. It does not avoid jargon, as a subject such as computing is riddled with it, but jargon is cut down to a minimum, and terms are carefully explained. Beware of anybody who tries to sell you a computer, and yet who cannot do it without resorting to attempting to 'blind you with science'. Ask for an explanation if you don't understand. If you don't understand the explanation, think twice about the kind of support that firm will give you.

Because different readers have very different needs, this book is organised in such a way that it does not have to be read from cover to cover. Naturally, there is a consistent flow if you read all 21 chapters in order. You may, though, want to miss out some chapters, either because you know enough about a topic, or because you do not need to know about a topic at that stage – you can always come back to a chapter later.

These observations are offered as an initial 'road map' to help you derive the most benefit from this book as your various interests develop or various decisions need to be made.

The first three chapters of this book will enable you to focus on some of the key issues of your purchasing decision. These are the least technical part of the book, because buying a computer is first and foremost about getting a job done, either something you already do which you want to do better, or about doing a new job which you need to think through. Once you cross the threshold of a computer shop, or start reading magazines, there is a danger that you will be seduced by the technology, so these chapters help you to marshal your thoughts.

One of the first issues in computing you will come across when you look seriously at actual machines is whether you will buy an 'IBM compatible' machine. Chapter 4 looks at what this term means, and whether it makes a difference.

You will have come across the terms 'hardware', for equipment, and 'software', for the programs which run on it. These terms, which started off as computing terms, have now migrated into more general, everyday use. Most advisers will emphasise that you must decide what you will do with the equipment before you decide what equipment you need. This book is no exception, and so the next seven chapters describe the software choices you may need to make. This does not mean that, once you have chosen your hardware, you cannot buy more software, but once you have purchased hardware your future options are usually limited.

Chapter 5 attempts to take an overview of issues that are common to all software choices, such as looking at what makes good software. It should help you to think more deeply about these issues than the sales literature tends to. This chapter rightly comes before an exploration of any specific types of software, but can be safely skipped over, or skim read, if you wish to look at a particular software area.

Chapters 6 to 11 cover a wide range of types of applications software, although some of your specialist interests may not be covered in the depth that you would need. You may need to look at the specialist press for ideas in those areas. These chapters are an attempt to cover the most popular software areas. They can be read in almost any order, or chapters can be omitted in your reading without losing the flow of the text. Inevitably, some chapters make reference to ideas introduced in previous chapters, most notably where spreadsheets are said to have elementary database features, and when desktop publishing builds on concepts both in graphics and word processing.

It is right that applications are dealt with before the equipment, and this book then looks at the tools for implementing those applications. Chapter 12 then looks at the main computer at the heart of your system. Much of this revolves around the central processor unit, or chip, on which the system is based. Chapter 13 describes the systems software, which breathes the life into the machine. This is different from other software described earlier, as it primarily carries out background work on which all the applications depend. It comes after the first chapter on hardware, as hardware choices affect the choice of system software.

Chapters 14 to 17 concentrate on different parts of the computer system, and can be read independently, and in any order. You can miss any of them out on a first reading without losing the flow of the text. These four chapters concentrate on the general issues involved, and then Chapter 18 illustrates some typical systems, as a guide rather than a recommendation of any of them.

The last three chapters look at the services provided by a supplier. There are aspects of your decision that are beyond the choice of hardware and software. Assuming that any of the ten possible systems you might buy will do the job required, a further choice has to be made about the forms of after-sales support that you might expect, and which you pay for either directly or indirectly. You are urged read these chapters regardless of which previous chapters you have skipped or read, and regardless of whether you are buying a complete new system or only part of one.

1

PLANNING YOUR PURCHASE

— Do you really need a computer? —

The first main decision you have to make when buying a computer system is whether to buy one at all. Judging from the fact that you are reading this book, it is a reasonable assumption to make that you consider the possibility quite likely. It is always worth considering, even at this late stage, whether a computer really will solve the problems you want it to. Have you actually decided what you will do with it when you have bought it?

When you are buying a CD player, it is pretty clear what you are going to do with it. There is some degree of choice. Do you want a portable system to carry round with you, or not? (There is an interesting analogy with computers there.) Although there are a few choices, if you are about to buy a CD player, I know what you will do with it. You may not know in detail which pieces of music you will play on it, but in broad terms, you are happy that you need it. The analogy with buying a computer breaks down at this point, though. A computer is a multi-purpose machine, not a single-purpose one like the CD player. Different people make very different uses of their computers. The aim of this chapter, then, is to convince you of the need to plan the purchase. Later chapters will explore the specific uses to which you might put your system.

—— Whose advice should you heed? ——

Other people are a valuable source of information when planning your approach to buying a computer. For many people, a computer will be the third most expensive thing they ever buy. If you have not bought a house or a car, it may even be the most expensive. If you let on to friends, relations, or business colleagues that you are thinking about buying a computer, they will either change the subject, or offer their advice. Their comments will inevitably arise from their own experience. This will probably mean that they will put forward very strong views either for or against particular products. By all means listen to this advice, but be objective about it. How recent is the person's experience? Is it related to the products currently available? Listening to advice from other people will, as a bare minimum, help you to identify some key issues that you need to address.

If you casually mention that you are thinking of buying a computer system, some people will not be able to resist giving you the benefit of their advice, and often they will use technical terms which baffle and confuse you. Unfortunately, this is a problem created by self-styled experts in any technical area. Most people who behave like this probably do not know as much as they would have you believe. You do not necessarily need to know lots of complicated terminology. It is the ideas that are important, particularly the ideas about what you want to do, rather than how it is done. The best response to the advice that your system 'must have such-and-such' is simply to ask 'Why must it?'. In this way you will either expose the charlatan or provoke an informed but understandable debate.

—— Hardware or software first? ——

Some people who give you the benefit of their advice may concentrate simply on the technology, and to those who are interested in it, the speed of technological advance is seductive. Yet to consider features of the equipment as the only factors in choosing a computer system (a term deliberately chosen to emphasise that you are buying more than just a computer), is to miss many important ingredients in your decision. Consider a few simple examples. What point is there in buying a computer with a superb sound system if all the software you will use does not make use of sound? You have to be careful that the tail does not wag the dog. Once you have committed yourself to buying a system with good sound, you will probably start looking round for software to justify your purchase. This involves you in even more expense to use a facility which you never knew you needed.

There is every reason to consider what you want to do with the system before you consider the actual equipment needed.

- What can I do with a limited budget? -

If you have decided to buy a computer system, you should set yourself a definite limit to what you will spend, and stick to it. It is very tempting to have 'just a bit more' at a little extra cost, and a sales force is trained to sell as many add-ons as possible to you. Extra sales are also based around seductive technology. All the things you are offered will be good and useful. A sharper colour monitor, a nicer shaped mouse, a printer with more features, and a larger hard disk will all be presented as worthwhile.

Setting a limit actually forces you to choose between desirable additional features, and gives you a sense of priorities. Don't forget that you can upgrade your system later. It is worth bringing the ability to upgrade into the conversation early, presenting this as a major factor in your choice, before the salesperson has chance to talk about adding extras. This then enables you to challenge each add-on, by asking whether it could be added later. In the computing world particularly, one benefit of leaving an extra feature as a possible future upgrade is that, should you decide that you do need it in the future, its price may well have tumbled.

— What should I include in the cost? —

It is important to bear in mind the full cost of making proper use of the system, both the initial cost and the running costs.

There will be initial outlay on:

- equipment (hardware) – computer, monitor, mouse, printer
- programs (software) – typically three or four items, such as word processor, database, spreadsheet, drawing package and accounts
- initial supplies – paper, ink, floppy disks
- manuals and books, needed in addition to those that come with purchases
- training, if you want it.

There will be recurring costs:

- regular consumables, like replacement paper, ink and extra disks
- repairs, which are difficult to predict
- electricity
- insurance, to protect your valuable investment.

——— What help can I have? ———

When making your initial purchase, you should also seek clear answers about where you will find support in using your system.

After the initial sales demonstration, and perhaps a brief training period, whatever manuals you have acquired are going to be your main means of support in day-to-day use of the package. It is vital, therefore, that manuals are understandable. Standards of layout, presentation, and the sort of language used are all important in finding your way around and understanding the features. Even as a prospective purchaser, you should be able to pick up the manual and understand its structure and how to navigate around it.

Although some advice from friends can be unsound, there are, however, great benefits in using other people as a sounding board for your ideas. It is quite likely that you know people who are already doing some of the things that you would like to do with a computer system. Having a friend who has been through some of the problems can be a great blessing.

It is useful to be able to use a system in practical everyday use at your own pace before you take the plunge. A sympathetic friend will let you spend far more time having a thorough look at a system than you could possibly have in a shop. A friend can show you the basics of a system, but you must keep reinforcing the idea that you do just want to look at the basic principles involved.

It is useful to know someone with the same system in case you have problems once you are using your new system. Has the friend experienced the same problem? Are you doing something wrong? Is there some equipment that is not working correctly? (If you try your printer on your friend's system and it still doesn't work, then you can be pretty sure it is broken.)

It is useful to have a friend for facilities in an emergency. If you do have problems with broken equipment, it may be sent away for repair. Experience shows that this will often happen at an awkward time, when you are in the middle of something important.

⎯⎯ Can I believe the literature? ⎯⎯

Most vendors will be happy to supply you with a wealth of well presented and informative sales literature. Of course, sales literature is aimed at marketing the product, not at explaining how it works; the literature will usually be written in generalities, rather than attempting to be rigorous in giving precise descriptions. If you cannot understand the sales literature, then what hope have you of understanding the manual?

When buying any product, you must, of course, be very wary of what you read. Sales literature is rarely inaccurate, but might not tell the whole story. Glossy leaflets abound with such words and phrases as 'quickest', 'most popular', 'newest', and 'unique'. You must ask yourself what words like this mean or whether they mean anything at all. Also, beware of claims about the number of functions: there are different ways of counting. For example, some program features can be requested using more than one command. If there are two ways of doing the same thing, is this one feature or two? If a spellchecker program has an option to check a single word or a whole document, is this one feature or two?

Literature will claim that systems and products are 'compatible' but this is a difficult word to define. If you have any doubts, ask for a system to be demonstrated. This should achieve two things. First it should prove to you that products really are compatible (or not, as the case may be). Secondly, you will see how easy it is to work things together. Something may be compatible, but so long-winded in use that it is almost worthless on a day-to-day basis.

Sales staff and literature will also talk about a computer being 'ready' for a particular new technology. This idea has arisen in the last few years because of the trend for announcing new products before they are launched, as a spoiling tactic for other manufacturers' products. New purchasers who have heard that a new product is on the horizon, though, may be reluctant to invest in the current technology if it is about to be surpassed. To avoid compromising today's sales for future ones, current machines may be designed so that they can be up-graded when the new technology is available. Buyers should beware, though, that few guarantees are given about price, and whilst future upgrades might be simple to carry out, they may involve throwing away the most expensive part of your current machine.

As part of your planning process you should collect and read litera-ture, particularly computer magazines. Most large newsagents sell a range of computer magazines, usually a dozen or more titles. This choice can, in itself, prove baffling. A quick browse through a few should give you some guidance on which to buy. At around a pound or two each, a few magazines are well worth the investment. Some people complain about the number of advertisements in some maga-zines, but actually this might be one of the things that you are looking for. Unless you are committed to a particular games machine, you will probably want to avoid several of the specialist magazines in the games area. In choosing which magazines to buy, you should try reading a few of the articles. Are they about topics that interest you? Do they avoid technical detail? Are they general enough for your interest? Are they written in a language that you can cope with? (To be useful to you, articles should not be too technical or refer to concepts that you have not come across.) Are you happy with the style of writing? (Perhaps you find the 'jokey' style of some of the writing distracts you from the content.)

Among the articles carried in magazines are reviews of new products. The latest computers, software and printers are particularly covered. These reviews are generally good guides and sometimes reviewers give ratings, which can be helpful for comparison. Many magazine reviews of software are based on so-called 'beta test' versions of software. These versions are produced by manufacturers after laboratory testing (alpha tests), and before going on general release. This method allows manufacturers to take their product to market quicker in a very competitive field. Remember, though, that bugs identified in reviews may well have been fixed before the product goes on general release. Of course, you might not wish to buy the very latest version of software, particularly if a review identifies the new features and you realise that you are not likely to use these. Indeed, the appearance of a new version, such as version 6.0, probably means that version 5 will become a lot cheaper, and if it does all that you want, you may well pick up a bargain.

Most of the main magazines carry out regular surveys comparing, for example, the 10 most popular spreadsheets, or presentation graphics programs or colour monitors. These are a powerful source of information, not necessarily in choosing a product, but in identifying exactly what products in that category can do. Many such surveys will include a table of features for easy comparison. Interestingly, some also include a comment about the packages' strongest and weakest points.

A book like this cannot describe all the latest developments of every aspect of technology. Computer magazines perform this task admirably and deliver the material in interesting and lively ways. Readers are recommended to look at *Computer Buyer, PC Direct, Personal Computer World* and *Windows User* as four good, varied examples of useful magazines. Most of the magazine companies provide a subscription service offering substantial discounts off cover prices of up to 40% for an annual subscription. Many magazines are also sold with free software supplied on disk and increasingly on CD-Rom. If you do not want the software, floppy disks can always be used as part of your general stock. Read the small print, though, as some of the software provided on cover disks may be shareware, for which a licence fee is payable should you carry on using the program.

— Will my local college or TEC help? —

Local colleges of further education usually run a wide range of courses. These are a lot more varied than the old 'night school' image of the old 'techs'. Of course, evening classes are still one of the options, but there is an increasing range of day-time or late afternoon sessions available. The style of course available is also very varied. A lot of courses now work on an open learning basis. First, you pay as you go, and only pay for sessions which you need. Secondly, you choose what areas you want to look at. In an initial briefing, you can be as specific or as general as you like in identifying your needs; it is then the tutor's role to identify suitable learning materials. So, you may want to spend several hours on one product, or you may wish to try out several different word processors to see which you like.

If you are choosing a computer for a business, it is worth approaching you local TEC (Training and Enterprise Council). It may be able to give advice itself, or to point in the right direction about who to talk to locally. Being in an impartial role, it can do this fairly without fear or favour. If the business is applying for finance through a bank, the bank may suggest or insist that particular advice is sought. Again, this is offered in a supportive capacity.

2

WHAT YOU MIGHT
— USE YOUR —
SYSTEM FOR

—— Keep your eye on the benefits ——

There is a vast range of jobs that a computer could do. Many of these are described in more detail in later chapters. The detailed applications need to be explored in depth before you make your final choice, but a good impression of the range of uses is an important starting point. You will need to become an enthusiast for the help a computer can give you, but you should also retain a healthy cynicism: not every job is best done by computer. Whilst we continue mainly to discuss the positive benefits of using computers, both individuals and organisations should consider the dangers and pitfalls that lie in wait for the unwary purchaser.

Later chapters of this book talk exclusively about what computers can do, rather than whether you need one at all. At this early stage, it is worth asking the really hard questions. In your domestic budget, it may be a choice between a new computer and double glazing; you have to be realistic. In a business, it might be a choice between a new photocopier and a computer; you have to be hard-nosed.

Vendors will offer you all sorts of products. Do you really need them? Will you really use them? Take, for example, a computer program that will help you with time management. It can help you prioritise tasks. It will print colour charts of your jobs, in order. It will remind you about jobs that are incomplete. It will remember appointments. It will do 101 other things. Now there is no question that the software works in a technical sense, but will it work for you? Perhaps, like me, you are perfectly happy with a few sheets of paper, say in a Filofax. Remember, for a computer to aid your time management, you have to enter every task and then tell the computer when it is complete. The equivalent method using my Filofax consists of writing the task down and crossing it out. The computer may produce the charts in full colour, but only if you have a colour printer. I am not saying that time management software is not good and reliable, nor that it is not useful for some people. I am not saying that doing the job on a computer might not make it more interesting. What I am illustrating is that the decision needs to be taken carefully and rationally, rather than in the heat of the moment, thinking, 'oh, yes, I could use that'.

——— Some basic terms defined ———

In essence a computer system consists of two parts. The 'hardware' is the physical equipment, such as the main computer, printer, disk drive and so on. 'Software' is the term for the programs you run on the hardware. The name software was coined because whilst it is stored on disk or in the computer, software is not a physical object. When you purchase software, you are buying or licensing a very complex set of codes or instructions for your computer. Producing the physical copy of the software onto floppy disks costs the software manufacturer very little. Most of the income from sales enables the manufacturer to recover the investment in developing the product, matching it to user needs, testing the product, writing documentation, consulting users about improvements, providing user support, and so on. Some of the income from selling software is reinvested in producing upgrades or new products. This is why some of us become very annoyed with those who illegally copy software without proper licences, as it deprives people of their rightful income and jeopardises future development.

There are two types of software. Applications programs are those that enable a particular use to be made of the computer, such as an accounting package, or a word processor, or drawing program. Users will choose the applications packages that suit their individual need, perhaps linking applications together. They are not likely to buy applications they do not need.

Systems software, on the other hand, is the term for those programs that 'breathe life' into the computer. These programs do not, in their own right, allow you to carry out the applications for which you bought the computer. Rather they allow access to the various parts of the system, so that, for example, signals to the printer and to the monitor are controlled. Systems software ensures that disk drives are organised properly so that files can be retrieved. Increasingly, systems software will ensure that a user can have several programs loaded into the computer, can launch and stop them at will, and carry on with something where it was paused. All these tasks are essential 'housekeeping' within a system, and are used in different combinations by the applications software, which could be described as 'the programs for which you really bought the computer'. Systems software is sometimes described as the 'glue' which holds the system together; it is essential, but not for what it does in its own right, but for what it helps other programs (the applications) achieve. Some well-known examples of system software are the MS-DOS operating system (in use for over 10 years now, in various versions), OS/2 from IBM, Microsoft Windows for the PC and System 7 for the Macintosh. Both Microsoft Windows and System 7 are supplied with some simple applications programs, but are essentially operating systems presented in a more graphical manner.

Most systems are now designed to be, as the jargon would have it, 'user friendly', carrying out as much as possible without user intervention. So, for example, a system can be arranged (or 'configured') so that it has an 'auto resume' feature, allowing you to carry on where you broke off without having to instruct the computer to reload the program. Whilst not in use, the contents of the computer memory are either stored on disk, or kept active by a battery or some other power supply.

Another optional configuration of many machines allows an 'autosave' feature which saves data to disk at periodic intervals without user intervention. This is also known as timed backup.

Computers are often set up in such a way that the same program is run each time the computer is switched on. (In MS-DOS this is achieved using the AUTOEXEC.BAT file; in OS/2 the equivalent is STARTUP.CMD.) Using such files, the computer runs through an established 'script' of commands, which could include launching the user automatically into an application such as word processing.

——————— **Be software driven** ———————

There is a huge range of hardware and software. Potential purchasers are well advised to try to remain realistic in stating what they really want the computer to do. It is important to let the software be the driving force in the choice of a system. Magazines and other media find it easier to compare hardware, by measuring features such as physical size, memory capacity, speed and so on. Software can be more difficult to compare, but the applications are at the heart of why you want the system. Within reason, choose your applications areas, and products within them, then look for hardware that will run the software. Among other things, this will probably narrow down the field of possible equipment to a more manageable range to look at in detail.

Many machines are described as IBM-compatible. This term is explained in more detail in Chapter 12. The history of computing is littered with standards which groups have proposed. Some standards have caught on. Most proposals have, with the passage of time, been superseded. Standards are important, because they enable a manufacturer to communicate complicated ideas with a guarantee that a system meets a standard. From the manufacturer's point of view, standards also make it more likely that equipment from different manufacturers will work together. Because they revolve mainly around physical and therefore measurable ideas, hardware standards are a lot more common than software standards. Equipment can be measured and tested for speed, accuracy, and so on. It is a lot more difficult to put your finger on what makes a good piece of software. Many of these issues are explored in more detail in Chapter 5.

At different stages in the development of computing, manufacturers have formed various alliances to work collaboratively. At one time, Lotus, Intel and Microsoft worked together on expanding the amount of computer memory available to software. A recent alliance has been formed to work around the PowerPC, including IBM, Motorola and Apple.

There are many specialist software packages on the market to perform tasks which are quite specific to a particular trade or profession, or to a particular industry. There are specialist companies which concentrate on supplying computer-based systems for tourism, the motor trade, advertising and so on. This makes for an added complication in your choice. If you want to be able to communicate with others in the same industry, it makes sense to have compatible equipment. If you want to be as good as your competitors, there is again a strong argument for buying the same kind of system. Others would argue that buying the same system means that you lose a potential competitive edge, and that what you really need is a different system which does 'all that' and more besides. You will have to use professional judgement when you view a demonstration of such a system, and decide whether it represents value for money.

Identify your core needs

You need to be ruthless with yourself and establish specific purposes to which you will put the computer when you acquire it. It is very easy to have vague notions that a computer is 'educational', or 'useful for the Guides', or 'where all the jobs are'. A proper analytical approach would identify the purpose of the purchase more clearly, so that in some senses it can be measured. Most people will be thinking about buying a system from a mixture of motives. It helps, therefore, to clarify to yourself what you would like to use the machine for, and what you need the machine for. Unless you do this, how will you know that your purchase has been successful? Some of the vaguer reasons for the purchase which you might not be able to measure will then come as a welcome bonus.

Some people might think about buying a computer because they hold a position in a club or society. Thousands of small groups depend on the hard work of volunteers to keep them going. Members of such groups, such as secretaries and treasurers, would find a computer helpful for keeping minutes, preparing correspondence, maintaining mailing lists, controlling accounts, designing leaflets and so on.

Another group of people making increasing use of computers is the clergy. In preparing orders of service, worship and other material, a computer can prove to be a real time-saver, reducing the paperwork and freeing the clergy to do the less desk-bound jobs.

——— Computer – boon or bane? ———

Whilst there are many benefits of computers to voluntary groups, there are also drawbacks. There is always a problem about where such a computer is sited. Wherever it is, access to the particular computer can be very limited to other members. This can mean that not only does all the work fall on a few members, but also there can be a fall-off in participation from other members. Arguments over access to resources can also lead to bitterness and resentment. Such an organisation might also become very dependent on one individual. If that individual chooses to leave, problems are created. Once the system has been computerised, a volunteer who cannot run the system in that way may be very reluctant to take up a post. If the parting is acrimonious, there can be a difficulty in ensuring information is passed across. Unless the running costs and the implications of the cost of repairs are thought about from the start, there are again many potential wrangles.

A computer might not always be the best answer to a problem. Computers can be effective, for example, in creating letters to chase debts for a company. Chasing debts is a real bug-bear for many small companies, yet is vital for cash flow, and ultimately survival. Many large companies have found that, after commissioning large scale feasibility studies about whether to have a computer, they have decided not to have one. Proper investigation can reveal, to large companies or small, that there is a better way of doing things which does not involve buying computers. In the case of debt collection, a manual system might be more cost effective, or targeting a limited number of debtors for regular personal visits might be more fruitful, if you compare properly the costs and the benefits.

Computers can bring tangible benefits, which for a business, usually means that a figure can be put on a saving. Computers might also bring intangible benefits, such as enhanced company image, or increased peace of mind, or in the home context might save time, bringing a better quality of life. Such benefits are very difficult to put a value on, but must be important considerations.

There can be obvious benefits in being able to carry on with a piece of work at home when there is opportunity. Some people would do this by taking home a laptop computer from work. Others would aim to buy a desktop computer for home which is compatible with the one at work. Some firms actively encourage the policy of buying laptops by, for example, purchasing one for any member of staff who wants one. They calculate that for a relatively small outlay, they earn the investment back very quickly in increased productivity. Some staff will then do extra work at home in their own time. Others will learn to use the equipment at home, saving on a training budget. Many workers will use the chance to carry on a piece of work at home where the chances of interruption by personal or telephone callers can be greatly reduced. In this way, an important report or presentation can be prepared much more quickly and effectively in a quiet environment.

Some people use their home computers for all their personal correspondence, such as letters to solicitors, the bank, the building society, Inland Revenue and so on. A computer makes the keeping of previous correspondence a simple task, either for reference in the future, or as a skeleton for a future letter.

Another argument used in favour of a home computer is that it will be useful for the children as well as the adults. There is no doubt that a good home computer, well used for the proper purposes, can be of great educational benefit to youngsters. Many would argue, though, that the use of computers has to be controlled and monitored, just like that of televisions. Many hours can be wasted on home computers playing aggressive games such as those of the 'zap the alien' variety.

Home computers can be used to stimulate a young person's flair for art, music, programming and so on. Parents need to show real interest, and make sure that the computer is being used to tackle interesting and imaginative projects. In later years of study, a home computer used as a word processor can help a student to a great extent, such as in project work at GCSE and beyond.

3

— MAKING CHOICES —

—— Will you be programming? ——

In the early days of computing, the terms computer user and programmer were almost synonymous. The mathematicians and scientists who wanted to use the computer would write the instructions, put them onto paper tape or cards, and queue up to use the computer. Even when computers first came into the home, one of the first uses tended to be programming. One of the great selling points of early home computers, and this is only 15 years ago, was how easy they were to program. Some had all the programming commands printed on the keys for ease of use; several automatically loaded up in the Basic programming language when you switched them on.

That scene has changed very quickly. Some people do use their home computer for programming, and this can be a worthwhile interest and challenge. Most people, though, will buy ready-written programs. If you can buy a program, for example, for your home accounts, for £20 or £30, you are unlikely to attempt to write your own, for a number of reasons. First, it will take you a very long time, and so would only be worthwhile if you wanted to gain other things on the way, like experience of programming. Secondly, your own product is unlikely to work as well as, or be as comprehensive as a commercial product. Thirdly, and perhaps most significantly, when you buy a commercial package, you receive comprehensive written materials, which include a user guide, and perhaps a reference book, a troubleshooting guide and possibly some example files. All this documentation is vital to make best use of the product. Most people who write their own software never produce such documentation, and later, as time goes by, forget some aspects of what a program does.

So, one of the greatest benefits of buying ready-written software is the detailed documentation which comes with it. Though it might not be referenced by many users, this often includes more technical details about the 'nuts and bolts' of how the system works for those who are interested in the technicalities.

The standard of manuals published in the last few years has improved considerably. The quality of manuals is an important factor in choosing which package to buy. In many cases, the features of rival products can be very similar, so it is the documentation which may set one product apart from the others. Though home users find it difficult to see a range of manuals before selecting a product, commercial companies, who are buying large numbers of the products have a huge influence, and this has pushed the quality ever upwards.

Whether you are choosing hardware or software, or even a central heating boiler, you will probably be looking for a number of similar things. The reputation of the company is important. The wide availability of the product normally suggests that you are not buying a relatively untested product. Good written documentation should enable you to use the product to the full. Seeing the product demonstrated builds your confidence in the product. Personal recommendation is another major factor, with product reviews coming as a second best.

— Who will help you with problems? —

You may well need support in your first few days of using a computer system. To set up your system, you may be carrying out several tasks which you will only ever need to do once, yet it is so vital to do them correctly. Some of these jobs are complicated by the copy protection which might exist with some products. Thankfully, many vendors will install initial software for you. This should not take long for an experienced dealer, and it will give you peace of mind.

When you first begin to encounter problems with a system, it is difficult to know whether you have a serious or a trivial problem. With more experience, you will probably be able to diagnose your problems, and either solve them, or find a way round them by doing something a different way.

With early problems, it can be hard to tell whether it is you or the computer system that is at fault. It is vital to try out your support system, whether it be your friend, the vendor or a hotline, within the first few weeks. Choose a problem where you think you know what the solution might be to avoid possible embarrassment of having bothered other people with a trivial problem.

—— What software will you need? ——

The advice regularly given to people about to buy a new computer system is that they should think about the software first, and only after that look for the hardware which suits. This approach ensures that you focus on the uses that will be made of your computer.

First, you need to think about the jobs you are likely to do. You also need to decide whether simple packages will suffice, or whether you need the more advanced features offered by the more expensive packages. The lure of clever hardware can tempt you to spend more than you really need to, and so can the lure of additional software features. Yes, of course, it would be nice to have a word processor which checks your grammar, and a spreadsheet capable of drawing three-dimensional pie charts, but how much will you actually use them? Of course, passing a drawing into a word processed document will improve it, but do you really need it?

These issues become even more complicated, because, increasingly, like a lot of other consumer products, it is hard to buy a simple version of something. If you walk into an electrical shop and ask for a simple radio, you will be offered one with automatic tuning, memory, perhaps a clock, and so on. These features might be available even at the bottom of the product range. A similar situation is beginning to emerge with computing products. Major manufacturers of software are attempting to undercut each other in price and to provide more features in their products at the same time.

In the UK, computer software and data are protected by a number of laws, including the Copyright Designs and Patents Act 1988, the Copyright (Computer Programs) Regulations 1992, and the Computer Misuse Act.

In the technical sense of the word, you do not normally 'buy' software, you purchase a licence to use it. The law allows the purchaser to make a necessary backup copy of software. Different software manufacturers, however, interpret this slightly differently. As you install software from floppy disks, some argue that the original disks are sufficient backup. Others would say that legitimate licence holders can always be sent a fresh set of disks in emergency. It is the purchase and registration of the licence that ensures the control of legitimate copies. Registration is usually a condition of user support and is used to establish a mailing list for minor upgrades to the software, such as bug fixes. If you trade in old software for a new product, this will normally lead to the cancellation of your previous licence. In other circumstances, however, it can be possible to sell second hand software licences to others, so long as you pass on all the paperwork. This is most likely to happen when a machine is sold second-hand with ready-installed software. Some software manufacturers take a very firm line against such sales, but most accept the sale as valid, and benefit from a new source of potential sales, particularly for upgrades.

Do you need to spend a lot on software?

An alternative channel of software sales has emerged in the last few years. This is the shareware market. The idea is that the product is easy to copy to help you to try it out. If you decide that you would like to use it, you register as a user by sending a registration fee to the author. Because products like these are not marketed in the same lavish way as those from major manufacturers, there is a huge saving. Once you become a registered user, the author may offer a proper manual at a reasonable price. The author may also send you details of updates to the software if the product is improved, or details of other products. Several companies supply shareware, and will send copies of software you are interested in for the cost of the disks, plus a small handling charge and postage.

It is not just programs themselves that are available through the shareware route. Ready-written macros and add-ins for spreadsheets, specialist dictionaries for word processors, and utilities for operating systems are also published in this way. The history of software is abundant with examples of products which were really only written for an individual's personal use but others then found useful. Some have turned out to be very popular. Examples include CP/M (an early microcomputer operating system), VisiCalc (the first spreadsheet), and dBase II.

Amongst the shareware products now available are simple and effective word processors. They perhaps do not do all the tasks which the top commercial packages now do, but they probably do what most of the top products did five years ago, at five per cent of the price. Features include spelling checkers, column editing, and arithmetic functions, as well as the usual headers, footers, mail merge, search and replace and so on. (See Chapter 6 for a detailed explanation of word processing features.) Many shareware word processors will be described as 'like' or 'compatible with' a well-known word processor. This might mean that they use exactly the same command structure, and that they can read files prepared using another package, and that they can produce files capable of being read by the other package. This compatibility almost certainly does not mean that all the commands are provided in the shareware, but those which are will work in the same way.

Shareware spreadsheets usually provide most or all the features of commercial spreadsheets. Features include a wide range of mathematical and accounting functions, formulae, and at least as large a theoretical maximum size for the worksheet as other packages. Though shareware software may support most of the common screen formats, you may need to check whether it supports the particular printer you will be using. Spreadsheet models are also marketed as shareware, providing for tasks such as loan repayment, mailing lists, and simple payroll.

Database shareware again may do most of the tasks which you would wish to use, whilst omitting the latest sophisticated features. Different degrees of compatibility may be provided with commercial products but features will probably include indexes, screen formats, sorting, searching, various report formats and record duplication.

Other shareware provides toolkits for programmers, a wide range of programming languages, educational programs and, of course, many, many games. There are also many speciality programs available as shareware, for professional and hobbyist users as diverse as cooks, musicians, and chess players.

The software market changes rapidly. At the leading edge of the market, many manufacturers bring out new versions of their packages about once a year. There is a constant leapfrogging of products as each manufacturer attempts to keep ahead of the field in terms of performance, range of features, user-friendliness and, to some extent, price. All this competition undoubtedly works in favour of the customer. If you want to buy the very best, these programs are getting better all the time. If you set your sights a little lower, then there are bargains to be had. Very reasonable prices are being asked for older versions of software.

Many manufacturers, realising the selling power of their brand name, produce simpler and cheaper versions of popular packages. You might decide, for example, to buy a slimmed-down version of the word processor which you use at work. Another example might be buying a simpler version of presentation graphics programs for your laptop to prepare presentations which you will use on a more powerful machine at the actual presentation.

Another source of cheap software is known as the software bundle. The term 'bundle' is now used in two slightly different, but related, senses in computing circles. The first meaning is to stress the idea that a number of packages are provided 'free' with the hardware. This will mean that software will come normally ready to use, with the packages installed *en masse* in the factory. This can be a good way to acquire a basic set of software. If some of the packages fail to meet your needs in the future, you can then make an informed choice about a state-of-the-art package. The second meaning of the term 'bundle' is that of the 'office bundle', a set of packages from the same manufacturer including a product in each of the major software categories. This idea is explored further in Chapter 11. The two uses of the term 'bundle' are, of course, related, because an office bundle might be the software that is bundled with hardware at the time of sale.

4

SHOULD I BUY A
—— PC-COMPATIBLE ——
MACHINE?

—————— Some basic issues ——————

Many factors come into play in choosing the right computer for your particular needs at home or in the office. As soon as you begin to read around the subject, you will be faced with opinions on whether you should buy a PC-compatible machine, meaning that it is designed on the lines of an IBM PC, or whether to choose another 'platform', such as the Apple Macintosh range (known colloquially as the 'Mac').

Comparisons between different machines are notoriously difficult. Various groups have attempted to establish benchmarks, which are tests of performance using particular programs and standard data. These might inadvertently produce better results for one machine than another. They may also test facilities that you may not use very often. The only fair comparison is to see the two machines working in the way which you will use them, yet this is almost impossible to arrange.

There has never been a simple answer to the question of which are the 'better' machines, and as the years go by, the choice has not become any easier, though the differences have generally become less important.

IBM produced its original PC in the early 1980s, and, as a deliberate policy was completely open about various aspects of the design. The range of computers has changed considerably over the years, but each successive model has been based on Intel chips. From the very early days of the IBM PC, there were many 'clones' which were produced by other manufacturers to behave in a similar way.

At the same time, Apple has developed its range of Macintosh computers, suited to similar types of users. Both the original Macintosh computers and IBM PCs have long since been superseded, yet many people still base their bias towards one machine or the other on historical differences rather than the current situation. In one sense this is understandable, as once an individual is committed to one 'platform', a lot of time is invested in learning how a system works, buying additional products, reading and learning. It is a brave choice for somebody buying a second system to move across either way, for fear of not being able to reuse existing files, documents, and utility programs acquired over the years. There is also a fear that much of the time already invested in one system will go to waste. These dilemmas, of course, do not affect the first time buyer.

Your opinion of a particular system will depend greatly on what you decide to use it for. If your main use will be fairly standard home and office applications, such as word processing and databases, then you will use one basis for comparison. The comparison would be very different if you were looking for a system handling reference information on CD, or which would record and play sound. There is a particular problem where computer games are concerned. If a computer works well with games, it becomes labelled with the tag 'games machine', as if a machine which is good for games cannot be good for other serious applications, too.

Some machines are designed for games only: these range from the hand-held machines into which a cartridge is plugged, to specialist CD-based systems designed for use with the domestic television. The generally accepted use of the term computer is that it is a general-purpose device that can carry out very different types of tasks. In contrast, other devices, such as games consoles are special purpose machines. They can use different games but cannot carry out other tasks apart from playing games.

– Similarities between Macs and PCs –

Both Macintosh and PC systems have developed rapidly over the last few years. Differences between the systems from the user's point of view are much less marked than they were.

Software, for example, used to have a very different feel on the different types of machines. Apple at one time was well ahead with its user interface, and the use of the mouse for all applications. The PC world has successfully narrowed the gap with the introduction of systems based on Microsoft Windows. It is now possible to run a PC with a very similar feel to a Mac with the added advantage, some would say, that PCs give the user direct access to MS-DOS and all its power. Apples, for some years, had the edge with desktop publishing systems. The gap has narrowed in this respect too, so that most of the packages are now available on both platforms.

In the other direction, Apple Macs were once criticised for the narrow range of software available. If users were familiar with a commercial PC package through work or some other system, it was frustrating not to be able to buy the same package for a Mac. With adaptation in most cases to suit the Mac user interface style, packages which have been popular for a number of years on PCs are now available in Mac versions.

In this way, good software and good software ideas have migrated both ways to the benefit of both platforms.

The swift mushrooming of the PC market in the early 'eighties was largely due to a design which meant that small growing companies could produce add-on features for early PC machines. IBM's design for the first PC was relatively conservative, being very reliable, but somewhat dated technology. There were opportunities in the market for other manufacturers to produce equipment which would improve performance, such as graphics cards, memory boards, and improved hard disk technologies. Many of these small companies, termed as 'third party suppliers' fell by the wayside, but some produced commercially successful products.

There were two main benefits from this approach. First, the successful products emerged through the process, yielding substantial profits to some entrepreneurs. IBM was then able to negotiate whether the next generation of PC's would incorporate the successful products, without having taken the initial risk. Secondly, third party suppliers undertook their own marketing, which reached all sorts of special interest markets, which IBM could not have hoped to do alone. Whilst the suppliers were advertising their own wares, of course, they were emphasising that their products were IBM compatible, reinforcing IBM's message.

Because IBM was using third parties to supply various components, mainly hardware, but also the operating system, it was open to other manufacturers to purchase the same components. This led to the rapid development of the 'clone', IBM-compatible copies from other manufacturers.

A similar pattern also emerged in the Apple Mac world, both in the development of add-on equipment, and in Apple's relationship with other suppliers. Early Apple machines enabled third party manufacturers to develop a comprehensive range of boards and peripherals. The early success of Apple II machines also owed a great deal to the development of the VisiCalc spreadsheet. Apple, too, has collaborated with other suppliers at various stages of the company's development. However, Apple has continued to be the sole manufacturer of Macintosh computers, although it does have plans to license its operating system.

Similar ideas are used on both Mac and PC systems for structuring the storage of data. Data is stored on files within each system. Files are organised in directories (PC) or folders (Mac), which are related through a tree structure. So, we have directories within directories, or folders within folders. These ideas are explained in detail in Chapter 13.

– Differences between Macs and PCs –

There are, of course, many differences between Apples and the PC-style machines. The differences, however, are nowadays more to do with incompatibility with each other than with the jobs that each can carry out. In just the same way, you would not expect a Ford car part to fit a Vauxhall car, or a diesel engine to run on petrol. You would not argue, though, that Fords or Vauxhalls, or petrol or diesel engines, had major differences in their abilities to get you from A to B.

For many years, the fundamental difference between Apple Mac and IBM PC-style systems was that they are built around completely different chip families. Chip technologies continue to develop rapidly, which is why we are seeing computers continually increasing in power and speed. Products from each chip manufacturer tend to leapfrog each other in sophistication. Various companies such as IBM have for many years produced chips for their own computers under licence from one of the major chip designers.

Computers termed as PCs, that is those based on the IBM style, are built around the Intel 80000 series, or family, of chips. This range is outlined in more detail in Chapter 12. Several generations of Apple computers, on the other hand, were built around the Motorola 68000 chip series (sometimes abbreviated to 68xxx, or 680x0). A shift is now taking place, with IBM and Apple collaborating with Motorola on a new range of chips called the PowerPC, described in Chapter 12.

Though the major ideas behind operating systems are not explained until Chapter 13, a rough idea of their role is necessary to appreciate some of the differences between makes of computers. An operating system is a program which is run within any computer usually as soon as it is switched on. This program interprets and carries out the user's instructions, enabling the user to state, for example, which applications are to be run. Because operating systems are at the lowest level, little or nothing can be done without them. Two computers with the same chip may use different operating systems, whereas versions of the same operating system are available for different chips.

When you buy a computer, you will need to buy a licensed operating system with it. Sometimes this comes on disk, and sometimes it is placed on a chip within the computer itself. Differences between the operating systems are therefore often proclaimed as key benefits of one supplier's system over another. These claims still have some validity, though applications are increasingly likely to be on sale for different systems. The newer machines can also often handle programs for several operating systems, either through add-on equipment, or through programs which simulate other's programs.

Apple describes many of the virtues of its system, of course, in advertising and brochures. Internally, Apples use built-in standard operating systems routines which are accessed by programmers to provide the user interface. As well as ensuring a more standardised approach, this also means that applications will take up less disk space, and will use less memory when running.

Because of the Mac's standard interface, many claims are made about its ease of use. Because common commands like 'print' and 'save' appear in the same places in the same menus in very different applications, it is suggested that learning time is greatly reduced, increasing productivity. Others might suggest that some of this ease of use leads to increased experimentation by users with features which are not strictly necessary in the workplace, leading to more unproductive work time.

Apple took a bold step in standardising printer drivers. This means that once a printer driver has been installed, all features of the printer can be used by any application. This contrasts with many MS-DOS applications, where drivers have to be written and supplied for each printer type for each application. A degree of standardisation on IBM compatible PCs was not achieved until the introduction of Microsoft Windows.

On the Mac, as part of the standard user interface design, a small 'Apple' icon is displayed in the top left corner of the screen. This enables a user, when in the middle of using any application, to access a number of commonly-used facilities.

Apple is also proud of its software which, with many applications, enables you to receive help about any command by pressing a single mouse button. Help appears in speech bubbles on the screen.

Great strides are being made in user interfaces all the time (see Chapter 5). The simplicity of some of the Apple dialogue is very appealing. In the latest version of the operating system, if, for example, your system has more than one printer, an icon is shown on the screen for each. To print a document, you simply pick it up on the screen and drag it to the appropriate printer icon. This is a far simpler idea than attempting to achieve the same by using text-based commands.

Mac keyboards include a command key, which has a picture of propeller. This is used in conjunction with another key to command the machine, usually to provide keyboard shortcuts for menu options. The uses of command key combinations are standardised, so all Mac applications support them. On early machines, this key was known as the 'Apple' key, as it had on it the Apple company's logo. The command key provides a real alternative so that most commands can be accessed either through the mouse or keyboard.

— Which system comes out on top? —

The Macintosh range came to prominence because it was the first computer to support PageMaker, the desktop publishing program from Aldus (now part of Adobe). In conjunction with the LaserWriter printer, an affordable office laser printer, PageMaker lead to the huge popularity of Macs in publishing. Despite the introduction of similar systems on PC machines, the initial supremacy of Macs in this area has never been lost.

Many would argue that Macs are superior in their sound, both as output, and for voice recognition and use of a microphone. More of these features come as standard on Macs than on cheap PC clones.

Mac enthusiasts would also say that Apple has the upper hand in developing multimedia systems, and that courseware can be prepared using Authorware on the Mac, and can then be transferred to a PC. Authoring on a Mac can also be done through software called 'HyperCard'.

Apple literature also argues that simple networking is easier to set up and use with a Macintosh. Apple would claim that while the system is not fast, it does enable one machine to talk to another, allowing access to other people's files. In a small organisation, this may be all that is needed. Elaborate and quick networks might not be needed. Macs have contained the elements necessary for this simple networking since 1984.

It is claimed that because Apples are so simple to use, in practice, purchasers need to call on technical support less often.

One concern expressed by potential purchasers of Apple systems is that they will become tied to the one supplier. This has benefits and drawbacks. Apple is clearly in control of aspects of systems such as the user interface, and can ensure that incompatible systems are not released. On the other hand, because Apple is firmly in control, some might regard this as inflexible.

In support of PC systems, many would argue that, because of the huge share of their market, PC machines are somewhat cheaper. Price comparisons are very difficult, and you must be careful to compare like with like. Even when this has been done, you also need to take into account whether you need all the features you are buying. Software prices on the different platforms are broadly comparable.

Ideally, you do need to take into account the costs of maintenance and support of your system. In many organisations now, the cost of repair of a computer is such that, if it doesn't work after a few years, it is thrown away. Home users might have to take a very different attitude.

Supporters of the PC route will claim that PCs have a greater range of software, particularly business software, available. The catalogue of Apple software is, however, rapidly catching up. In particular, PC supporters will quote the widespread use of MS-DOS as the established operating system. This has a number of advantages, in that there are more knowledgeable people about to ask for advice, it is easier to pass files to friends or colleagues, and there is more literature on the subject. This argument is sometimes caricatured by saying PCs are popular because they are popular.

Within the PC platform there is a wide choice of manufacturer, which certainly leads to more product variety. However, manufacturers may rise and fall, leaving users less well supported. Price cutting within the PC trade has financial benefits to customers, but the downside has been the lack of stability of some firms.

Some would argue that the PC platform allows the use of either Microsoft Windows, mirroring the Mac interface, or MS-DOS directly, providing a quicker route to some computer management tasks. This might be particularly true if users mainly wished to use text-driven programs.

The PC platform still retains its popularity with corporate users, partly because they have been committed to the PC for some time. This commitment can represent a huge investment for many organisations, which may also have well-developed arrangements for support and training.

In counteracting concerns about incompatibility between PCs and Macs, Mac supporters would argue that Apple File Exchange, a Mac utility, allows users to convert data files between Mac and PC formats. This is very helpful particularly if the same software has been bought for both machines. This principle applies only to the data, though. Software bought for one type of machine does not normally run on the other. AppleShare PC also allows a PC to be included in an AppleTalk network with Macs.

These differences are again being narrowed through the working together of Apple and IBM on the PowerPC. PowerMacs can run Windows, although this is only in a relatively slow emulation mode.

A brief look at machines that are neither Macs nor PCs

The Commodore Amiga uses the same Motorola 68000 chip family as many Apples, but is not compatible with Apple systems, because it uses a different operating system (see Chapter 13).

The Amiga 500 is geared to home use, and includes speech synthesis, four-channel stereo, and 4096 colours. Because of this, the Amiga is a popular machine, and is particularly suited to games playing, musical applications and multimedia. Other Amiga models include the 2000, which is geared for office use, including Computer Aided Design (CAD) and desktop publishing. The 3000 has enhanced graphics and a window-oriented user interface, known as Workbench.

Atari produces both dedicated games machines and computers. The Atari range was the first to use MIDI for music (see Chapter 15). Models include the 520ST, 1040STE, and the MEGA STE.

Acorn was originally made famous through its partnership with the BBC on the BBC micro. At that time, it made substantial inroads in both the education and home markets. It launched the Archimedes range in 1987, using a technology known as RISC, which has since become much more widespread. (See Chapter 12 for a more detailed explanation of RISC.) Since that time, Acorn has generally used its own chip technology designed in house, and its own operating system (RISC OS). Many of the models accept add-on modules which allow access to DOS and Windows. In some areas Acorn works in partnership with Apple, and uses the title 'ARM' for its machines with various model numbers. 'ARM' stands for 'Advanced RISC Machines'.

———————— Tips and wrinkles ————————

When choosing between systems, always take into account all the costs. Most advertisers omit VAT in adverts, except in the small print. You must compare like with like, however. Does the cost quoted include the monitor and the keyboard? (The prices of these are sometimes omitted because the user has a choice.) Will you need to buy a video card? (Apple literature, for example, boasts that video cards supporting several standards are built into their systems, avoiding extra expense.)

Though many people will volunteer a view about which system is 'best', ask yourself whether the view is based on the current differences between systems, or on factors that are no longer relevant.

The differences in hardware don't matter so long as when you buy your initial system, you ask 'will it all work together?' When you buy an enhancement, you need to ask 'will this work with my existing system?'

5

QUALITY: THE HUMAN–COMPUTER INTERACTION

Why is HCI important?

The way through which you, as a user, carry out a dialogue with a program to make selections, to save data, to produce print-outs and so on is through the 'user interface'. The subject of examining how users interact with computer systems has been given the title 'human-computer interaction', often abbreviated to HCI.

Computer product advertising, and some software reviews, will make very bold claims for a product, using terms like 'easy to use', 'intuitive', or the ever-present 'user-friendly'. The marketing industry has also produced some computer jargon, such as 'WYSIWYG' (meaning 'what you see is what you get', pronounced 'wizzy-wig'). Yet very few of these terms have precise meanings. Perhaps this provides a useful barrier for the advertisers to hide behind. For example, with WYSIWYG word processors, it is unlikely that what is displayed on the screen will be exactly what you have printed. For this to happen, the screen display must be exactly the same size as the paper you are using, and the screen resolution must be the same as the printer you will be using.

Many people confuse the idea of 'easy to use' with that of being 'easy to learn'. These are not the same at all. A product may be designed such that a few elementary and well used features are easy to learn.

This might be provided, though, at the cost that more sophisticated features, which nevertheless some people will use frequently, are made very complex.

In many cases, the good use of colour, varying brightness, flashing symbols, pictorial images and so on will, in moderation, help communication. There is much discussion in the specialist press, and in academic circles, about standards for user interfaces. Whilst most professionals would agree that standards are desirable, there is a real problem. Within the well-recognised categories of software (see Chapters 6 to 11), many of the packages provide very similar features. These will probably, nevertheless, be provided in very different ways. If the functionality of different products is virtually the same, and the prices are very similar, the main differences between packages are likely to be the way things are done – in other words the HCI. Manufacturers have rightly been jealous of their interface designs, and have at times resorted to legal action to defend their design ideas. The 'feel' of a program is becoming an increasingly important selling point. This can turn up as a similarity to other well-known products, or as resemblance to previous versions of the same software, with which existing users are probably very happy. Experiments have shown that users will attribute all sorts of qualities ('easy to use', 'easy to learn') to the first product they are introduced to, however good, bad or indifferent it may seem to others.

It is easy for people, such as the writers of manuals, who are regular users of computers, to forget how much specialist language ('jargon') is used in a computer context. For example, in a computer context, in manuals or other user guides, the term 'abort' is used to describe abandoning a function or program without saving the data. Unless this term is explained, users might find themselves in difficulty. Similarly, a new user might need the term 'cursor' explaining, particularly as various cursors such as text cursors and mouse cursors take very different forms. On the other hand, if a manual or an on-screen dialogue explain all these basic ideas in great detail, an experienced user is likely to become very frustrated.

The term 'user friendly' is not a simple one to define. Indeed, different users may require different behaviour from the simplest of activities. When a word search is being used on a word processor, the screen could be regularly updated to show how the text is being worked through. This would show very vividly that the search is taking place, but it would actually slow down the search, as processing time would be used to update the screen. So, whilst regular updating of the screen would be reassuring for the novice user, the slower operation would frustrate the experienced user. The choice of approach could be presented to the user, but many users do not want to have to set a whole number of options.

In addition to the alphabetic, numeric and other keys found on a standard keyboard, a computer keyboard has a number of other keys. These other keys include 'BACKSPACE' (often represented by a reverse arrow), a 'Break' key, a 'DEL' key, a 'HOME' key and so on. In the use of a program, each of these keys might have a specific meaning. Once you have used several different programs, you might be able to guess what those meanings are, but without experience, it is very difficult to know. For users, the problem is made more difficult when these keys have different roles in different programs.

The 'Break' key, for example, is almost always used to abandon an operation. In one context, say a word search in a word processor, it might mean abandon the search and continue editing the document. In another context, though, it might mean abandon running the program completely. Inexperienced users are unlikely to have an intuitive feel for what the program is likely to do.

In one program, where a file of information contains the equivalent of several screens of information, in one case pressing the 'HOME' key might return the user to the start of the file. In another program it might move the cursor to the top of the current page. In yet another case, it might only move the cursor to the beginning of the current line.

The 'INS' key may be used to switch an application between 'insert text' and 'overwrite text' mode. In other applications, though, pressing the 'INS' key might simply indicate that text is to be inserted at the cursor position. Other keys, such as 'BACKSPACE' achieve different things in different circumstances. In many applications, it will delete the character immediately to the left of the cursor. The 'DEL' key, on the other hand, may delete the character at the current cursor position, and the character immediately to the right will move across to take its place. The 'DEL' key in this mode is therefore described as 'deleting forward'.

There is also a series of conventions in computer documentation, such as the use of ^ (the caret symbol) in a manual or as part of an on-screen instruction to signify that the 'CTRL' key should be held down at the same time as the following character. Thus ^S means that the user must press 'CTRL' and 'S' at the same time. Because this notation is so common, it is rarely explained, yet no new user is likely to guess what it means, and the better manuals will explain conventions such as these.

In some packages, it makes a difference whether the user types characters as capitals or lower case. In other applications, it makes no difference at all. Again, experience will teach users which case is more likely. To a new user, however, the difference is confusing, and so is the term used to describe the idea, that input is 'case sensitive'.

The quality of user dialogue and documentation are very important, yet very few demonstrations of software give you a fair picture. Sales staff may be very good at showing you what to do when things are going right. They might be less good at saying what to do when things go wrong. Yet how the program behaves when things go wrong is a major element in determining what is a good piece of software.

User types

Just because defining terms in the study of human-computer interaction is difficult does not mean that users do not know what they like or find useful. We must be particularly careful not to assume that different users have the same needs. In different contexts, I might be classified as a different type of user. I am fairly proficient at using several different word processors. I know the features that I am likely to use regularly. I can pick up a word processor which I have never used and will immediately look for all the important features. If, on the other hand, I was introduced to some new accounting software, particularly if it used accounting conventions and terms unfamiliar to me, I would require a very different kind of dialogue. I would expect to be guided slowly through the features, receiving explanations of concepts which an accountant, however unfamiliar he or she is with computers, would not need explaining. So there are not only different categories of users, but the level of competence depends on the application.

Most programs provide you with a help facility, so that by pressing a single key, you can ask for an explanation. The function key 'F1' is used within many packages to access help, though others use the '?'

key, or a different function key, or an appropriate on-screen icon. The 'help' message that is then displayed will then explain to you what choices you can make at that point, and what will happen if you select each option. Where the help relates directly to the current choice, it is described as context-sensitive. Whilst help is being obtained, other program activity is normally suspended, and the screen is 'frozen' in the state which applied when 'help' was chosen. This gives the user confidence that the program can be re-activated when the appropriate help has been obtained. With many systems you can also request help on any aspects of the facilities within the package. This kind of help is not a replacement for a manual, but if you are adept at using the help, you may be able to look up a detail (such as the exact format of a formula) quicker than in a manual.

Many packages now allow you to use keyboard function keys for the selection of options within a package. There may be two or three ways of selecting many of the well-used features. For unfamiliar users, function keys have the drawback that their use is not easily remembered, as there is no simple way of relating a function key number to the various options. For regular users of one or more packages, however, there is usually some consistency in the way function keys are used by different packages, particularly between products from the same software manufacturer. The number and position of function keys can differ, some keyboards having 10 function keys, others having 12. The use of 'F1' for help, has become widespread but not universal. Other function keys can be put to whatever use the software author decides. Function keys are also used along with the CTRL, SHIFT and ALT keys to provide quick access to even more features.

Where a package makes use of function keys, a plastic template may be provided to place round the function keys to indicate their use within that package. Different colours may be used to denote the use of function keys with CTRL, SHIFT or ALT.

Many packages use the 'ESC' key to abandon the choice of an option. So if, for example, you choose 'print a file', and then realise that this is not what you want to do (perhaps the printer is not switched on), you press 'ESC' to go back to the previous menu. It is worth checking, though, whether 'ESC' works this way on a particular package, or whether you abandon an action in some other way.

Programs are now beginning to be adapted to individual user needs. For example, I regularly mis-time pressing the 'SHIFT' key, so that the second letter of a word is in upper case rather than the first letter. Yet my word processor works through and suggests a lot of other possibilities, usually with different letters, before suggesting that my mistake (the reason it can't find the word in its dictionary) is that the second letter is in the wrong case. Now, it may be that for other users, other mistakes or more likely. A sophisticated package will adapt the order of choices offered in the light of experience of my previous errors. The building in of such 'intelligence' to programs is only in its infancy.

Some packages provide a wide range of options which allow you to 'customise' the program to your own taste. You can set, for example, the rate at which the cursor flashes, the response rate of the mouse buttons, the screen colours and so on. This has a major advantage, but two major disadvantages. It is an advantage to be able to set up a system to behave exactly as you like it. This is all part of helping you to feel in control of the system as a user. You might be genuinely slow in using mouse buttons, so adapting the system is useful. On the downside, though, it is common to see users wasting a lot of time 'playing' with a system, trying out all the different ways of tuning the system, rather than getting on with using the system for the job for which it was intended. Another drawback is that, if the computer system is shared by several people, the settings that you have chosen might be very unsuitable for another user, and the other users will not know which combination of settings they will come across next. New users may not know how to alter the settings, or they may not want to waste time changing them all.

─────── Screen considerations ───────

Some programs use colour very imaginatively in their design. Different colours can be used to distinguish between types of information. You should be wary if you have only a monochrome monitor, though. Colours which look very different might be very similar when presented as shades of grey. This will cause real problems if, for example, the dialogue or the help refers to the actual colours, or if colour backgrounds and text are used together.

With some colour programs, the combination of colours can be altered by the user. This might be important, as personal tastes differ as well as an individual's ability to distinguish different colours. If you are even slightly colour-blind, you could have real difficulties using some programs.

A lot of research has been carried out into good screen design, and a number of principles have been put forward.

It is important for a program to avoid crowding the screen with too much information (known as 'visual overload'). For example, the use of bold characters, flashing text or symbols, reverse, underlining and half-intensity text on a single screen may be too much to follow.

The design of screen dialogues is more of a job for a communications specialist than for a programming expert. Many programmers seem to be carried away by the range of techniques they can produce, and seem to feel that they must produce them all at once! Many simple rules can be applied to screen design, such as placing larger text at the top of the screen rather than at the bottom if a mix of sizes is to be used. The choice of typefaces is also important. The number of typefaces used at any one time should be limited. Similarly, it has been shown that lower case text is easier to read. Those seeking to understand good simple screen or report design could do a lot worse than browse through magazine advertisements, which are specifically designed to be eye-catching and easy to read.

Computer dialogues need to be consistent in style. This idea is often used by a manufacturer to sell further products in a range to users because they have a comfortable and familiar 'feel' like others in the range. Consistency will involve using the same areas of the screen for similar purposes. So if a particular type of box appears on the screen, the user will know from experience that it is a warning, or an error message, or a confirmation message from its appearance, without reading the text. Commands are normally displayed either on the top few lines or bottom few lines of a screen. Instructions to the user might appear within a box in the centre of the screen, or on the bottom few lines. Many packages also include messages such as a status line, telling the user the current status of the program.

To a new user a screen which many regular users would find familiar may feel very crowded. A typical word processor screen, for example, might include on its top line of display the name of the current file, details of the cursor position (page, line, column number), and a symbol to denote insert mode, and another one to denote whether text justification is on or off. The next line might include the main menu, and a further line could contain the text ruler. These ideas might all be new to a user, and in combination, the effect could be very disconcerting. A new user will find it hard to know which messages are important and may need acting upon, and which are merely for information.

One manner in which programs can differ considerably is in the amount of feedback given to a user. Often, confirmation messages help users feel comfortable, whether they are new to the package or not. A simple message such as 'File is being saved, each dot represents 4000 characters', with a series of dots, can reassure users that the right thing is happening. Other similar effects are achieved using an on-screen egg-timer, a clock, or a bar which gradually changes colour. Reassuring messages are particularly important when an unavoidable delay takes place before a user can select another option. The fact that something is happening on screen can discourage a user from thinking that a new input must be given.

Types of dialogue

Command-driven systems

One form of computer dialogue has been used ever since programs were first written for other people to use. It depends on the user typing in a coded instruction line according to a set of rules. This system is known as the command line approach. When you are satisfied that you have designed and entered all the aspects necessary, for example to generate your report, you press 'ENTER' at the end of a command such as 'LIST CUSTOMERS WITH SALES > 1000'. The program will then attempt to service your request. This style of dialogue has been common since the early days of computing when, to use a computer at all, you had to be familiar with programming.

It is fashionable to suggest that, nowadays, we have developed 'beyond' this approach. For regular users of a system, though, the command line approach has a number of benefits. Amongst these benefits are the capacity to specify exactly what you want, including some sophisticated options, in a single command. If, for example, you were a librarian, regularly interrogating a database of sources, the forms of search would become second nature to you. The command line approach relies on the user knowing quite a lot about the form of commands ('syntax'). If you are using a system regularly, you will probably attend a training course and read manuals and other literature on the subject. As a frequent user of a program, you might find yourself very frustrated if you have to specify each aspect of your search through a different menu.

Command driven programs can be made more helpful in a number of ways. First, help screens can be incorporated just as easily as in any other system. If the program recognises an attempt to use a particular command which fails because of incorrect use, the program might actually ask whether you would like to see a help screen in that particular subject. Secondly, command driven programs can store previously used commands, so that if a user wishes to use a command again, either directly, or after a little editing, the command can be recalled for this purpose. Thirdly, if a command is slightly incorrect, the program might be able to suggest valid commands which are fairly similar to the user's attempt, which the user can either use or ignore. For accomplished users, the days of command line dialogues are not over.

Menu-driven systems

The second type of user dialogue is the menu-driven system. In this dialogue style, familiar to those who have used Fastext on television, or bank cash machines, a set of options is placed before the user who then selects one of the options. Depending upon the first choice, a further set of options is presented, which may lead to yet another set and so on, until the exact detail has been entered.

There are different ways of selecting from a menu. For example, to make a choice from a menu, you might:

- Press a button corresponding to your choice. On bank cash machines, buttons are placed on either side of the screen next to the choices. On a Fastext television the different colour buttons correspond to the choices. On a touch sensitive screen the user will point to the requested option.

- Type the number or letter indicated against the choice (perhaps in conjunction with the 'ALT' or 'CTRL' key), using the keyboard. The command might be selected through its initial letter, or some other highlighted letter.

- Move the cursor across or down a menu, using a key, such as 'TAB', space or a cursor key, so that your choice is highlighted, and then press 'ENTER'.

Some programs allow users a choice of working with one of these methods or a combination. It is also helpful if the menu style is consistent, so that, for example, the choice of 'exit' is given the same key allocation in every menu, such as '0', '9', or 'X'. It is worth pointing out that when a menu is displayed, the normal arrangement is that if a valid selection is made, the effect is immediate; if an invalid choice is made, then the entry is ignored. In this sense, either way, a menu system generates an immediate response.

Some systems are entirely menu-driven in that all commands are given in the form of menus. In other systems, menus are used only for particular tasks. In a typical word processor, for example, the text of a document is entered 'directly' onto one part of the screen. The user switches over to menu operation by using the 'ALT' key in combination with the requested facility from the menu. In some spreadsheets, formulae are entered on the grid of cells; a specific request has to be issued so that the system changes mode and the menu is displayed. In several spreadsheets, for example, users must press '/' to gain access to the menu.

Many programs involve the use of sub-menus within menus, so that the choice of one entry from a menu leads to the display of another menu from which a choice should be made. The terms 'pull down' and 'pop up' menus are used in this context. There are slight inconsistencies in the way some people use these terms.

A 'pull down' menu system is one which generates a sub-menu from a request from the main menu, which you will often see as a row across the top of the screen. The sub-menu would normally appear immediately below the main menu selection which generated it, and selections can then be made from this sub-menu. It is now most common for main menus to be displayed at the top of the screen, but a similar arrangement could be made with a menu at the bottom of the screen. Some purists would say that the term 'pull down' should only be used for the Macintosh style of menu, where the sub-menu is only displayed while a mouse button is depressed, so that by dragging the menu is pulled down. Such people would use the term 'drop down' for menus which remain displayed without mouse action.

A 'pop up' menu is one which appears on request, whatever you may be doing at the time. It will appear in a box on the screen, temporarily obscuring part of the current display. Such pop up menus do not necessarily appear in the same place every time. When you choose an option from the menu, another menu will pop up, normally next to the original. Thus, the series of menus, allows you to see the set of steps which you had gone through.

Both 'pull down' and 'pop up' menus allow you to backtrack through the levels, or layers, of menus. Often this is achieved by the use of 'ESC' to cancel the current menu and to allow you to return to the previous one.

Menus described so far require the user to select one of the displayed options. One variation of this system is to design menus where several options can be selected together (where tasks or options are not mutually exclusive). In this case a separate command is included in the list to enable the user to implement the choices, labelled 'go', 'execute' or in some similar way.

Icon-driven systems

The third approach to dialogue is to use a more visual approach, using a symbol for each feature. This approach accounts for much of the appeal of Apple Macintosh computers, and is the approach also taken by Microsoft Windows. Simplified pictures, called icons, are displayed on the screen, which a user can select, often through pointing and clicking with a mouse. In this way, a picture of a disk drive is used to denote the operation of selecting that drive. A picture of a printer might represent the printing of a document.

Such a system is known as a graphical user interface, abbreviated to GUI (pronounced 'gooey'). This more visually based approach to dialogues is especially suited to systems which make use of a mouse or some other pointing device, which then allows many tasks to be carried out without recourse to the keyboard.

Icon-based screen dialogues can be designed to be completely independent of language, so can be used across language barriers. Text-based menus, dialogues and instructions have to be translated, of course.

One drawback of icons is that their meaning isn't always obvious. Does an icon of a printer mean 'print', or does it mean 'select a printer from a number which are available'? Does a capital 'T' to represent text input imply that all text entered will be represented in capital letters?

It can be difficult, too, to design icons to convey a precise meaning. How, for example, would you design two separate icons, one to mean 'spellcheck a whole document', the other to mean 'spellcheck a single word'? If you can not design different representative pictures, you may have to resort to some words, which defeats much of the point of using pictures in preference to words. Does the waste basket (trash can) analogy or metaphor really hold – you can always retrieve something from a waste basket; should the symbol really be a paper shredder?

The desktop world of Macintosh computers and Microsoft Windows has mushroomed rapidly, and many of the visual ideas have been given names. The idea, however, is that users will intuitively feel they know how to use symbols, and if they don't, they are encouraged to experiment on screen. For example, the term 'button' is used to mean an on-screen icon which can be 'pressed'; the term is used to contrast with a key on the keyboard.

'Radio buttons' on the screen are represented as circular buttons. If the centre is filled, this means the feature has been selected, otherwise the centre is not filled. The convention is that, from a row of radio buttons, you must have one and only one selection. If you select a new option, by clicking on it, the old one is automatically deselected. For example, a printout may be in portrait or landscape mode. You must have one, but you can't have both. The analogy is with the wavelength selector on a conventional radio: you cannot be tuned to FM, AM and LW all at the same time.

In contrast, a check box is used for a selectable option, where several choices can be made in any combination. In Microsoft Windows, a square is used to denote a check box, and a cross is displayed in the box when an option is selected. Again selection and deselection are achieved by clicking. In this case, however, clicking on one box has no effect on the others.

Other settings for which there is a wide range of possible values can be changed using an on-screen slider mechanism. By using the mouse, a slider can be moved within a scale of settings to determine, for example, the brightness of colour, or the contrast, or the sound volume, or the speed of an activity.

Various terms have been coined to help users distinguish between the operation they wish to do, and what they want to do it to. Some writers use the terms 'objects' and 'actions'; others refer to 'select' and 'submit'; others still refer to 'operands' and 'operations'. Confusion and frustration are caused to users if they are unclear whether the object or the action should be specified first. There is no single or simple convention on this. In one case, you will specify that you wish to save or load a file and are then asked its name. In another, you must specify which text you wish to format before selecting the bold format option.

Other operations can be carried out on objects using a mouse or similar technology. By holding a mouse button down you can move an object around a GUI screen, which is known as 'dragging'. You can drag and then drop an item, using the mouse button rather like a magnet; when the button is pressed it will attract objects, when it is released, the object will no longer be attracted and will be left behind. Some systems show an icon of a hand, as a 'grabber hand' which can pick up and relocate objects on the screen. In applications such as graphics programs, a rectangular frame might be shown around an image to show its location for grabbing; this frame or parts of it are sometimes known as 'handles'.

Most users will be more than happy to use a graphical screen without needing to know the technical terms such as 'radio buttons' or 'handle'. New users are encouraged by the visual environment to try ideas out. For examples, cells on a spreadsheet can be picked up and stretched. Naturally, if this works, you will have confidence that you can always use the same method to put it back to how it was previously. Problems are caused for example when some features require the use of keyboard 'SHIFT' or 'CTRL' keys with mouse buttons. Many users would not think to try out such commands without prompting.

Many applications allow users to pass data from one application to another, using a device known as a clipboard. Much effort is currently being expended by software developers to make this transfer as easy as possible, so that, for example, graphics can be transferred from a drawing program to a word processor, or pie charts from a spreadsheet can be used within electronic mail.

Graphical interfaces also support a number of means of letting you keep track of where you are. A scroll arrow is an icon containing an arrow pointing left, right, up or down. By selecting the correct arrow, you can move in any direction within the spreadsheet, page layout or whatever. A thumb mark or elevator is a box within a slider used to show how far through a document you are, either vertically or horizontally. Where a screen is displaying details of several programs, documents or menu options which may be active at any one time, the currently selected one is normally shown through highlighting in some way. A highlight bar is a line on a screen menu which is shown in reverse or in a special colour to denote that it is the current choice. An on-screen button may have a different colour border to show that it is currently selected. Other systems use half intensity for options that are not chosen or active.

Scrolling menus enable a list to be displayed which has too many entries to be shown at once. The first few choices are displayed, with scroll arrows to allow you to move through the list. Some authors use the term 'menu' to denote any list from which you choose, whether it is a list of actions or objects.

Graphical interfaces also need to give messages to the user. Such systems use a variety of dialogue boxes. These may for example give a warning or may be explanations of errors. It is popular for such boxes to provide buttons to confirm that you have read them; they may include options to ignore the problem or cancel the operation.

Good user dialogue

The principles of good user dialogue should apply whatever the form used, whether it be command based, menu-driven or a graphical interface.

Programs should communicate clearly to the user what they are doing. If, for example, a spelling checker is requested from the middle of a document, there is a decision to be made when the end of the document is reached whether checking should continue at the beginning of the document. Some word processors will ask the user to choose at this point. One issue that is overlooked, however, by many software designers is that most users don't mind whether the system carries on from the beginning, stops, or gives them the choice, so long as it tells them what it is doing.

Good messages to the user should use concrete terms rather than abstract ideas. So it is better for the error message to say 'your file name contains nine letters, and you are only allowed to use up to eight', than the more abstract, and easier to implement 'maximum of eight characters only'. Messages should be designed to inform you about what you need to know rather than telling you off for getting it wrong!

Similarly, well-designed messages can be used to reassure the user that the correct action is taking place. After a request to print a file, an appropriate message would ask for the name of the file to print. After a request to save, the message would ask about the file name for saving. In this way, those who have made the correct choice receive confirmation, and those who have gone wrong receive a reminder without having been told off. Many users prefer this more subtle approach to being asked 'are you sure you want to print?' every time.

Good dialogues also allow experienced users to use short cuts in data entry. A good example is provided by many spreadsheets. Formulae are entered into a large number of cells. Users can operate by typing formulae in full, and this is how many new users will begin. Options often exist, though, which enable references to cells to be entered simply by pointing to the relevant entry, and its cell reference is then incorporated into the formula. This short-cut method provides an advantage to the experienced without slowing down the new user.

Short cuts, though, are not always the easiest to use. Take for example, the user who wishes to select the fifth entry in a menu. This could be selected, in our example, by typing the 'CTRL' key with the initial letter of the command. An alternative might be to press the 'down arrow' symbol four times. Some users would prefer the 'down arrow' option, because if they are unfamiliar with the keyboard, that takes less looking for.

It is often suggested that a good program remembers the user's chosen values from one session to another. This question is not as clear-cut as many people would have you believe. Yes, you would like the system to remember which printer you were using, as you are likely to use the same printer again next time. If, however, you choose an unusual feature, say printing your spreadsheet sideways, you would probably be very frustrated if, on subsequent use of the package, perhaps with a different model, the setting for sideways printing remained. Having a 'feel' for the differences between the two examples above, and hundreds of others, is part of the art of software design.

Good dialogues also allow users to carry out tasks in the order that they choose, rather than having a set pattern forced on them. This encourages users to experiment with features, and to work more creatively. Perhaps the user wants to develop a spreadsheet without a heading, or a word processed document without formatting. If combinations of commands only work in a particular order, a user might become very frustrated. If they do only work in a set order, however, the best dialogues will explain why things have not worked, and clarify what the user must do.

Well-designed systems will also give users control over the messages they receive. Often the system is initially set up to provide detailed messages to naive users, but a good system will allow more experienced users to reduce the level of detail given during the dialogue.

There are a number of useful features which some packages provide:

- 'Are you sure?' options check that you mean what you have said before irrevocably writing over a file or re-formatting – these are useful safeguards against accidental choice of the wrong option.

- An 'undo' option cancels the last action carried out – this is useful for reversing major mistakes, though some people would argue that the existence of a safety net makes users less wary of making mistakes in the first place.

- An automatic back-up, saves a copy of a file every ten minutes or so without you having to request it.

- a warning is given if you attempt to print something that you haven't yet saved to disk – some packages force you to save before you can print.

- a reminder is given if you try to quit without saving an active file which has been changed (in some applications, you might have several active files at any one time).

—— Other quality considerations ——

Popular packages often evolve through several upgrades, usually distinguished by a version or generation number. To attract existing users to move up to the next generation of the product, software manufacturers will often keep features from previous versions of the software. This they do even if the new version allows the task to be done in a different and better way. This allows an existing user to carry on doing something in a familiar way, whilst new users will learn a new style of using the package. On first impressions, this can be confusing, and users new and old might ask 'why are there many ways of doing exactly the same thing?'

Many packages help the user by anticipating the possible answers to questions. Some programs make sensible suggestions about the most likely choice you will make. For example, if you select the option to save a file, the existing file name may be suggested. If this is what you want, you simply choose 'ENTER', otherwise you type in the new file name. Other examples include searching for the same word in the text again, outputting to the same printer type as before and so on. Such guesses by the computer rely on suggesting the last entry used with that feature. Such suggestions don't delay you if they are wrong, but they speed things up if they are correct.

A development of this 'suggestion' idea is that all possible options are displayed, either automatically, or upon user request (perhaps through a function key). This idea works well when a limited set of options is available, such as a selection of printers which can be used. The idea also works reasonably well when a number of options are likely. When loading a file, for example, the file name must come from the set of existing file names, so this list can be displayed. When you are saving a file, if an existing name is to be chosen, for overwriting the file, then the choice can be made from a list. If a new file is to be created, the file name will, of course, have to be entered.

Most software packages operate some sort of system of file backup. At the elementary level, when you save a new version of a file, the previous copy is retained, with a different name (with many MS-DOS products, the same file name is used with a BAK extension). Should something subsequently go seriously wrong, at least the previous version can then be retrieved. Many packages can also be customised so that if the user has not made a copy for perhaps 15 minutes, then the software automatically triggers the saving of the file. This can only work, of course, if a file name has been chosen.

Without manuals, it is almost impossible to exploit all the potential of a package. The term 'package' was originally used to emphasise that you are buying more than a program.

Manuals fulfil a variety of tasks, for different types of users. Amongst the sections provided in a single manual or a set of manuals could be:

- an installation guide, aspects of which are examined in Chapter 21
- a training guide to help new users, covering the frequently used and essential features, describing the main concepts behind the use of the package
- a detailed guide, explaining every command and its use, usually grouped into chapters of similar commands
- a reference manual, giving technical definitions of every command and feature, usually in alphabetical order, with an index
- a upgrade guide for people who have used previous versions of the software, explaining where the new version differs
- a technical guide for those who want to explore the package in more depth, customise it and so on (perhaps in a technical appendix)
- an index to the documentation as a whole
- a quick reference card or guide which gives a summary of the main commands, without explanation, as a reminder for regular users who know what they want to do, but can't recall the command to do it.

Many packages now include a manual or a set of manuals running to 600 pages or more. Writing manuals is a difficult job, because different readers are looking for very different things from their manuals. At one extreme, there is the complete novice, who wants to use a program without having used a computer or the type of software before. At the other extreme is the person who has used very similar products before, and so knows exactly what he or she wants to do, and simply wants a clear, short explanation of how to do it.

If you really want to get the best out of a piece of software, you will not find all that you want in any set of published manuals. There are many books written about most of the popular packages. Some are aimed at the type of user – naive, or experienced with computers but not this application area, or familiar with the type of software but not the equipment, and so on. Others may be aimed at your particular interest or career – spreadsheet books may, for example, include sample models for quantity surveyors, or accountants. With most well-known packages, there will be several dozen books from which to choose. It is perhaps best to become familiar with the basics of the package by using the manufacturer's manuals, and then to look round book stores and libraries for books which suit your circumstances. A little knowledge of a package will give you a good idea of the depth and speed at which a book covers the topics.

—— Ten tips on software quality ——

- Everybody means something different by the term 'user-friendly'.

- Menus can be very helpful to allow you to see what can be done, but too many layers of menu will slow you down when you know what you want to do.

- The manual will probably be written for all machines on which the software will run. This could mean various parts of the manual are not relevant, and that features are used in different ways on different machines.

- An 'undo' feature in a package is not just a safety net; it positively encourages experimentation with the whole range of facilities, and so makes learning easier.

- The shortest way to achieve an operation is not always the most well used by operators.

- You might be reading something into an icon which was not intended.

- With a good dialogue, the user feels in control, and is told what is going on.

- Messages should not be patronising, nor should they tell you off; they should say what you can do, and offer you advice.

- Dialogues should not insist that you do things in a particular way if there are several possible approaches.

- A system which has a familiar 'look and feel' will help a user to feel more comfortable and confident.

6

WORD
PROCESSING

The basic idea

Most people buying a computer system will want to carry out some form of word processing on it. It is frequently claimed that the availability of accessible simple word processing was the main spur to the mushrooming of the use of computers, both in the office and in the home. Many new computer systems are sold with a word processor already installed 'free'.

Word processing packages provide facilities to enter, store, retrieve, manipulate and print text. As time goes by, most of the packages are tending to have many of the same features, and, indeed, increasingly look very similar. As with any segment of the market, manufacturers are keen to provide all the features provided by their rivals, and a few more, and to implement them in a way that they see as quicker or more convenient.

Word processing packages vary in price from under £20 to over £300 for a fully featured top-of-the-range product. The prices of the most sophisticated products continue to fall, however, even as their numbers of features increase. Research shows that many advanced features within word processing packages go unused or are underused. You may not have paid very much extra for these extra unused features. Your only worry might be that the fully featured products take up too much of your disk space, particularly when dictionaries and other reference files are installed.

Many early word processing products were aimed at a particular type of computer, or even a specific make. This situation has now changed, with several of the big players in the market producing versions of their products for each of the main platforms: DOS, Microsoft Windows and Macintosh. Increasingly, these different versions have the same look and feel, but clearly you must buy the right one for your computer.

Word processing was substantially changed by the widespread availability of the mouse. There are still several major word processors available in versions which do not use mice, but most DOS packages make good use of the mouse for selection from menus, for highlighting text to be manipulated, for quick movement within text, and so on.

With Microsoft Windows versions and Macintosh versions, it really goes without saying that mouse manipulation and control are essential elements around which the interface is built.

– Features that they all (usually) have –

All word processors will allow you to enter text, save it to disk (usually keeping a backup copy for you), and print a document. Portions of text within a document can be cut, copied and pasted, enabling movement or duplication of sections of text. The way that text is marked for cutting and other operations differs between packages, most markedly between those that are purely keyboard based (where no mouse is involved), and those that provide a mouse based marking system. Once marked for manipulation a section or block of text is generally highlighted in some way. Several mouse-based word processors will allow you to identify a section of text, pick it up, and place it elsewhere within the document. This feature is termed 'drag and drop' and allows simple editing without recourse to the menus at all.

Word processors allow you to adapt the layout of a document, so you can look at the same basic text with a number of different formats. By doing this, you can choose the most appropriate layout. Control over poor appearance is available in several packages where paragraphs are not split between pages (either automatically, or under user control). In particular, most users seek to avoid paragraphs which leave just a few words of a paragraph on a second page. Among the layout commands will usually be the ability to print alternate pages with a different offset, so that space is left for holes to be punched or for sheets to be bound. An odd numbered page needs indentation at the left, and an even page at the right.

Most modern word processors allow users access to a wide range of text fonts. 'WYSIWYG' packages display the text as it would actually be printed, so that the display is true to the font style, and is bold and italic when these features are selected. Some word processors do not meet this definition of 'WYSIWYG' but still support a variety of fonts for printing. Many print fonts appear to their best advantage when output is proportionally spaced. This means that characters are not printed as a series of columns as would have happened on an old typewriter or as appears on many screens. Instead, the space allowed for each letter depends upon its width, and the spaces between letters are adjusted so that they are as equal to each other as possible.

Because there is no precise definition of 'WYSIWYG' some manufacturers describe a product as 'true WYSIWYG' when others would not. Some packages are limited by the display mode used so that they are unable to display alternative fonts or true on-screen proportional spacing. Potential purchasers will have to decide how important 'true' WYSIWYG is to them.

Many word processors include security features, such as reminding or forcing the user to save a document before printing, loading a new file or leaving the program. To some users these are irritants, as they may not wish to save, but most users will tell you that there has been a time when such a feature has helped them avoid the loss of a great deal of valuable work.

As with most packages, word processors normally allow for types of undo facilities, so that the effects of commands can be reversed. Many support a single level of undo (the last command only), although others sport four levels, or even 100. Some word processors encourage users to use the undo to make copies of text. The text is marked, then deleted. To move this text, you then move the cursor to its new position and select undo. Critics would say that this is a dangerous form of user interface, as users are so error-prone.

The user's current position within a text is indicated by a cursor. Movement through the text is controlled through manipulation of the cursor control keys, and, on mouse-driven systems, through on-screen symbols. Movement commands usually include transfer to the top or bottom of the current screen, or of the complete document. Text addition and deletion take place at the current cursor position. Deletion options may include deletion forward or backwards of a character, a word, a line or even a sentence.

On screen, text automatically moves onto a new line once the text is too long to fit the line margins. This takes place under automatic program control, with text flowing down or up when text is added or deleted anywhere in a paragraph. The main unit of text recognised by a word processor is the paragraph, which the user will end with the 'ENTER' key.

Paragraph formats can be specified, such as right-justified, where extra space is put within the line by the package so that the right-hand edges of each line are lined up. Other paragraph formats include ragged right, so that no extra spaces are entered at all. Users might also specify that a paragraph is indented within the page by a particular amount, or that part of a paragraph, perhaps the first line, is. Most packages provide a set of standard paragraph layouts which can be selected, either through menus selected by keyboard or mouse, or through on-screen icons selected with a mouse. Some packages support automatic hyphenation of words at the end of a line, to improve the appearance of the text. The software can choose an appropriate point within a word to insert the hyphen.

Most word processors allow the user to choose different printers. Codes to exploit the printer's features are held in file called a printer driver. (Most packages come with over 100 printer drivers.) Users can also choose different paper sizes (so long as the printer can take different paper sizes).

As well as manipulating text in blocks of several lines of text over the full width of the paper, most packages allow you to specify a rectangular block of text for manipulation. This is known as a rectangular cut, or column mode.

Headers and footers are standard lines of text which appear on each page at the top and bottom respectively. Headers and footers can be one or more lines long, incorporating features such as dates, times and page numbers. Though not normally displayed as part of the text being edited, headers and footers can normally be seen when a print preview is requested so that the screen shows precisely what will be printed. Header and footer features will normally allow for the inclusion of the page number and the total number of pages in the document.

Search features allow you to search through a text for a specified word or phrase. Various options will allow you to specify that upper or lower case characters are to be ignored, that whole words only are to be looked for, and whether the search is forwards or backwards. A fuzzy search allows the user to specify that part of the text string for which the program is to look might be any character. Fuzzy searches are usually established through a wild card character, so '?' might represent any character. A 'replace' feature develops this idea further so that words can be changed either automatically, or under user control. It is possible that a user might want to search for items other than text, such as for formatting commands (bold characters, for instance). Some word processors support this as well.

A spellchecker feature works by checking every word in a document against a standard dictionary of commonly used words, typically over 100 000 words. If a word used in a document is not in the standard dictionary, either the word is correctly spelt, but is not in the dictionary provided, or alternatively an error has been made. The program will suggest alternative spellings for words that it does not recognise. Users can have one or more personal dictionaries on disk, so that words that are not contained in the main dictionary can be remembered. The two most common forms of words that would not be contained in a standard dictionary are proper names (of people and places), and technical vocabulary. A word processor can be configured to examine several dictionaries, in a specified order, as part of the spellchecker process. Specialist dictionaries can be bought for particular users, such as doctors, chemists, politicians and so on. Foreign language dictionaries can also be installed. Potential purchasers should look carefully at the dictionaries which they are buying – their vocabularies range from 10 000 words to over 200 000. Depending on your circumstances, you might find that the former is too low and the latter too slow. Also, beware that American dictionaries will have substantial differences from English ones.

Some recent word processors make automatic adjustments to text as it is typed in, so that simple spelling mistakes are corrected without user intervention as the text is entered. This can only take place where there is little doubt what was intended, such as cases where letters were accidentally inverted, and produce a word that is not recognised.

A word count feature enables you to know how many words have been used in a document or a specified part of it. Word count features aren't always entirely comparable, because of the different ways they treat entries such as numbers and some characters such as paragraph bullet points.

At times when you are editing documents, you will want to be able to look at several documents at once – often two, and occasionally more than two. This happens when you are trying to move parts of one document into another. At other times, you want to look at completely different parts of the same document. To allow either of these, many word processors provide a facility to open several 'windows'. Users can then manipulate the text in each of the windows, and move text between the windows.

——— Extra features to look for ———

A mailmerge facility allows you to prepare a standard document, such as a letter, into which various items need to be slotted, such as a company name, and address, an amount outstanding, and a deadline date. Another file is separately built up containing the appropriate details of name, address and so on for each document that is to be produced. When you run the mailmerge feature, a document is printed for each entry on the list, with the appropriate details in the correct positions. By building up a whole set of different documents and a whole set of mailing lists, the same letter can be sent to members of different groups. Conditional mailmerging allows entries to be included in the documents if particular conditions are satisfied by the data for that entry. Mailmerging has been given something of a bad name by some companies that insist on sending you 'personalised' letters more regularly than you would like. It is a good idea to use a print preview before you print a long set of letters. A simple mistake, such as the omission of one item in somebody's details can mean that all subsequent documents are produced with entries misplaced.

A thesaurus in a word processor, suggests word of similar meaning. By choosing a word in your document and invoking the thesaurus, you can see alternative words meaning almost the same. You can then choose one of those words, or keep the original. A thesaurus is a helpful tool for writers to improve and vary the English they use in a document. The size of the thesaurus is important. If it is too short it will not offer enough ideas; if it is too long it will be slower and take up a lot of disk space. A less comprehensive thesaurus might, for example, hold words similar in meaning only to one form of a word, say 'change', rather than also containing 'changed'. Alternatives to 'change' will give useful suggestions for alternatives to 'changed', but you will probably have to retype the 'ed' on the new word.

Most users will, after some experience in using a word processor, settle on a number of preferred document formats. The preferred style will reflect the subject content, the audience and so on. These styles can usually be stored within a word processor. There are generally options to store the style of a paragraph or of a whole document. (Some manufacturers use the alternative term 'template'.) A number of pre-prepared styles may be supplied with the original package. By calling up the styles, users can work to a standard. This might be particularly important in a business, where a consistent presentation is very important both to give a feel of a house style and to fit pre-printed stationery. Whole documents can also be re-shaped by the single action of changing a style sheet. Style sheets allow large-scale changes to be made to a document without the need to pick out each paragraph, heading or other part which needs changing.

Writers sometimes want to use a footnote so that a separate explanation of an idea can be given, normally at the foot of the page. This then avoids the main text being broken up, or the flow of ideas lost. The addition or deletion of further footnotes causes the word processor to renumber them accordingly. Endnotes are a similar idea, but the actual text of endnotes is included at the end of a chapter or a document.

An indexing feature within a word processor allows you to specify the words and phrases within a text to be included in the final index. When all such words or phrases have been marked, an index including page numbers can be built up by the computer. Benefits are to be gained if changes then have to be made, and the index has to be rebuilt. The same job done by hand is time-consuming, tedious and error-prone.

A similar feature for the start of a document is a table of contents. If extra text is added within a document, the table of contents can be quickly rebuilt.

Reports can be made a lot clearer by using paragraph numbers. Many word processing packages provide a feature that does this. Variations on this theme allow Arabic or Roman numerals, and sub-paragraph numbering as 1.1, 1.2, 1.3 and so on. Whatever system is used, automatic renumbering usually takes place when paragraphs are added or deleted.

One other paragraphing feature on some word processors allows for a bullet point to be placed at the start of several different paragraphs. The bullet point might be one of a number of non-alphabetic characters, and users usually have a choice of bullet character.

Text boxing allows a passage of text to be enclosed within a box of lines. This means that boxed text can be produced without users having laboriously to type individual characters. Further benefits are gained if the text is altered, as text boxes are generally redrawn by the package itself. Most word processors allow a wide choice of boxing styles, with different thickness of border, double borders, shadows behind the boxes and shading of the box background.

Windows and Macintosh word processors allow graphics to be included easily (see later chapters). Some DOS-based word processors also allow for graphics to be included in a document, from a drawing package or from a spreadsheet. Though the output might work perfectly well when sent to the printer, there can be some problems with features like print preview, where a graphic might simply be represented by a box for the space it will occupy.

Simple mathematical functions are provided within some word processors, so that the four basic arithmetical operations can be carried out without the need to use a calculator, physically or on-screen. Such features can be very useful when, for example, word processing a balance sheet, or a quotation for a job. A column of figures might be added in a few keystrokes.

Simple table features in many word processors allow columns and rows to be included. Some have sufficient spreadsheet-like capabilities that users argue they don't need a full-blown spreadsheet. Table features allow not only mathematics to be carried out, but also ensure correct layout on the printer with columns exactly aligned even when proportional spacing is used. Sometimes users carefully line text up on the screen without a table facility, and then find that because of uneven character widths, the text is not lined up on the printer. Table handling also allows for the printing of grids, exchanging of columns and sorting. With mouse-driven programs, the size of the table can be adjusted using mouse control.

Most word processors also allow the user access to the current date to incorporate within documents. Some provide user control over the particular date format used, such as whether the day of the week is included, and whether the month is shown as a word or number. The date function is particularly useful for letters, but can be useful in reports as well. Probably less useful, but as easy to use, is a time function enabling the current time to be incorporated in a document, again in various formats.

An improved impression of a document is gained by the reader if the characters are carefully spaced across the page. Most word processors will justify text. Additional features in some word processors allow text to be kerned and the leading can be altered. 'Kerning' allows for the horizontal adjustment of text within a line, and 'leading' the vertical distance between lines. These techniques are explained in Chapter 10, but apply equally to the more advanced word processors.

———— Other special features ————

A macro feature allows the user to specify a phrase of text which is then recalled whenever it is needed by using one or two keys. This allows for shortcuts in typing. Many systems come with some in-built macros, such as the word 'sincerely'; the date and time may also be accessed with macros. Users can define their own commonly used phrases such as a name, address, employer and so on. A macro can also be used in some systems to store a commonly used set of keystrokes for commands, such as 'move to start of previous paragraph' if such commands are not in-built. A macro might be useful, for example, so that with a simple set of key strokes, the company heading and address is loaded, and the date is inserted ready for a letter to be typed.

Many mouse-based word processors include one or more lines of icons allowing the user to select a feature without having to work through the menus. A typical row (or 'bar') of icons might contain up to 20 symbols representing frequently used features. Different manufacturers have chosen different sets of icons, but there are a number of commonly used ideas. Typical icons would include 'open file', 'save file', 'print', 'undo', 'cut', 'copy', 'bold', 'italic', 'underline', 'centre text', 'spellcheck' and 'thesaurus'. The icon bar is given different names in various packages, such as 'SmartIcons' in Ami Pro, 'Toolbars' in Microsoft Word and 'Button Bar' in WordPerfect.

Normally features on an icon bar are also available through the menu system, and may also be accessible through keyboard shortcuts (for example using ALT key combinations). When these options are combined with the option to access the menu through the mouse, there are typically at least three ways of calling many of the commands. Recent versions of word processors also allow you to create additional entries in the icon bar, and even to have different icon bars for different contexts. This is a useful extension of the macro idea described earlier.

Another feature which improves the usability of a word processor is the use of on-screen colour, whether the final text is to be in colour or not. In some packages, the position of the cursor is remembered so that when you re-load the document, you come back to where you left off.

Another productivity tool allows you to record various details about the file with it, but not as part of the file text. For example, Word for Windows asks for details of the author and the topic. When you are loading a file, you can look for documents not only according to file name and date, but also by author and topic. WordPerfect includes a QuickFinder which can search specified areas or the whole disk for a word or phrase as another way of finding the document that you want. One other short-cut offered for file loading is the listing of the last few documents edited, typically the last four, as entries on the file menu.

Spellchecker dictionaries are made available in a number of languages, and these are easy to select from the menu system. When a word processor is first supplied, you may receive a number of foreign language dictionaries. You should choose the languages carefully at installation – to include them all would take up an inordinate amount of disk space. Check the manual carefully to ensure that additional languages can be installed later if you so wish. If a language has not been installed, then the word processor will either not offer the language on the menu, or will offer it but then display an error message when the relevant file cannot be found.

Some spellchecker features allow a third type of dictionary along with the standard dictionary and a personal dictionary. This is an exceptions dictionary, in which can be held correct spellings which you wish to have reported every time. For example the word 'fro' is a word which I use only very occasionally. If I type 'fro' it is more likely that I intended to type 'for' and mistyped it. It is useful if software can point this out to me when it happens.

Style and grammar checkers will read through a piece of text and offer advice on how to improve your writing. They will pick up the use of a plural verb with a single noun, the use of 'their is', and other mistakes, which are not picked up by a spellchecker. Other poor phrasing, like the use of 'in order to', and 'a lot of', and jargon are also detected. Advice is also given about overuse of particular sentence construction, such as passive verbs. The better style and grammar checkers allow you to specify the form of writing you are using. (Is it a business letter, a report, or a letter to a relative, for example?) This should help to overcome the annoyance of having the same advice given many times about particular grammar styles rather than rules.

Another innovation, as a writer's tool, is to include a measure of text readability. Various formulae have been developed over the years to measure how easy it is to read written text. These formulae depend on factors such as the number of syllables in words, the length of sentences, the frequency of passive verbs and other factors. Two of the most frequently used measures are the Gunning Fog Index and the Fleisch Readability Formula. Each produces a numeric rating with higher numbers indicating harder to read text, but you will have to read the manuals for explanations of precisely what your rating means.

Many word processors now allow for the insertion of graphics within a document, with consequent extra features such as the ability to flow text around a graphic. Word processors differ in the extent to which graphics can be manipulated once they have been imported. Many do not allow you to edit the graphic, though you may be able to resize it and move it or give it a frame. Features such as these have been incorporated by word processor manufacturers as a way of narrowing the gap between word processing and desktop publishing.

Other text formatting features include the ability to 'bend' text so that it can be arched up or down, as well as being presented in one of about 50 different typefaces. These features too are an attempt to narrow the same gap.

——— Specialist word processing ———

Some users need to use an international character set. Some early word processors supported international characters by use of an on-screen table from which a letter could be selected. This may be suitable for the occasional extended character. For regular use, however, many word processors can be customised so that particular key combinations will provide accents over characters. Some systems go further and support foreign keyboard layouts, again after running a simple customising program.

An outliner enables you to control text through headings. Items of text of any length can be associated with each of the headings. Using key commands, you can look either at the whole text, or at just the headings, or the text associated with some headings can be hidden while that with others is not. You can then edit the document by moving headings around, and the associated text is moved with the headings. This allows you to edit a large document while keeping a good overview of its whole structure. The same principle can be applied to sub-sections within a section. Allied with automatic paragraph numbering and renumbering, this can be a very powerful tool for report drafting and re-drafting.

Various packages offer revision marking of text. This allows a second reader to read through somebody else's draft and enter suggested changes. The originator can then read through and decide whether to accept the suggested changes or not. Revision marks are easier to follow if they are presented in colour, in much the same way as handwritten comments on paper text are. A single user might also find revision marking useful to show somebody else a set of proposed changes. It can be very frustrating attempting to read a revised document such as a new policy or contract where it is clear that only a few changes have been made, but you cannot see what they are.

In many contexts, document security is important, and many packages now provide protection, such as password-only access, and encryption of text, so that text is held in coded form which cannot be read without being decoded. There is obviously little point in having password security on a file if access to the raw text can be gained from the operating system. Encryption will mean, of course, that the package will not be able to search the disk for files containing particular words.

Some word processor users want very specialist features within their package, such as symbols greater in size than a single character in mathematical or scientific notation. There are a number of specialist packages on the market to meet these needs. It is particularly important when handling complex formulae which may stretch over several rows (with division signs and so on), that it is possible to specify that several rows be treated as one when editing, otherwise alignment of symbols or parts of symbols can go wrong. Where specialist products have tapped into a niche market, you will often find that the big players in the market will respond by incorporating similar features in their own products.

Other specialist features which some word processors provide include envelope printing, equation editing, and charting. Much of the sales literature will be devoted to such features if a manufacturer feels that it has something unusual to offer.

Clearly many users will invest hundreds of hours in preparing documents within a particular word processor. Should they wish to switch to another product, or to pass a document to somebody who uses another product, the file will probably not be compatible. Each word processor manufacturer, therefore, will provide a set of routines allowing you to convert a document written in another word processor to their own. In early versions, the conversion would take place outside the word processor. In more recent products, the converter is called from within the word processing package. Users should, however, beware that this process is not always as smooth as is sometimes suggested. The main body of text will normally pass accurately, but what will happen to formatting commands? Will foreign characters pass over successfully? What will happen to footnotes and endnotes? Will all the layout commands pass properly?

———————— To DTP or WP? ————————

People regularly ask whether it is necessary to buy desktop publishing software, now that word processing is, as we have seen, so sophisticated. You will see in Chapter 10 what desktop publishing programs can achieve. There is no simple answer to the question whether you need word processing, desktop publishing or both. As soon as we point out a difference between most word processors and desktop publishing, somebody will point out a product on the 'wrong' side of the divide with just the feature we were talking about. Anyway, if there isn't now, there soon will be. The differences between the two software categories really fall into two main groups.

First, each category has its own specialisms which it generally does better. So, word processors are usually better at grammar checking, have large thesauri and so on. Desktop publishing packages are usually better for page layout, text kerning, colour separation of images, producing higher resolution images and so on. Even these distinctions are blurred by some of the latest products in each category.

The second difference is not so much what they can do, but the ease with which they can do it. A word processor might be able to present text at any angle, but can the text be edited once it is at an angle? (The change could be made by going back to the original text and then slanting it again, but this is time-consuming.) A word processor might provide a kerning facility, but is this automatic, or does it require user intervention? An image might be inserted in a document with text flowing around it, but what happens to the text if you then wish to move the image? Will a word search include all text? Will it include headlines? Will it include text within graphics? You might think that you would obtain a good idea from asking the right questions about a package's features. The problem is choosing the right question. In these cases, it is often not a case of asking whether a task can be carried out, but how easy it is. That sort of question is very difficult to frame in order to provoke a useful answer.

—— Some typical products ——

Locoscript Professional 2 Plus, for DOS, is the latest version of the word processor made popular by the Amstrad PCW. Its popularity owes a lot to the large numbers of users who learnt their word processing on a PCW. It is low priced and represents good value, including a spellchecker and thesaurus, but no grammar checker. It includes all the common features of word processors, including a mailmerge which uses its own integrated database for lists of names and addresses. Users who operate the system regularly like it a lot, whilst some new users might find it takes some getting used to. Most users would describe it as a good straightforward product, providing all they need.

At the more expensive end of the price range are several DOS dedicated word processors, such as Microsoft Word 6.0, WordPerfect 6.0 and WordStar 7.0. These could be described as the heavyweights of word processing, and have each been around for about ten years, with new improved versions being released each year. Each provides the full range of the main features described here, supporting several hundred printers, and requiring about 384 K of memory. Each also provides most of the more advanced features. If there are particular combinations of advanced features which you might feel are vital for you, then these might help to narrow down the range of products,. An important factor in your choice may well be how comfortable you feel with the user interface, as clearly some interfaces suit some people better than others.

At the budget end of the Windows word processor market, there are a number of products for around, including Lotus Write 2.0 and WordStar for Windows 2.0. Unless there are particular advanced features which you would make consistent use of, you might ask yourself why you should buy all the power if you are not going to use it. Indeed, some of the features which five years ago were considered to be 'advanced' are now included in packages in this lower price range.

The heavyweight contenders in the Windows arena are Lotus Ami Pro 3.0, Microsoft Word for Windows 6.0, and WordPerfect for Windows 6.0. Each has tried to outdo the other with advanced features such as macros, drag-and-drop, and even support for the others' keystrokes. Each supports the many fonts and printers that can be used within Windows. Again, personal preference is likely to be a deciding factor.

In the Mac software world, a key market leader has always been Claris. Its word processor is MacWrite Pro 1.5. This includes features such as tables, text wrap around graphics, and spellchecker and thesaurus in several languages.

Other Mac products include WordPerfect 3.0, and Microsoft Word 6.0, which their publishers say bringing the benefits of time-tested DOS applications to the Mac platform. There is a similar migration in the other direction with Claris products for Windows.

If you do not want to pay the considerable price of a dedicated word processor you may well be satisfied with an integrated package, such as one of those described in Chapter 11. In deciding whether to buy a dedicated word processor, it might be useful to ask the dealer what you would have with the dedicated product which you would not have with the integrated package from the same manufacturer.

7

DATABASES

The basic idea

A database program stores a variety of information about a set of items, such as details of all CDs in your collection, or the members of your local church, or particulars of business contacts. Having stored various data relating to each item in your set, you can then choose to list chosen items in different orders, select those meeting certain rules, print a label for each item and so on. Be careful that people sometimes use the term 'database' to refer to the data itself, and sometimes to refer to the program that manipulates the data.

A database package allows you build up a file, which consists of records, each made up of a number of fields.

A field is an individual item of information, such as a name, a code number or an address.

A record is made up of a number of related fields, so that, for example, a name, address and telephone number for an individual or a company might make up one record. The data is given meaning by relating separate fields together. For example, an address only has a use when it is somebody's address.

A file is made up of many separate records. A collection of details about all a company's employees would be stored in a file, consisting of one record for each employee, with each record being made up of various field.

———— Some technical terms ————

Over the years a large number of technical terms has been coined in the database world.

In much of the literature, you will come across the terms 'flat file' and 'relational' databases. The term 'flatfile' is used to describe a system that does not allow the interconnection between files. It is similar to an index card system where a set of record cards is stored in a box. For many applications, this approach is all that is needed, to produce mailing lists, to store data on items in a collection, and so on.

If, however, one record has to be linked to records in another file, permanent links should be made so that, for example, several orders in one file are linked to the relevant customer in another file. The term 'relational' is now used to describe any system in which files may need to be related together in ways which need not be determined from the start.

The idea of relating files together is useful, for example, so that when one supplier provides you with 40 different items of stock, your stock control system does not hold 40 copies of the same name, address and telephone number. Space is saved by only storing a single copy of the data, but more importantly, should the address or telephone number change, you will only have to make one amendment to data. In larger business systems, particularly, the potential of data conflict is a major headache in systems design, for once you have two versions of the same information, you are unlikely to know which is the old data and which is correct.

The experienced user of a relational database is able to relate data together in ways that were not anticipated. A typical operation would be to generate a new file with records from one file linking one field in an original file with a field in another. If the values for the field in the original file will match up with only one in the second file, this generates at most the number of records in the original file, and is called a one-to-one relationship. If the original relates to several possible values in the second file, this is called a one-to-many relationship. An example of a one-to-one relationship would be linking customers to a regional office (every address will be in exactly one region). An example of a one-to-many relationship would be linking customers to freelance representatives in their area (there may be many representatives in each area). Where files are joined in this way, many new records will be generated, though these may not necessarily be permanently stored on disk.

The choice of database package and the design of record layouts are vital processes which must be right from the start. A tremendous amount of work can be wasted in entering data in the wrong format in a database which cannot then be reshaped. When similar mistakes are made with other packages, such as a word processor or a spreadsheet, there is usually some way of readjusting the data, or of getting round the problem another way. The database situation is rather different. A file may be designed with 12 fields, say, for contacts in a particular town. If you later discover that you want to search for a particular person's name, or for particular attributes associated with those contacts, then the search becomes exceedingly complex, as all 12 have to be searched every time. If you have invested many hours in entering the data in one form, there is no easy way to reshape it into another.

Some authors also distinguish between data description which allows the user to define and the forms of data to be held, and data manipulation which allows the data to be processed in various forms. All database users will be involved in data manipulation, but not necessarily in data description. Others distinguish between those commands that are designer tools and those that are user tools.

Database users were slower to take up products which use a graphical environment than users of spreadsheets and word processors, but a number of graphical databases are now well established. Amongst the on-screen tools used are buttons similar to those on a video cassette recorder allowing a user to step through one record at a time, rewind to the beginning (first record), fast forward to the last record, and so on. Other graphical interfaces use the scroll bar familiar from other applications. In relational database packages which use a graphical environment, the relationships between files can be established by use of a mouse with a pointing, dragging and clicking technique, which is a far simpler form of dialogue than its text-based equivalent.

Types of data

Databases allow the type of data within a field to be chosen from a number of field types, such as:

- integer numbers, allowing values that are whole numbers only within a nominated range (the range of values will be limited by the design of the package)

- decimal numbers, allowing the storage of fractional numbers (perhaps storing about ten significant digits, and allowing very large and very small numbers)

- text, allowing a series of characters

- logical or Boolean values (stored as true or false, or yes or no)

- date (stored in a standard format, but able to be displayed in a variety of ways, varying the order of the three elements, using text or numbers for the month, and so on)

- memo, allowing a free format input for descriptions or details which will not normally be searched. In many cases, such descriptive fields will be too long for inclusion on a screen with other fields, so the first line will be shown, with a drop-down icon used to reveal the rest of the memo. In some cases memo fields can be formatted with various text and layout attributes to improve the appearance

- picture fields, allowing the user to nominate an exact shape of an entry, such as 9999-9999-9999-9999 describing a credit card field as four four-digit numbers separated by dashes

- user lists, where a complete list of possible values is entered, so that each time a user can select from a list (an example would be CD, cassette or vinyl)

- objects imported from other applications, such as a graphic or a sound file.

Once the database package has been instructed on the format and type of data to be stored, there will normally be a data entry screen. For quick data entry, a table with one record per row would probably suffice, but more normally a data entry screen will be defined.

All data entry to a database involves the entry of data corresponding to the independent fields of the record. Early products concentrated on the definition of records and their manipulation. In recent years, however, much has been done to improve the presentation of the data screens. This process is known generally as screen painting. Questions can now be substituted for the field names. Entries on the form can be spaced appropriately, using different distances between entries and different fonts and sizes for characters. On graphically based systems other more visual techniques are used. Radio buttons allow a choice from a limited number of possibilities in a 'user list', all of which are displayed. Drop down pick lists can be used for a choice from a list where the whole list cannot be displayed on the screen, but the possible values can be looked through with the aid of a scrollable list. Memo fields may be displayed by showing just their first line.

Most data entry systems provide a form of data validation as data is entered. Unsatisfactory data entered is immediately rejected, and an error message is displayed. Most packages will check that data is in the correct format, as specified in the data description. Other rules can be enforced, such as insisting that a specified field cannot be left blank, or that an entry in a field must be unique (so duplicates are checked for on data entry). Some packages provide the designer tools that specify that an entry must be within a particular range.

Data entry might also involve the amendment or deletion of records. Again, some validation may be included within this. In a relational database, a more complex rule, known as 'referential integrity' involves the package looking in other tables to ensure that a record is not deleted if other records relate to it. For example, you should not delete a customer's details when there are still outstanding invoices in another file.

Manipulating data

Some fields of a database might not be entered by the user, but might be calculated from other fields within a record, using some kind of formula. Fields of this kind need not necessarily be stored permanently, as the computer can calculate them when they are needed. Another term which is sometimes used for calculated fields is 'dependent' fields, in contrast to user-entered fields, which are 'independent'. If a field is entirely dependent on others, then it will need to be recalculated when the original data changes. In some packages, this is automatic; in others it must be requested by the user. In the best packages, the user can turn the automatic recalculation on or off.

A key field is a field that uniquely identifies a record from all the others in a file. Common examples are serial numbers and customer account numbers. In many data processing problems, one of the first tasks is to determine whether there is a unique field already available or whether some kind of unique identifying number will have to be added to control the system. Data will repeatedly be retrieved with this unique key value.

Modern database packages are very flexible, so that, for example, if a user decides that a new field is needed in each record this can be added later. (Early databases made such changes possible, but only after a series of operations involving renaming files, copying them with blank entries which only then could be altered.) Adding a new field to each record is achieved by editing the data structure. When a new field is added to each record, it will be blank, so the user will either define its value through a formula, or go through all the records adding a value for the field.

When data has been entered, you may wish to view the contents of the file, and possibly change entries. One method of record access involves displaying one record at a time on screen. Any fields that have to be altered can be edited on the screen, and then saved in their amended form. The second method of editing is to display many records at one time, normally with one record per line. Editing is carried out in a similar way, allowing the user to move between records on the same screen. Where records are longer than, say, 80 characters, the fields will scroll across as the cursor is moved.

Some databases provide a facility to view records without editing. This feature is useful for avoiding accidental changes to data. It is an essential feature if your system is to incorporate security, particularly with a multi-user system, where you may want to allow some people to access data but not to alter it.

The user dialogue design of databases contrasts with that of most other packages concerning on-screen data changes. If you attempt to leave a spreadsheet or word processor without saving changes, you will receive a warning message, and may at that point make the changes permanent. Most database packages do not provide this option because normally they save data changes immediately; therefore there is never a difference between the data displayed and that stored.

Users will wish to add or delete whole records in a database. To improve user flexibility, a request for the deletion of a record does not immediately delete a record, but instead just marks it for deletion. From this point it is treated as if it were not there, but if a user discovers that the record was deleted by mistake, then it can be recovered using some other function. There will be a point at which records marked for deletion will need to be deleted physically, enabling storage space to be re-used, and this will be carried out under user control. Obviously, this will make all the other operations that much faster, as fewer records are then stored for use.

The order in which you retrieve data can be altered. This can be done either in a physical or a logical manner. The physical method involves sorting the data into order, whereby a simple user command initiates a re-ordering of the file. The more flexible alternative is to build a logical index, which the program can then use to retrieve the data as if it were in a different order. Apart from saving time in physically moving records, indexes are useful because you can build several different indexes in the same file, so that you can work through records in a number of different orders, depending on the need at the time. In particular, different reports might require records in different orders. Once an index has been built, most database packages will now keep the index automatically up to date, reflecting deletions, additions and amendments as they occur. A sorted system cannot easily achieve this.

Indexes may be built based on the values in several fields, and this is essential if the field on which an index is to be built is not unique. Consider, for example, building an index in order of surname. Several people might have the same surname. A rule can be used that, where the surnames are the same, a secondary field is used to resolve the conflict, namely the forename.

Reports

A major purpose of a database is to generate useful reports, either displayed on the screen, or printed out. A report will be based on search criteria, that is the condition that you are searching for. An example might be 'all the customers who owe over £50', or 'all the people over 40', or 'all the female employees who have a car and live less than ten miles away'. Conditions can be combined, using the operations of 'AND', 'OR' and 'NOT'. These are normally explained well in manuals. 'AND' allows you to specify that a number of conditions must all be fulfilled. 'OR' combines conditions such that any one being true means that the record will pass the test. 'NOT' allows a test to be reversed. In combination, these operations will allow very complex searches to be carried out. Sales literature will usually boast of the most complex conditions which can be set up in searches, which can be off-putting to a new user.

Two terms which are bandied about in database sales literature are SQL and QBE. SQL stands for Structured Query Language, which was first developed for IBM mainframes, and is an attempt to standardise the process of interrogating databases. Databases which support SQL are available on mainframes, minicomputers and personal computers, and the argument is that, once the format of queries has been learnt, it can then be used on a wide range of platforms. SQL uses a very text-oriented approach. QBE stands for Query By Example, and was again developed for IBM mainframe systems. A framework showing the various fields is displayed, and search conditions are entered against the fields. Values entered can seek exact matches or ranges of values and can be logically combined with 'AND' and 'OR' operations. Proponents of SQL would point out that SQL commands can be stored and edited, which is a lot more difficult with QBE.

As well as specifying a search condition, you can usually specify which records are to be searched, so that only those records in one particular section of the file are examined. So, if an index has been built, and customers are in regional order, you can specify that only that region is to be counted within a particular search. This restriction on the operation is usually called the scope of the search. Of course, the scope of a search could be the whole file, but experience might show that such operations are unnecessarily slow, if the computer is examining several thousand records which you know will not be the ones for which you are looking.

Report formats can be specified, so that record matching the criteria are printed across the page as one record per line, or you might decide to present records with one field per line. The person specifying the search can usually choose which fields from the records are printed, in which format, and in which order. Summary features allow reports to include totals of particular fields, averages, maximum values, minimum values, and standard deviation. Records can be grouped within a report, so that sub-totals are produced for each category or group part way through the report. Reports can also include headings carrying over on each page, page numbers, and control over margins, in much the same way as in word processing.

Address labels will generally be produced using a version of the report generating software.

Database packages normally come with extensive 'help' files, so that the user can have on-screen explanations of what can be done.

——— Database programming ———

Many database packages allow for a series of instructions to be stored so that they can be recalled. Many of these packages therefore come with an inbuilt programming language, which includes all the formal language structures, such as loops and conditional statements. Because many personal computer databases, such as FoxBase and Clipper, work with commands of a similar form to the various dBase products, a generic title of xBase has been coined for such products. Early database systems used an interpreter which took one line of program at a time, worked out what it should do, and then carried the instruction out. This is a useful tool when developing applications. When a system is to be used in earnest, however, an interpreter will slow things down considerably. Database compilers are provided, therefore, which allow programs written in languages like xBase to be turned into fast running machine code. An added advantage of this system is that compiled applications can be run without the original full database development system. The user only needs what is termed a run-time system, which manufacturers sell at a lower price.

Multi-user systems

Compatibility of databases is a major selling point for many of the packages, and compatibility is more far-reaching for database packages than for other applications such as word processing. A user may wish to import data held in a format used by a different database by converting formats. There may be times, however, when data needs to be examined and used in its current format without conversion, such as when using somebody else's data either from disk or through a network. Therefore many database packages boast a range of formats which they can manipulate.

Another form of database manipulation involves cross-tabulation of data. A user might wish to search a database looking for two fields, producing a grid recording the occurrence of combinations of different values for the two fields. This process will create a table in a spreadsheet form for subsequent analysis.

Many databases are designed for use over a network in a multi-user environment. This will normally mean that the package must allow for the locking of data at various levels. Data can be kept confidential to particular users by using a password system. Particular fields might only be accessible to special users who have a different use category. Systems can be designed, for example, to allow users access to view data but not to change it. When data is being used over a network, however, there are security implications beyond privacy. It would not normally be helpful if two users were accessing the same record and both attempted to alter it at the same time. A feature known as record locking used on some systems is designed to ensure that while many people can view a record at the same time, only one can have the privileges to alter the data at any one time (usually on a first-come, first-served basis). A blunter instrument to crack this problem is file locking which means that once one person has control of a file, nobody else can make any alterations anywhere in the file until control is relinquished by the first person.

———— Some typical products ————

In the DOS market, one of the products which has been around the longest is Borland's dBase IV 2.0 . It requires a minimum of 2 MB of memory, and can handle 40 open files at once. It supports its own programming language, mimicked by a number of other similar products. Whilst it works using an interpreter, a compiler is available as an optional extra. Record locking is available, as is the import of files in various other formats, though competitors would claim that not as many file formats are supported as in some products.

Microsoft FoxBase+ 2.1 is another xBase product. It has a similar huge maximum number of records per file (measured in millions). Another DOS product in this category is Clipper from CA .

Users who have stayed loyal to the xBase camp would argue that there are a lot of third-party products, skills and literature available because these products have been around for so long.

For the Windows market, there are a number of budget products, such as Lotus Approach 3.0, and Borland Paradox for Windows 4.5. Each requires a minimum of 2 MB, with Approach allowing a maximum of 18 files open, and Paradox 60. Most users are unlikely to handle more than 18 files at once! Approach does not contain a programming language, but it does support screen and report painting. The reverse is true for Paradox. Both support DDE, OLE (see Chapter 13) and record locking.

At the higher priced end of the Windows market are DataEase Express for Windows, Microsoft FoxPro 2.6, and Microsoft Access 2.0.

DataEase is the Windows version of a DOS database which has been popular for a number of years. It allows 100 open files, with text fields having a maximum of 4000 characters. It supports macros, but has no programming language in its own right. It supports DDE and OLE, through which sound can be supported as a field of a record.

FoxPro for Windows has a loyal following, particularly amongst those who previously used similar products under DOS. This also proves to be an advantage if users need to transfer programs from a previous xBase environment, which could be a huge time saver. It requires a minimum memory of 4 MB, and allows 225 open files. It includes both programming language and macros. Its supporters claim that it is very user-friendly.

Microsoft Access requires a minimum of 8 MB, and allows 32 open files. Its programming language, Access Basic, has the advantage of familiarity to many programmers brought up on traditional Basic. Access benefits from the Microsoft approach of providing Wizards, which are step-by-step guides helping users to create quick designs. The help system is also highly praised, as it makes use of explanatory screens called 'Cue Cards'. Another strength is its ability to carry out comprehensive validation on data entry.

A number of the DOS and Windows databases, such as FoxPro 2.5 are also available on the Mac platform. A similar migration has taken place in the opposite direction. Claris Filemaker Pro 2.1 is said to have an easy-to-use graphical data entry system It has good report-generating facilities. Operations can be automated using scripting, which includes insertion of elements through point-and-click. Some users would find the abilities to import files, particularly indexes, in other formats, limited. Claris Filemaker might appeal particularly to those who work in an organisation with a mixture of PCs and Macs.

As with most other applications, potential purchasers of a dedicated database might like to consider whether the purchase is necessary, or whether an integrated package might provide sufficient facilities (see Chapter 11).

8

—— SPREADSHEETS ——

—— The basic idea of a spreadsheet ——

A spreadsheet package is designed to allow you to manipulate data held as a series of rows and columns within a grid layout. Each entry within a spreadsheet is uniquely identified by giving details of the row and column that it is in, called its cell reference. The values in the cells are related together, and this inter-relation gives spreadsheets their real power.

At any one time, there is a limit to the amount of a spreadsheet that can be shown on a screen. On a normal 14 inch screen about 20 rows can be shown, and perhaps eight columns. Spreadsheets allow users to view different cells by moving a cursor which indicates the current cell. One line of the screen display usually shows the contents of the current cell. Some spreadsheets have a 'zoom' facility to allow more cells to be seen on the screen, though with each cell smaller.

A cell in a spreadsheet will contain one of a number of types of entry. A data entry is a number entered for manipulation. A formula allows simple or complex relationships to be established between cells, by including in the formula reference to the other cells. Text entries are used for headings, labels and explanations, and cannot be manipulated in the same way as data entries. Some spreadsheets allow for a fourth type of entry, called a logical entry, which can have the value TRUE or FALSE.

The strength of a spreadsheet package is that, once a model has been built using one set of figures, a different set of figures can be entered to see how changes will affect the overall picture. This powerful idea led to spreadsheets being described as 'what if?' programs, because the user can experiment with a model, and find out what happens in different circumstances.

A whole range of commands is available through the menu to allow the user to manipulate a spreadsheet. Most obviously, commands are provided to save a spreadsheet model to disk, to load it back and to print it. When printing, there will be a number of options such as printing out all or part of a model, printing in condensed characters, in different type fonts, and printing sideways.

There are two types of printout available. A data printout provides the results for a particular set of data. A model printout provides the formulae that lie behind the cells. This model printout would usually only be a requirement of the person building the model in the first place, and not of the day-to-day user of a model that has already been built. Model printouts might either be in table format (matching the layout of the data model), or as one cell entry per row, as some formulae might be very long. Before a printout is obtained, a print preview can be checked, so that the user can see what it will look like.

Formulae can be built up and adjusted in a number of ways. Rather than the user having to type each cell reference in a formula, cell references can generally be entered by pointing the cursor at the relevant cell, either through cursor control keys or the mouse.

A spreadsheet package is able to copy formulae, and to do this intelligently. Formulae are normally adjusted as they are copied to allow for their use in different rows or columns. Normally a formula might be used to relate cells within a column, such as the final entry being the sum of the ones above in the table. A similar formula is needed at the bottom of every other column relating entries in that column together. The spreadsheet software is therefore geared to change all references in the formula to a particular column as it is copied across. The parallel situation of copying row formulae into other rows is just the same, with row numbers being automatically adjusted. If users do not want formulae to be adjusted, they simply have to tell the computer so.

Copying on mouse-driven systems can be achieved through a 'drag and drop' approach. The cell or cells to be copied are highlighted, and then with a mouse button depressed the area to be filled is high-lighted. A further development of automatic cell entry adjustment is called 'autofill', which allows the computer to make an 'intelligent' guess at further entries. So if one text entry holds 'January', and it is to be expanded across, further entries will be displayed with the following months. Of course, if the 'guess' is not the correct one, the user has lost nothing, and simply must make the entries by hand. A similar facility exists when formulae are dragged across with adjustments being made.

More complex formulae arrangements can be made by giving a range of cells a name, so that a meaningful name can be used in a formula, with operations on the whole range of numbers. Typical range formulae allow the use of functions which add up the elements in a range, find the largest value, find the average and so on.

Formulae, once entered, can be edited, either to improve or correct the model. Editing has to be carried out on a single cell at a time. Editing should be considerably quicker than having to re-enter a complete formula. Clearly, if a range of cells has the same error, it is best to correct one of them and then copy it to the others.

When models are being developed, you might want to add rows or columns to fit in additional information. This involves moving entries, which the computer will do for you, and at the same time it will adjust all the cell references and ranges that refer to cells that have moved. Similar adjustments are made if rows or columns are deleted.

Display settings can be altered to improve the appearance of a model. Most spreadsheets allow the user to choose a number of different fonts and sizes for entries. This then allows headings and results, for example, to be emphasised. The width of columns can also be altered in order to display longer numbers or text. Some also allow the user to adjust the height of rows, so that either taller fonts can be used, or text spread over more than one line. Some programs automatically adjust the cell height if a taller font is chosen. By adjusting the height or width to zero, or by selecting a 'hide' command, rows or columns can be hidden. On some spreadsheets there is a command allowing the user to set the cell width to that of the longest current entry in the column.

Various display formats can be selected for cells, so that numeric values can be displayed as rounded to the nearest whole number, or to two decimal places, or to some other format. Some users are confused by this, thinking that changing the format changes what is actually held in the cell. In most systems, the information is held with the same accuracy whatever the display format. Display formats for text allow users to display text at the left edge of, the right edge of, or in the centre of the column.

Whenever a cell value is changed by a user, there will be other values which depend on that value through formulae. These values will therefore need to be recalculated. There may well then be a knock-on effect, with other values then being dependent upon those changed values and so on. This process is called recalculation. With a complicated spreadsheet, this can necessitate a whole chain of recalculations. This process of multiple recalculation will obviously be necessary in order to compute accurate values. Sometimes, though, a user might want to change a whole series of values before a meaningful recalculation can take place. The process of entering a new set of data might be considerably slowed down if a meaningless recalculation takes place after each new entry. For this reason, many spreadsheet packages allow the user to turn the recalculation facility off, and to request recalculation only when it is wanted.

A good spreadsheet will also give the user choice over recalculation order, so that values are either calculated a row at a time or a column at a time. Depending on the style in which the spreadsheet has been written, this can make a difference to the values worked out.

Once a user has built a model, various protection features can be used, so that accidental changes are not made. When you design a spreadsheet you should have clearly separated areas, one for users to enter the values on which calculations are to be based, another for interim calculations and a third for adequate display of the results. If somebody else is going to use your model, he or she will normally only need to alter the first of these three areas. Cell protection can include locking of cells or hiding of cells. Neither of these methods, of course, is foolproof. If a user knows how to unlock cells or reveal hidden cells, the original can be corrupted. Users, though, who have that much knowledge should realise that they need to take care not to corrupt the work.

——— Other features to look for ———

Many more features can be found in sophisticated packages. In recent years the number of features has snowballed as each manufacturer adds extra commands in an attempt to sneak ahead of the field.

A whole set of functions which carry out calculations on sets of values is supplied with each of the spreadsheets now on sale. Some have as many as 300 different functions available. Many of these functions, such as average, standard deviation, the integer part of a number and the square root, are probably of use to a wide range of users. Others, such as Bessel functions for engineers, hexadecimal numbers for electronics, and future values for accountants are of more specialist appeal.

To improve the appearance of a spreadsheet, boxes can be drawn around an area of cells. Various border lines can be selected for boxes, and several shadings can be selected. Many of these design features are only available on systems that use as Microsoft Windows or on Macintosh but not on those using a pure text environment.

In a graphical environment it is also possible to provide on-screen buttons for some of the most commonly used features. One of these is summation of a range of cells. Again using 'intelligent' guesses, some spreadsheets, when told that cell is to contain a sum, can supply a suggested range which again saves the user some input.

As with word processors, the appearance of a well-presented spreadsheet can be marred by a few simple spelling mistakes. Several spreadsheet packages now incorporate spellchecker features.

Date features are also very important for many spreadsheet applications. Such features might include turning a date into the corresponding day of the week, calculating the number of days between two dates, or adding a given number of days to one date to produce another, and the ability to display dates in different formats. Access is also available to the current date, with dates usually being held as integers. Similar functions are available to access and manipulate times.

Simple alternative choices can be set up with conditional statements. These are normally in a form which says 'if this condition is true, calculate the value in this way, otherwise calculate it in that way'. Conditions, known as Boolean values, can also be manipulated through some specific functions, either for inclusion in conditional statements or as entries in their own right.

Sort facilities allow a spreadsheet package to rearrange data in order. When sorting the rows of a table, the user will need to specify an area which is to be affected by the sort. This will include a column whose values will be sorted and associated columns which will move in concert with them. Identical facilities will allow columns to be sorted by specifying which rows are to be involved. Users should beware that once data is sorted it may not be possible to return data to its original order unless it has previously been stored as a separate file.

Many financial problems involve values that depend upon which band of values a particular entry falls in. In a manual system, a person would look up this information through a table. A similar look-up table feature is provided with many spreadsheets. A cell formula can be set up which will contain a value from a table consisting of two columns. The first would contain the upper limit of each range, and next to it, in the next column would be the value or rate to be used for entries in that range. Such a system would be ideal, for example, in calculating tax rates, interest or national insurance, where the percentage rate changes depending upon the range into which another value falls.

Even before the advent of Microsoft Windows, the concept of a window within a spreadsheet was born. This allowed users to see different parts of the same spreadsheet or different spreadsheets on the same screen. Values could also be moved between them. The terminology has now become more complex, with some systems referring to panes as well as windows, and facilities allowing the synchronisation of their movement. Multitasking systems also allow several versions of the same package to run at the same time for swopping in and out. All these can be used as different ways of achieving the same things. Most spreadsheet models will be bigger than the screen display allows. The screen display can be adapted so that the user sees the original input data and the final results, without the screen being cluttered by intermediate calculations.

———— Even more features ————

The spreadsheet concept is, by its very nature, a two dimensional concept. One category of values, say the types of goods sold, will form the rows of a spreadsheet. Another category will form the columns, say sales areas within the country. In this way, a spreadsheet might be prepared for a particular month. A similar spreadsheet might be needed for next month, and the month after. At the end of a quarter or year, the complete totals may be needed. This could involve seventeen different spreadsheets, with virtually identical formulae and layout. A number of features are provided by many spreadsheets to handle such a situation.

A set of spreadsheets which are similar in this way can be declared as a set (called something like a 'workbook'). The user can nominate which values can vary between versions and which are fixed. Different versions within the set can be given titles, with versions being accessed through a system of tags rather like those distinguishing sections of a Filofax. Some versions in the set can be generated as totals from others in the set. This process is known as consolidation.

Another popular use for the grouping of spreadsheets is to enable a number of possible scenarios to be examined. In particular, three spreadsheets might be identical in their calculations, but the initial assumptions about variable factors may differ. Three common scenarios to be explored are the best case (most optimistic assumptions), the worst case (most pessimistic), and the most likely case. These three versions are most conveniently held as a set so that, under user control, if a change is made to the controlling spreadsheet's manner of calculation or other entries, this is automatically reflected in each scenario.

The capacity for a computer to perform many calculations very quickly can be seen in the 'goal seeking' feature available on some spreadsheets. These facilities allow a user to carry out tasks such as optimisation or linear programming. In essence, a spreadsheet is built with multiple cell dependencies. The user can then specify that the computer should step through a whole variety of situations. The goal is to find a particular value for a nominated cell (usually one which is at the end of a long chain of dependencies) by varying the values in another cell (usually a data entry cell). These systems are aided by the user offering an initial sensible guess at the value which is being sought, as this reduces the time taken. The basic principle of such a system is that the computer works out the answer for one guess, then another; then by examining which value was closer to the desired answer, it generates yet another guess and rejects the worst guess so far. This process will (normally) converge on a correct solution as the two best guesses come closer and closer together. Schemes like these are very useful for equation solving and interest calculations.

An alternative or additional approach to handling compound sets of data is provided in some spreadsheets by an outlining command. This allows one row, for example, to be marked as a summary line. Other lines which then work towards making up that line can be 'collapsed', so that they are temporarily hidden. In this way several sub-totals, each calculated from several values, may make up a grand total. Outlining allows the user to hide all but the sub-totals and grand totals, or to expand the original values back for manipulation. Collapsing need not, of course, be limited to the number of levels described here. Data might be collapsed either to allow the user to see the global picture or for reasons of confidentiality. An outlined spreadsheet on screen can look very odd to a user because the row numbers will be anything but the normal consecutive ones; row numbers for collapsed lines will be missing. Collapsing through an outline might be particularly useful for a printout. Before the advent of outlining, it was common to see a worksheet with various rows copied down to the bottom of a spreadsheet simply to build up only those parts that were to be printed.

Array operations allow an operation to be carried out on every element of an area of several rows and columns. Examples include checking whether a specific value is in a table, counting the number of entries of a particular value in a table, and placing a set of entries in rank order. These are all achieved by a process called iteration over the whole table. These features are very useful in statistical analysis.

Auditing features allow somebody who is writing a spreadsheet to search for errors. Whilst most users are clear that programs written with languages like Pascal and C must be tested before use, fewer people seem to insist on having their spreadsheets tested. Auditing allows a user to nominate a cell and then see all the cells which depend on that value. Alternatively, you could look at all the cells on which the nominated cell depends. Tools are provided so that you can see errors or possible errors. One typical error is reference within a formula to blank cells. Another error is a circular reference, which means that a cell depends for its value on its own value, which is clearly impractical, and usually unintentional.

As with many other software packages nowadays, manufacturers of spreadsheets pride themselves on producing products which are compatible with other products in the same category, and which can be linked to other types of software. Each major spreadsheet comes from a different manufacturer, so they tend to use different file formats. In leading spreadsheet literature, you will see reference to a number of well-used formats, and most packages are able to import files designed for other spreadsheets. This, of course, is a major selling point, so that purchasers who change from one supplier to another do not lose the value of investment in models built up over the years. The model will be passed over into a new format. There are some problems of detail, though, most obviously if you have used a function in one spreadsheet which is not available in the one you are translating to. The better translators will point out compatibility problems to the user. The other point to watch for is to ensure that your new package is able to translate from the correct version of your old package. Some of the latest spreadsheets even go as far as allowing you to use menus and enter data as if the product were some other spreadsheet. This means that all the training time invested in users using one interface does not go to waste.

Links from other types of software to a spreadsheet have always been a key feature. In particular, the ability to import from a database has been incorporated by many manufacturers. Each database record will be entered as a row of your new spreadsheet. It remains to be seen whether such discussions become theoretical, because of the much more open approach to links through graphical environments.

When it comes to outputting data, the picture is more variable. Some spreadsheet manufacturers do not want to encourage you to export data in a form for another spreadsheet, whereas others positively encourage it. Some output from spreadsheets might also be possible in common database formats, exporting each line of the spreadsheet as a record.

Several powerful spreadsheets now boast a wide range of database functions. These allow the user to carry out the most simple database activities. Data is normally entered as one row per record, but spreadsheets will normally only support flat-file databases (see Chapter 7). Records (rows) can then be sorted or extracted. Extraction normally works by establishing test criteria and a range of records to be tested. The records that match the test criteria are then copied to another area of the spreadsheet. Extraction criteria can use complex combinations of logical conditions. Other database functions allow the user to find the sum, average, maximum or minimum number of records that match given criteria. Spreadsheet manufacturers would argue that they supply all the functions which most people use on a database anyway.

A facility known as 'data parse' in some spreadsheets allows data held in a wide range of forms to be read, and the spreadsheet will make the best guess at splitting the items into columns. In this way, data held for a payroll, for example, might be read, and so long as there was a clear character separating each record, the data, being of a consistent layout, would be read into columns of the spreadsheet. If your data is odd and does not carry over properly then, as the manuals would have it, you have lost nothing.

Most spreadsheets provide a wide range of graphics capabilities. Spreadsheet packages will generally lack the range of graphics commands of the specialist graphics packages, but the spreadsheet programs benefit from a wider range of types of calculation from which graphics can be produced.

Spreadsheets will usually present data in the form of line graphs (a series of dots joined together on a two-dimensional grid), bar graphs (blocks of various heights reflecting values produced), and pie charts (where the size of each slice reflects its share of the whole). Each diagram will be able to include labels, legends and titles for explanation purposes, with colours varied at the user's control.

More advanced graphics features may also be included, such as three dimensional diagrams, graphs which use polar co-ordinates, contour surfaces in three dimensions, and wireframe diagrams. Three dimensional graphs are used to plot a set of values for two factors which vary, such as a set of bars for sales for different areas for different years. The views of a three-dimensional diagram can be altered in some packages by rotation, so that it can be looked at from different angles.

Many spreadsheets use a dialogue through which a user selects precisely what form of diagram is required. There may be as many as five stages in this selection. Users may have to nominate an area of data, choose a chart type, choose a style of diagram within the type, nominate whether data runs across or down, and then add labels in various places. When a subsequent chart is to be created, the program will suggest each of these values staying the same, so the user can work through the same dialogue, only changing those values which are necessary.

———— Taking it even further ————

In using a spreadsheet, you will find yourself repeating the same set of instructions. A 'macro' allows you to store a series of commands for future use. In this way programs of macro instructions can be stored as part of a spreadsheet for future use. The form in which macros are built and stored is explained in great detail in spreadsheet manuals. Macros are normally stored with one command per cell.

Instead of writing your own macros, however, you may well wish to purchase ready-written macros. By buying such 'off the shelf' solutions to particular problems, you are buying a ready-to-use tested version of a spreadsheet. If you buy a ready-made macro and set of skeleton models, all you need to do is to learn how to use them properly. Many users therefore only need to learn how to run a macro rather than how to write one.

Some macro programs actually allow programmers to set up their own menus which appear in place of the normal spreadsheet ones. This approach allows for better design aimed at the needs of a particular user, who may not even realise that a spreadsheet is being used. One example might be an on-screen calendar system with various specific menus for working forwards or backwards through months and years. The user may not realise that the screen display, a month at a time, is built around a spreadsheet. Another advantage of the use of amended menus is that many of the normal features of the spreadsheet can be hidden from the user if access to them is not really essential.

Many of the leading spreadsheet packages are very powerful and include a huge number of facilities. Though computer memories are now available with huge capacities, there is no point loading a whole range of facilities which you will not use. The increased size of packages and the decrease in speed that this can bring are particularly noticeable where several applications are loaded at once in a desktop environment. This is one of the reasons for the development with some spreadsheets of add-in programs. Add-in programs are supplied as a particular file type and add further commands to the menus or extend the range of other features. A second reason for the use of add-ins is to customise a generic spreadsheet to a specific user's context. A third motive for spreadsheet producers is that by encouraging third party suppliers to produce compatible products as add-ins, and making the process easy, development of the spreadsheet market continues.

Many spreadsheets using a graphical desktop interface provide one or more on-screen buttons which launch powerful sections of programs. One example already quoted is the launch of graphical commands. Other single buttons provide features such as context sensitive tips. These are different from help screens, which give general descriptions of features. The new breed of 'tip' facilities actually anticipates and suggests what you probably want to do next, or even suggest what you might be doing wrong. ('Are you sure you want to do it this way. It is more usual to do it this way.')

Spreadsheets are available with the usual level of security, password protection and encryption options relevant to any software area. Spreadsheet data can be particularly sensitive if it contains information about company finances, and, other than when it is in use, such data might need to be encrypted, stored on floppy disk only, or both.

—— A new breed of spreadsheet ——

In the last couple of years, new products described as 'dynamic spreadsheets' have been launched. Their approach is substantially different, to the extent that some people would claim that dynamic spreadsheets should be considered as a separate software category of their own.

Dynamic spreadsheets are built around the notion that many complex businesses or other problems are based around considerably more than three variable factors. This means that even the grouping of spreadsheets and consolidation are not sufficient. When you have built a spreadsheet with particular rows and columns, and then versions (for a third variable), in a traditional spreadsheet you must persevere with one particular view of the data. Dynamic spreadsheets allow you to 'pivot' the data, so that you can show data of more dimensions and change the way it is grouped. It can be described as looking at several different aspects of the same dice. This powerful facility does mean that, upon loading, a dynamic spreadsheet looks very different, as models are built up by creating the categories of values that are to be stored. For example, a four-dimensional system could involve the four categories of months of the year, type of product, area of sales and customer type. So, for each of these four categories, data needs to be held for any combination of possible values. Different views would then allow, for example, a table of sales to be cross-tabulated by customer type in each sales area. The data, by pivoting, could be represented by product for each month of the year.

—— Some sample spreadsheets ——

DOS spreadsheets are sold at two broad price levels. In an effort to compete with other products in the market, a number of spreadsheets which had formerly been at the higher end of the price range have become much cheaper. Amongst these are CA SuperCalc 5.5, and Borland Quattro Pro 4.0. Both of these support spreadsheets of nearly 10 000 rows and 256 or so columns. SuperCalc will support three-dimensional spreadsheet models, will support Lotus 1-2-3 menus, and produces a wide range of graphics of nine basic types. It also provides spreadsheet auditing facilities through the Test command, and a versatile flat-file database facility. Quattro Pro for DOS is able to read files created by Borland Paradox.

Lotus 1-2-3 is a long-established spreadsheet program, which gained an initial domination in the market, so many users are familiar with its style and commands. Macros have always been an important part of 1-2-3, to the extent that many other manufacturers produce spreadsheets which read 1-2-3 macros as well as 1-2-3 data files. A thriving market for third party macros was established. There are now two versions of 1-2-3 available. 1-2-3 Go is a beginners version, which provides all the features that many users will ever need and is mid-priced. The latest version of the full-blown edition is Lotus 1-2-3 version 3.4a, which costs much more, but which provides a very large number of different graph types, and integration with other Lotus applications.

One shareware product, As-Easy-As, was designed to be very similar to 1-2-3, but as a much cheaper product. It provides many similar features and as many functions, plus a simple manual with a lot of help screens. It only allows one file to be open at any time (as did earlier versions of Lotus 1-2-3).

In the Windows sector, there are a number of key products. Borland Quattro Pro for Windows 5.0 is one low-priced spreadsheet which users consider to be good for graphics, applications generation and consolidation of several spreadsheets.

At the upper end of the price range, Microsoft produces Excel 4.0. It is noted for its wide range of font styles and sizes, with the manual making particular emphasis on how useful this is for visually impaired people. It integrates with Microsoft Word and PowerPoint. One key advantage is that it uses the same file format for Windows and the Macintosh, allowing easy transfer for organisations using both platforms. Its 'Wizards' take you step by step through complex tasks. It includes a Scenario Manager, and a Customisable Toolbar to make frequently used features easily accessible. It boasts 310 functions.

Lotus produces both 1-2-3 for Windows 4.01, and Improv 2.0. The former is the latest version of the very popular 1-2-3. The latter has been seen to set the pace in dynamic spreadsheeting, allowing operations such a pivoting, and has a large number of functions.

9

——— GRAPHICS ———

- Different types of graphics packages -

Nowadays, most users will want to create some form of graphics to enliven documents, displays and presentations. Graphics programs have moved beyond the sphere of the hobbyist because of higher resolution, sharper colours and the wide acceptance of the use of the mouse. Many people now use ready-made artwork to save time and improve the appearance of their work. Graphics are now used both in desktop publishing and to some extent in word processing. Packages which are normally termed 'graphics programs' are those in which the user can originate artwork and can make major revisions to pictures.

Graphics programs are crudely divided into four main categories. These are:

- painting or illustrating programs, primarily designed to computerise the process of freehand drawing

- drawing programs, which allow the user to build up complex line drawings using tools and shapes which can be combined

- photo-retouching programs, which enable a user to take a scanned image and adapt it for use on its own or in combination with other images

- presentation graphics programs, which allow a user to build up a sequence of slides or moving images for display.

Two problems arise, however, when attempting to make these distinctions too rigid. First, you will find common features in several of these categories, perhaps implemented in more or less sophisticated versions. Thus the categories are not entirely separate. Secondly, some of the more advanced packages contain programs from several of these categories, as a single 'graphics package' may contain various different programs.

The difference between painting and drawing packages

'Painting' packages allow the user to use a series of tools to create a picture on screen which is stored as a complete set of cells, with the contents of each screen cell being remembered. This 'raster' or 'bit-mapped' approach allows the on-screen manipulation of graphics so that the image can be made to look exactly right. This approach is very heavy on memory usage, even for simple pictures (with some savings through compression, described later). The entire background, for example, even if it is all the same colour, will be stored bit by bit. The method is ideally suited, however, for users who are good at freehand drawing, as they can produce their own unique images in a form that can be stored and manipulated.

'Drawing' packages, on the other hand, allow the manipulation of pictures made up of a series of shapes. These can be placed on the screen, moved, stretched, made to change colour and so on. Information is held on each shape separately and any picture consists of the combination of shapes on it. This approach is sometimes referred to as 'vector graphics'.

The two approaches are quite different. Because it uses on-screen bit manipulation the 'painting' approach may mean that the resolution of drawings is limited by the resolution of the screen. Any printing of such 'paintings' can, at best, be at the same resolution as the screen, and so shapes can appear with jagged edges. 'Drawings' on the other hand can be rescaled for the printer in use at the time, and are not limited by screen resolution. In some cases, 'drawing' programs are capable of supporting resolutions of over 25 000 dots per inch.

In practical use, systems of either type can be given fairly similar appearances. Both will support a 'fill' feature, for example, which will change the colour inside a specified area with a colour or pattern. Differences might be seen, though, in the detailed execution of the command. Filling a fixed shape in a 'drawing' will be carried out through calculation from the detail of the shape. With a 'painting' individual pixels will mark the boundary, and the shape will be filled by 'bleeding' the coloured 'ink' outwards until it reaches cells which form the border. Interesting effects occur if the border has a gap in it, as the 'ink' seeps out.

—— Features to look for in painting ——

Most painting programs rely on the use of a mouse or trackerball, though a few are able to use other devices such as a graphics tablet. The graphics tablet, with its precise stylus, is necessary if very accurate drawing has to be carried out.

A typical painting screen will use most of the screen as a drawing area, with various 'tools' placed around the edges of the screen. An area of the screen is normally reserved for the palette of ink colours which can be selected. Normally only a limited range of colours can be displayed at one time; others becoming available by cycling through different versions of the palette.

Another part of the screen will be used for the painting tools, such as a paintbrush, a spray can, a stipple brush, a pencil, scissors, an eraser and so on. The user selects the correct tool, and usually the mouse cursor will change to reflect the tool chosen. Other tools will normally include a text icon, so that text can be placed within a drawing. A zoom feature allows the possibility of manipulating part of a drawing in fine detail, even at the level of one picture cell ('pixel').

If a shape is provided on a painting package (such as an oval or a rectangle), the shape cannot later be changed as a single entity. Shapes must be erased using the on-screen eraser, and then drawn again.

Simple image manipulation features, such as inverting a part of a picture in a rectangular area, cropping the edges of an image and copying an area are usually provided.

—— Features to look for in drawing ——

As well as being differentiated from painting packages by the form of the storage, drawing programs usually provide more shapes and more tasks which can be carried out with those shapes.

Rotation of part of an image might be provided, through any specified angle. Drawings can be enlarged or reduced. Replication allows an image to be copied such that further changes in the original are then reflected in the copies.

CAD (computer aided design) programs are a specialist version of drawing programs which allow very precise control of dimensions and positions. This is particularly important in engineering and design, as designs may then be fed into computer-controlled manufacturing equipment.

Because drawing images are held as vectors, work produced can give the viewer too much of a computerised feel, with drawings looking too precise, though in many cases precision is essential.

Many sophisticated design tools are available on drawing packages, and in particular, many support three-dimensional drawing.

Three dimensional work can be achieved using wireframe diagrams, showing just the edges of a shape. A much better visual effect is produced when objects are drawn using techniques which make them appear solid. Some packages allow the user to work in wireframe mode so that the screen image can be refreshed more quickly, and then switch to 'preview' mode to see the 'solid' three-dimensional mode.

Three dimensional drawings can be enhanced using features such as allowing the user to control and place a light source within the picture to produce correct shadowing and reflections. In some instances perspective is also supported.

Solid modelling, available mainly on CAD systems, is much more sophisticated than wireframe or surface modelling. In solid modelling, the software must ensure that all surfaces meet. In addition, solid models can be sliced, and no two shapes are allowed to occupy the same space. In wireframe systems, one object can be seen inside another where appropriate.

_ Features to look for in any graphics _ package

One tool which is available to help a user of a graphics package is the background grid, which is not part of the final drawing but can be used for guidance.

Much is said and written about the number of colours supported by a painting or drawing package. Huge numbers are now quoted, with packages increasingly supporting a system called 24 bit colour (see Chapter 12), which gives 16.7 million different colours. Other users may be satisfied with 256 different colours, though this can lead to washed out pictures, for example where you want to represent the subtleties of flesh tones, or to give a two-dimensional picture depth.

There are several different forms in which colour drawings can be represented, and most graphics packages will support several of them. These systems are known as:

- HSL (Hue, Saturation and Light), where the colour hue is represented by an angle around a colour wheel of varying colours, the saturation is the amount of gray mixed in, and light is the amount of brightness. It is also known as HSV (V for value), and HSB (B for brightness).

- RGB (Red, Green, Blue), familiar through television and monitor technology.

- CMYK (Cyan, Magenta, Yellow and BlacK), occasionally written CMYB, which are the four colours required in colour separation printing.

If hardware is incapable of displaying colours to the precision to which they are held, the software, detecting this, will make the best approximation it can.

Graphics packages will allow manipulation of images which are of different shapes. The two traditional layouts are 'landscape', where the image is wider than it is high, as on most computer monitors, and 'portrait' which is higher than it is wide. As various toolbars are displayed around the screen, generally at the side and at the top, the proportions of a landscape picture fit the screen well. With portrait style, some waste of space will occur at the side of the screen, though, in the better packages, the various toolbars are pre-programmed for the remaining space. Some packages allow the user choice over where to place toolbars, which are then said to 'float'.

Curves drawn in graphics programs can often be smoothed under program control to give a more professional look. Much of the literature describes the principle of Bezier curves. This is a system whereby a simple curve is represented at each end by a tangent. The curve can be manipulated by rotating a tangent to alter the curvature, or changing the length of the tangent to deform the shape. More complex curves are represented by more tangents along their length. Most of the manuals will encourage the user to try this facility out. It is much easier to get a feel for how graphics programs work by trying them in practice than to read about them.

Tools for drawing various shapes are normally provided, and these will generally include rectangles and ellipses. These are drawn by selecting the correct tool, then clicking once for one corner of the rectangle and again after moving the mouse for the opposite corner. When an ellipse is drawn it will be specified in the same way, with the two clicks denoting the opposite corners of the rectangle within which the ellipse will be drawn. A square is a special case of a rectangle, and the circle of an ellipse, and these are usually obtained by using a keyboard key along with the mouse buttons.

Items within a graphics package are generally moved or changed using what is called a 'handle'. This involves displaying on screen a device which outlines the boundaries of the shape. In drawing packages this would generally apply to a shape as drawn, and the handle can usually be obtained by pointing and clicking on any part of the shape. In a painting package, an outline must usually be drawn around the part of the image to be manipulated.

Items within a graphics package can be grouped, so that they can be manipulated together. This enables them to be moved, enlarged, reduced and so on in conjunction with each other. Screens of graphics are often also layered, so that individual objects or groups of objects can be shown either above or below others. Commands are provided to move layers up or down, which can make a huge difference to which layer obscures which. Other features may allow a layer of graphics or individual shapes to be transparent or opaque.

– Input and output of scanned images –

There are two main ways in which the printed version of a scanned image may be made to look more life-like. Traditional printing methods print monochrome images using dots of varying size to produce darker and lighter areas. Denser areas of larger dots are used to produce dark shades and less dense areas of smaller dots are used for lighter shades. Computer printers are only able to print dots of the same size, so computers use simulated halftones through a process known as dithering, using more or less of the fixed sized dots for gray effects, but this inevitably leads to distortions.

The alternative method for representing monochrome images is to use representations of gray on what is called gray-scale, which is able to store details of, say, 16 shades of gray ranging from black to white. Gray-scale monitors can represent such an image very well. If the gray-scales are stored, then printers such as a PostScript printer will convert gray-scale to dot patterns with a variable black-to-white ratio in the manner best suitable for the resolution of the target printer.

——— Photo-retouching software ———

If you are intending to use scanned images, particularly as part of a composite image with artwork, it is desirable to be able retouch the image in a number of ways. When you buy a scanner, you will usually buy appropriate scanning software with it, but this will only accept the image as seen. Scanned images, particularly photographs, may have imperfections for a number of reasons, such as under- or over-exposure, or may have large areas of solid colour.

Retouching allows the user to overcome many of the imperfections, and to improve on the image. The brightness, contrast, or the strength of the colours of an image may all be altered. The process is not very different from altering the settings on a television. The edges of an image, or a selected area of it, can be softened or sharpened, smeared or blurred, allowing it to be blended more easily onto another image, or to stand out more.

Retouching can allow you to overcome imperfections in original artwork, such as the 'red eye' so common on photographs taken with a flash. Special effects can also be incorporated so that an image can be marbled, stuccoed or cracked at will.

Another technique, called posterisation, describes the process of reducing the image to one made up of a few strong colours. Spherising allows an image to be wrapped around a shape, such a sphere to create special effects.

——————— Ready-made artwork ———————

With most graphics packages, and with most shareware catalogues, whole libraries of readymade pictures, generally called 'clip art', are available. Specialist libraries are provided for almost every profession or hobby from architecture to wargaming. Besides this, pictures or photographs can be scanned in. Once loaded, of course, pictures from either source can be stretched, manipulated or distorted.

When you are choosing a library and tools to manipulate it, you need to distinguish clearly between those images that can be broken down into their various components for manipulation in a drawing program, and those that can only be treated as paintings, even within drawing programs.

Most manufacturers of packages, or companies selling clip art will quote the number of images in the library. This is not the only factor you should take into account in distinguishing them, though. First, those libraries that involve images made up of various components provide much more variety through the use of those elements. Secondly, without a good index or other form of organisation, clip art libraries become painfully slow to use. Page titles, which are often used for file names, are of limited use. Thus 'OFFICE1' or 'OFFICE2' do not tell you very much. Some clip art libraries come complete with a printed catalogue of all images. This perhaps forms some sort of protection against piracy; the files on disk are much less useful without a manual or catalogue.

Character writing

Similar caution is needed when judging the number and type of fonts available for text. Different software suppliers might count the number of fonts differently. First the figure for the number of fonts supported can be very misleading. Does the supplier treat variations such as italic fonts as separate or part of the same font? Secondly, after text has been manipulated on the screen, such as stretching, warping or fitting to a curve, can it still be edited?

Some packages allow text which has been incorporated into a graphic to be spellchecked, and others also have a thesaurus available.

Graphics compression

The storage of graphics files can take up a tremendous amount of disk space. Ordinary file compression (such as the 'disk doublers') can have some effect on this. Several methods are used to reduce file use by graphics programs even further. The details of how each system works need not concern the user. What you must ensure, however, is that the systems that you use are compatible.

File compression is also used in the transmission of graphics data. The more compact the data is made, the quicker the transmission, and therefore the cheaper it becomes. Users of bulletin boards have been quick to exploit compression techniques.

Compression techniques work in a variety of ways, each seeking to represent repeated values in as efficient a way as possible. Many graphics screens have considerable repetition, particularly if you consider the background of a picture.

The two types of compression are described by the terms 'lossy' or 'unlossy'. The former allows most pictures to be compressed more but with a small but acceptable loss in accuracy of the drawing (almost unseen to the human eye), whereas the latter ensures that there is no degradation of the image.

—— Presentation graphics software ——

Presentation graphics software (sometimes referred to by the initials 'PG') enables the user to produce a set of images for a presentation, such as charts, graphs and lists. These images can then be shown to an audience through a series of slides on a large computer screen, or through a conventional or overhead projector.

Most professional people find the preparation of a talk or presentation a daunting prospect, and much can rest on the outcome, such as the awarding of a contract or the selection of an individual. Good PG software will help to ease the process of preparation, and can help to boost the confidence of the individual giving the presentation. It is beyond question that a well-prepared computer-based presentation will have an audience sitting up and paying attention. On the other hand, a poorly prepared and poorly managed presentation is a real turn-off.

Many of the early PG software products were geared towards the production of 35 mm slides for use in a conventional slide prjector. At one time this was the only reliable way to turn computer-generated images into something which could be seen by a large audience. Specialist firms would be used to turn images held on floppy disk into 35 mm slides. This process was reltively expensive, and introduced delays into the job of preparing a presentation. It was difficult to use up-to-the-minute information if slides had to be submitted a week before their use.

Recent years, however, have seen the development both of laptop computers and projection panels which can be used on a conventional overhead projector. These two items, both relatively portable, can now be used for very effective presentations. There are times, however, when it is more convenient to use 35 mm slides or pre-prepared acetate slides for an overhead projector, as these are much more portable. A presentation given from a laptop is able to be topical, can use dynamic on-screen techniques to remove one slide and replace it with another, and can include animation. None of these features is available where it is a necessary to produce hard copy materials for a presentation.

Many of the PG packages allow the user to select a slide presentation style. Users who are unfamiliar with the package are helped by having a limited number of suggested styles presented, from which they can choose. This is a much quicker process than asking a long series of questions about formats. In a large corporation, standards may be set for a 'house style' in all images presented on behalf of the organisation. Pre-prepared styles are useful here, too, in helping staff stick to guidelines (such as choice of fonts, limiting the number of type sizes, spacing, bordering and so on).

Standard features

Presentation graphics packages vary in their detail, most notably in the style of user interface, but also in the range of features. There are, however, a number of standard slide types which almost all PG packages support, the main differences usually simply being in the number of variations provided within each category.

Typical slide types include title charts, bullets charts, graphs, tables and organisation charts:

- Title charts are slides consisting entirely of text, perhaps with a preset background. Typically the screen is divided into three areas, described as headline, body text and footnotes. The whole of the text within each area is usually given a font type and size (and perhaps colour). It is usual to use the largest size at the top and the smallest at the bottom. Simple editing of the text is allowed, but this may not even include word-wrap to move text between lines. Title slides normally allow for a fixed number of lines of text within each area, with the sizes of the areas being adjusted in line with the text sizes. Text can be centred within each line.

- Bullet charts allow the display of a series of related points, each preceded by a filled circle, a square, or some other symbol. Bullet charts will also usually have a single line headline, and may have a footnote for explanation. Further options may allow for the different points to be numbered (in Arabic or Latin numerals). The different bulleted points will normally be separated by blank lines. Secondary bullets may also be allowed so that a series of sub-points can be made within each point.

- Graphs can be drawn from a simple grid of data. Graph types include pie charts, bar charts, line graphs and high-low charts. Each of these can be used with a variety of headings, titles, labels, and keys to be displayed. Within each category there may be ten or a dozen variations, allowing for exploded pie charts, percentage bar charts, varieties of shading and so on. Manufacturers (and reviewers) will quote a figure for the number of different graph types available. This raw figure is frequently not a good guide, as there may be six or ten different pie charts which are all very similar; other manufacturers may quote a figure of only one style for varying pie chart types. Readers should be particularly careful to study claims that various charts are three dimensional. This may mean that genuine 3D graphs are available (with three variables X, Y and Z), or it may mean simply that normal 2D graphs are given depth with shading. Some PG packages include sophisticated graph types such as polar co-ordinates, regression and log graphs, but you must ask yourself how regularly you would use these.

- Tables in various styles may be supported for the presentation of rows and columns of figures. Choices can be made about the style of column and row headings, and of the type of grid shown, which might be horizontal lines only, vertical lines only, or both, or neither. Numerical values can be aligned within a table. Ranges of values, such as negative numbers can be shown in a different style (such as a different colour).

- Organisation charts allow the various levels of a hierarchy to be shown. This style of chart is not just useful for showing the structure of a company, but also to show how the various components of a problem, or a design, are broken down. This aspect of the software normally allows for differing numbers of layers of boxes to be shown. Box and text sizes are then adjusted to fill the screen whilst leaving reasonable space between boxes both horizontally and vertically. Text within boxes can be aligned at the top, the middle, or the bottom. Various types of shadows may be added to the boxes.

Better looking slides

A number of features of PG packages are applicable whatever the type of slide. A background drawing may be selected, for example, and may be included on every slide. Thus every slide can be shown against the same background, such as sky, or a graded shading. The background picture might be more adventurous, and might include a company logo, the presenter's name, or even the details of the particular presentation and date, giving the appearance that attention has been paid to detail. A number of standard background drawings may be supplied with a package. Other backgrounds may be imported from graphics packages. Individual details may then be added, such as the date.

It is desirable to produce a series of slides with a similar format. Some packages allow the choice of a master template, the contents of which will be incorporated into all the slides in a designated set. A change in the master will then be reflected in the rest of the set.

Many PG packages have a facility to check the spelling of a slide or a set of slides. Nothing is more embarrassing at a major presentation than discovering too late that a slide, or even a set of slides, has a glaring error.

Sorting out sets of slides

Various features within a PG package are designed to help with the editing and sequencing of sets of slides.

A slide sorter enables a user to build up a sequence of slides which can then be viewed, either in full, or in a series of thumbnail pictures. The careful preparation of a talk will usually involve the resequencing of slides several times. An outliner is a purely text-based alternative, which allows the user to look at the text parts of slides only, either as a series of titles, or showing the full text. Entries in this list can then be expanded from title to full text and back again for ease of organising.

Some packages allow for slides to be built up gradually within a demonstration, such as revealing one bullet point at a time. Previous points may then be grayed out on the screen. Other packages allow for slides which consist of other objects, such as an exploded technical illustration, to be built up layer by layer.

Transition effects can be built into a presentation. Whilst technical vocabularies for the various features differ, many packages allow an existing slide to be removed from the screen and a new one to be presented in a variety of ways. Techniques include 'wiping' (moving a line across from one of the four sides of the screen), 'fading', and 'dissolving' the screen by removing pixels from all over the picture at random.

Control sections for presentations allow for manual or automatic replacement of one slide by another. Another useful feature allows the user to skip back to previous slides, either one at a time, or to a numbered slide.

Some packages allow for the preparation of a run-time version of a particular presentation. The code generated can be run without the main package. Such a presentation then can be copied without infringement so that the same presentation can be given in different places, or placed onto a portable computer.

Further specialist features

If you have specific uses of your presentation graphics software in mind then there are a number of additional specialist features that might be worth looking for.

All PG software will prepare slides for printing. Complex on-screen effects cannot always be reproduced on monochrome printers. There are two main reasons for this. First, the number of gray scales on a printer will be limited. Graduated fills, for example, may need simplifying for a print-out. Secondly, of course, colour effects lose much of their impact when reproduced in monochrome. Good colour contrasts do not always work in shades of gray.

When slides are printed, however, there are two saving graces. One is that most audiences will not mind if the set of printed slides does not match the displayed set in style (but would notice a difference in content). Secondly, print-outs may only be for your own use as presenter. Many of the packages are capable of printing a set of slides with several per page, as reference material for the presenter. The points about loss of detail made above apply even more when pictures are scaled down.

If you are producing slides for high-quality colour printing, it is worth finding out which colour reproduction system your printer will be using. Some PG packages, for example, support the separation of colours into CMYK format or for the use of spot colours in the standard Pantone shades; others do not.

In some circumstances, the use of sound can help a presentation. Again, some PG packages have a sound feature, many do not.

Some presentations will require the use of specialist symbols, such as mathematical or Greek characters. The ability to access these, and their ease of manipulation would be something to look for if this kind of work was anticipated on a regular basis.

Animation tools are also becoming available on some PG systems. Some would judge these unnecessary; it will depend on your uses.

Links with other software

All the principles of linking different software packages apply in the PG context. You may well wish to import items from a word processor, a spreadsheet (either for turning into graphs on slides, or to import ready-made graphs) or a graphics drawing package. The principles of OLE and DDE apply to this software area as much as to any other combination of packages used together (see Chapter 13). Many of the key PG packages are available in DOS or Windows forms.

——— Some sample systems ———

The following are just some examples of the many drawing, painting and presentation graphics programs available. 1st Design from GST Software Products is aimed at beginners. It supports 16 million colours, and rotation of both text and pictures. The package includes Postscript support, but not colour separation.

PC Paintbrush Plus from Softkey is the latest version of the package which was for several years bundled with Windows. As well as pull-down menus, icons are provided for the most commonly-used features. There are 27 tools on the tool palette, including eight different drawing implements. Further choices are offered from a ribbon allowing tools to be applied with up to six different styles. The program allows more than one image window to be open at the same time. The package comes complete with a clip art library, but this is mainly black and white line drawings.

Corel Draw from Frontline Distribution is still available in three different versions. The higher the version number, the higher the price. CorelDraw 3.0 provides over 14 000 clip art images and dozens of slide templates. Spellchecker and thesaurus are included, and the package supports 24 bit colour and over 250 fonts. It is available both on Windows and Macintosh systems. It supports a wide range of transition effects for presentations. Its three dimensional features include the use of perspective and extrusion, and Corel Draw has a comprehensive help system.

Corel Draw 4 0 consists of a number of modules: a vector drawing program, CorelTrace which converts scanned bitmapped images into vector images, CorelShow for presentations, CorelChart for graphs, Corelphoto-Paint for creating and editing bitmapped images, and CorelMosaic for cataloguing and searching for images. Version 4.0 also includes CorelMove for animation. Its 18 000 pieces of clip art are provided on CD, along with 750 fonts.

CorelDraw 5.0 (on floppy disk and CD, or on CD only) incorporates Ventura Desktop Publisher. A price differential exists between the two distribution modes emphasising the size of the package, and the saving to a manufacturer in using CD only. Though the system will work with a minimum of 8 MB, 16 MB is recommended. The minimum disk space requirement is 38 MB, though the full installation takes 50 MB. As well as having more features than version 4.0, the number of items of clip art and typefaces is again greater.

Aldus FreeHand allows users to create a wide range of hand-drawn effects. It supports 24 bit colour and colour separation, picture and text rotation, and shapes text to fit curves. It also incorporates 99 levels of undo. It allows the use of multiple pages in multiple sizes.

Harvard Graphics is a presentation graphics package from Software Publishing Corporation. It is available as Version 3 for DOS, with Harvard Graphics for Windows now in Version 2. The DOS version will run in just 640 kB of memory and allows slides to be prepared of five basic types (text, organisation, pie, XY and drawing). There are many variations within these, so that overall there are 161 graph types.

Microsoft PowerPoint 4 is a presentation graphics package that runs under Windows, requiring 4 MB of memory, and is also available on the Macintosh. It includes an outliner, originally developed by Microsoft for Word, which enables a user to see the contents of several slides at once, and to sort and edit them. The various levels of headings and sub-headings are clearly shown. This feature can be particularly useful when converting text from a word processed document into slides. A thousand items of clip art are provided, as is support for sound and video. Stand-alone slide shows can also be created. PowerPoint is also sold as part of the Microsoft Office bundle.

ClarisImpact is available for a wide range of models of Macintoshes. It combines three main environments: drawings, reports and presentations. It provides eight pre-designed chart types, and various diagrams such as hierarchy, flowcharts and networks. Its timeline charts provide Gantt charts and calendar functions. A Slide Manager allows the easy organisation and reorganisation of slides for a presentation. Its report generation includes margins, tabs, columns and footnotes as well a as spellchecker. Files can be imported for any of these applications from formats such as MacWrite, MacDraw, and Microsoft Word and Excel. Multimedia support is provided.

10

DESKTOP PUBLISHING

—— What is desktop publishing? ——

Desktop publishing packages are used to prepare layouts for printing incorporating various sizes and type of fonts, graphics and other incidental layout features. Many packages are designed so that they can be used by somebody who does not have particular skills as a graphic artist or in layout. The final computer-produced document is then used as an original for whatever printing technique is chosen. The abbreviation DTP is used for the term desktop publishing.

Many word processing packages now incorporate features which only DTP packages had at one time. These include multiple columns, incorporation of graphics, use of background tints, and line and box drawing. DTP packages, in continuing to retain their market share now incorporate many more features. Some users may claim to be able to do everything necessary with a word processor and therefore they do not need DTP. This may be the case, but apart from additional features, one other difference is the ease with which effects can be achieved in DTP compared with word processing.

More than almost any other software category, what the user can achieve is limited first by the sophistication of the package chosen and secondly by the specialist equipment used. DTP packages range in price from well under £100 to over a thousand pounds, and products at each level within the overall price range fulfil different needs. Users who wish to use sophisticated features such as full colour printing will have to buy specialist equipment. They will also be limited to DTP packages at the top of the range which are able to make the most of the equipment.

DTP features

Although most DTP packages include their own text editor, it would be more normal to prepare text first in a word processor, as this would be more efficient at manipulating text. A completed text would then be imported by the DTP program. Most DTP packages will read text from a wide variety of word processors. The ability to import from many word processors is important because you need to be able to take text from your own word processor, and you may be passed documents from other people in different formats. This is regularly the situation, for example, for a voluntary editor of a magazine for a special interest or local group. People are willing to contribute, but only in a format they can produce.

It is important to look at the way text is imported. At worst, the imported text might lose all formatting, such as character formatting and fonts. You must read the specification of the DTP package carefully to see what will be done with fonts available in the word processor but not supported in your DTP package. The imported text will be reformatted to fit the new column width and text style. DTP packages differ, for example, in the extent to which they retain formats such as page breaks, bulleted text and other features of text prepared in a word processor.

Various design rules can be selected by the user. Terms such as 'template' are used to describe details of the layout within the page, such as the margins on the four sides of the paper, the number of columns, the gap between columns (gutter), and the way the printable area is divided. Areas can be reserved, so that graphics, photographs and different types of text, such as body text, headings and sub-headings can be incorporated.

The screen display will normally help in layout by incorporating a number of features that will not be printed. These include guidelines for the edge of the text as well as the edge of the paper, an indication of where columns lie, and guidelines to show the middle of the sheet horizontally and vertically. A grid is also defined for the page layout, which may or may not be made visible. This grid can then be used to line up various elements of a document with each other. Frequently, an area reserved for text or a graphic might be lined up using a command such as 'snap to grid'. This enables you to place a box roughly on the screen, with the computer placing it more precisely using the nearest gridlines. Not only can the display of the gridlines be turned off, but the program can be instructed not to use them if you want to control exact lining up yourself.

Many DTP packages allow you to view more than one page of a document at once for editing purposes, though naturally much detail cannot be seen on the screen display when this is done.

Rules are incorporated within most packages to determine how close the edge of one area will come to the edge of another. These rules can be varied by the user, but are normally based on experience of good layout. Once areas of the page have been set aside, they can be given various background tints, and text or a graphic can be placed into them. At times, you might want to use a graphic background over which text is placed. Various notations are used for the operation of placing an object such as text or a graphic in a box, the most vivid of which is the idea of 'pouring' the item into the reserved space. This process usually includes allowing text to flow around a document.

If an item does not fill the space precisely, it may be shrunk or expanded to fit. This may work well for a graphic which is slightly the wrong size or shape, and the user may simply 'crop' the picture by shaving off parts (on screen, of course!) so that it does fit. With most graphic images it would not be appropriate to change the proportions of height to width: with precise diagrams, or photographs, the effects could lead to unhelpful distortions. If, on the other hand, text does not fit into a designated box, it may be appropriate to enlarge or reduce the typeface to make it fit. Otherwise, if the text is far too long, the overflow can be retained and poured into a box on another page. Some packages in these circumstances will include a message within the article saying 'continued on page 3', and on page 3 will say 'continued from page 1'. Similarly, the program should give the user a warning if text from some imported document has not been incorporated; the solution might be as simple as adding a new page between two existing pages.

The term 'style' is generally used to describe the format given to a paragraph of text with selections made for the font, size, indentation and line spacing. Once paragraph styles have been defined, they can be stored so that the same style can be applied to any number of paragraphs. Users can usually give names to their chosen styles, with several ready-made styles being available for use or adaptation. When a user pulls down the menu to apply a style a list of available styles is normally displayed. In the most flexible system you can 'pick up' a style from one paragraph, and drag and drop it across so that it is applied to another paragraph.

Once it has been loaded, text can be altered so that the gap between characters is altered ('kerning'), the distance between rows altered ('leading'), and the spacing of a line of text changed ('tracking'). Many specialist terms associated with DTP are borrowed from the typesetting world. Manuals are full of these terms, such as the measure of distance, in 'points'. Kerning involves altering the space between letters on the same line of text either to bring them together or move them apart. Kerning is most often used to reduce the space between letters to improve the appearance and readability of text. Automatic kerning allows the space reduction to take place without user intervention, as details are stored of which pairs of letters this can be carried out on. Manual kerning is laborious, but can be used to make minor adjustments so that text will fit the space available.

Character formats can also be selected. DTP packages have traditionally supported more fonts and more variations within each font than most word processing packages. As well as the traditional bold, italic and underline, other font variations such as shadow and outline fonts are available with some DTP packages. Outline fonts can be particularly useful if text is to be placed on a tinted background.

Scalable fonts

The use of scalable fonts is not restricted to DTP packages. They are described here rather than in chapters on graphics, spreadsheets or printers as a matter of convenience.

Scalable fonts can be enlarged to any size (up to a very large limit) without producing distortions or jagged edges. The most common method of achieving this is to use an outline which contains an algorithm for generating the correct bitmaps when the character is displayed on the screen or is to be produced on a printer. The bitmap generation is done either by a special card in the computer or by logic in the printer.

There is a considerable saving of storage space with scalable fonts, compared with bitmapped fonts, where it is necessary to store each size and variation separately.

One example of a scalable font is TrueType, which does not require a printer with special in-built font logic. This, it is claimed, makes documents much more portable between different systems as TrueType fonts will print on almost all printers.

DTP packages first popularised the use of scalable font systems, in particular Adobe PostScript The ability of your DTP package to support scalable fonts should be a major factor in your choice, as this will mean that the screen display will show fonts in any size without distortion. Modern DTP packages generally support both TrueType and PostScript. During a typical DTP session you might examine the same document on screen with three or four different magnifications, depending on the task in hand. With a scalable font, each display will show the typeface as accurately as possible, which helps you in carrying out the various tasks. The screen display and printer display will each produce the best available character shapes, as clearly differences between the resolutions of screen and printer cannot be overcome.

Many desktop printers incorporate a large amount of in-built processing power. A Page Description Language (PDL) is a specialist programming language which can be used to pass instructions as ASCII text from a computer to an output device, such as a laser printer or an industry-standard typesetting machine. These instructions are then used by the interpreter built into the printer or other output device. A PDL allows the computer to describe the objects which are to be placed on the printed page, rather than passing an image dot by dot in a bit-mapped way. This helps to speed up the print processing. Instructions in the PDL give details of the font chosen, its size, direction and so on. The image is then built up within the laser printer's memory and the full page is printed upon completion of the signalling. PDLs are designed to be device-independent. So you can prepare a single output which can then be interpreted by a laser printer or a high-end typesetting machine, and in each case produce the best image possible from the equipment.

The PostScript PDL was devised and patented by Adobe Systems Inc., and was first used in the Apple Laserwriter in 1985. Other manufacturers, like Hewlett-Packard, have their own PDLs, in this case PCL. Xerox uses the Interpress PDL. To exploit the full range of features of a printer with a particular PDL, it is essential to have software which sends signals in that particular language. Fortunately, most recent software boasts PostScript support.

For printers which do not support PostScript or another PDL, such as those which do not print a page at a time, software called an emulator can be bought. This takes a file in PostScript or some other form, and converts it within the computer to the form needed by the specific printer, and then sends the signals in that form.

Graphics

Graphics can be loaded into a DTP package from a painting or drawing program. If an image from a painting program is to be magnified, since it is formatted as a series of dots, all that can be done to magnify it is to increase the size of the dots, so images can begin to look chunky. Imports from drawing programs, as long as they are interpreted to the maximum precision that the system can handle, generally give sharper graphics. Graphics manipulation within a DTP package usually allows for image flipping, resizing, duplicating, rotating, and cropping. Many DTP programs come with clipart libraries of 1000 or more images.

The idea of a graphics style is used in some packages, in a close parallel to text style. When a graphic has been given a number of attributes, such as a choice of line style and fill type, this can be stored and then applied to another drawing. This approach then allows all the graphics in a given document, whatever their original source, to have the same 'look and feel'.

The real test of the versatility of a DTP package comes when we start looking at changes to the document. Many allow, for example, for the flow of text around a graphic. If you move the graphic slightly, some DTP packages adjust the text to fill the new space around it. Text might be incorporated and then slanted, but after it has been manipulated, it can still be edited.

Print previews in DTP are similar to those in word processing. Similar techniques such as greeking are used when text is too small to see. Redrawing graphics, even at a reduced size, can be time-consuming, and since print previews are generally used to obtain an overall impression, it is quickest if graphics are shown simply as shaded areas.

Many DTP packages come with a ready-supplied set of templates, giving page layouts for a variety of types of documents, and a number of paragraph formats. If these sets are comprehensive enough many users will rarely use others, though instructions are usually given in how to build your own templates and styles.

———— Specialist features ————

Some of the more specialist features may only be available in a few DTP programs. For example, only some support drop capitals. This involves presenting the first character of the first word as a large letter, perhaps covering two, three or four rows; the rest of the text is reshaped accordingly. Other packages control 'widows and orphans' so that paragraphs are not split inappropriately between pages. In a market as competitive as that for DTP software, it will usually be the case that if one product becomes successful, rival products in the range will include similar features to remain competitive.

Most DTP programs support some form of colour, and like graphics programs, they vary in the number of colours supported. The twin prices to pay for a greater range of colours are financial and in terms of memory taken up by larger codes for more colours.

DTP output will regularly be to a laser printer, with either 300 dots per inch sufficing, or 600 dots per inch being used. Much higher resolution can be obtained by outputting files through an image setter. Such equipment is very expensive, but there are many bureaus that provide an output service for desktop publishers. If a company is thinking of making regular use of such features, it is essential to seek the advice of printing contractors to ensure compatibility of systems from the start.

———— Best practice in DTP ————

If you are going to take up DTP seriously, it is worth reading around the subject. This should enable you to learn from the acquired knowledge of several centuries of publishing. Critics claim that it is very easy to spot an inexperienced user of DTP, through tell-tale signs of rank bad practice. Examples include trying to fill up the whole page leaving too little white space, and using the wrong fonts on reverse text. (For example, serif fonts in reverse tend to lack clear edges through ink bleeding.) Inexperienced users also forget to kern large typefaces, or do it badly, and use far too many different fonts and sizes on the same sheet.

One colleague suggested to me that she could trace back to the time her children's school bought DTP software from the letters sent home. Almost every week, she could give an account of the new features and fonts which the staff had discovered, as they just had to be incorporated into the latest letter. DTP and many other packages provide huge numbers of features, but users must remember that they do not have to use them all!

Managers also express concern that DTP packages encourage professional people to waste time producing something that a graphic designer could have done a lot better. Staff seem to like trying out different features and making that tiny adjustment here, there and everywhere. If computers generally can be said to soak up time because they fascinate some people who forget the overall aim of the job, DTP can be said to do this more than most applications.

Most users have a fundamental grasp of what a good page layout looks like when they see one, but need guiding into using the principles behind good design. All too often, a DTP package might simply make it very easy to produce bad layout. Many people who would not claim to be page design experts will have picked up, almost subconsciously, ideas about page layout from all the advertisements and magazines they have seen. Others, who do not naturally pay attention to detail, might not.

——— Further reading on DTP ———

Books such as 'Teach Yourself Desktop Publishing' give lots of good ideas on how to exploit the wide range of features with care and style.

Manuals for DTP software differ greatly in how much time they spend in helping users address concepts of good design. The better ones give a good deal of material on this matter, including lots of examples.

Some sample systems

PagePlus 3.0 from Serif is a Windows package which has been well received in the press as a well-featured product at the lower end of the price range. It supports a wide range of imports from word processors, as well as a number of graphics formats. It supports PostScript and TrueType, with scalable fonts. It supports RGB and CMYK, and Pantone colours. It does not support halftone screening. Three different user ability levels are available, with the lowest giving regular prompts while the user constructs a document.

The mid-priced Microsoft Publisher 2.0 runs under Windows and is document-based rather than page-based. It includes clipart and text flow around graphics, but no word count. It supports most popular word processor formats and most graphics formats. It supports TrueType and 19 different fonts, but does not support many of the colour printing features of its rivals. It helps users through common tasks with Wizards which give a step by step approach to guide inexperienced users.

At the upper end of the market, Aldus PageMaker 5.0 is available on both Macintosh and Windows platforms, requiring a minimum of 4 MB of memory and 40 MB of disk space on a PC. As would be expected of a product at the top end of the range, it has a dazzling array of features, including support for many file formats. Also included are incremental rotation of text and graphics and colour separations. Several documents can be open at the same time. A reduced version of PageMaker, called PageMaker Classic is available at a much lower price, providing many of the key components that helped to gain PageMaker its market dominance in the late 1980s.

The other industry standard package is QuarkXPress, which, like its major competitor PageMaker, has a huge range of facilities. It is available for both Macintosh and Windows computers.

Some people will argue that occasional users will have difficulties with the top of the range desktop publishing packages, as they have so many features which are difficult to remember for infrequent use.

11
—— OTHER SOFTWARE ——

—— Project management software ——

Project management software is designed to allow you to enter the details of all the aspects that make up a project, such as the tasks, the resources and the deadlines. This information can then be used to present the information as a variety of different charts, and can highlight those tasks that are critical to finishing the project on time. Once changes to the relationships between tasks are entered, the effect of a change in one task on others can be seen.

Project management is a sophisticated science and in complex situations, experienced managers are needed. The term 'project management software' could be regarded as a misnomer. This software simply records a plan and provides tools to manipulate that plan. Though it is a cliché to say it, in computing, the software is only as good as the information that is entered. The software will not point out, for example, that a vital task has been missed out, or that task dependencies have been incorrectly entered.

Project management software allows you to enter the details of a series of tasks, including dependencies, such that a task might not commence until other tasks are completed, and it will then take a certain minimum amount of time. Projects also require resources, such as staff, materials and equipment, to be available, and these have to be shared across tasks. The availability of resources can change as a project develops. Equipment might break down. Staff might leave or take a holiday. The effects of any such changes can be seen by feeding the new information into the software. Questions can be answered, such as: 'What if I take two days leave at this point; will it affect the whole project?'

Once the data is entered, the user can manipulate it to explore, for example, which are the critical tasks. These are the tasks which, if delayed, would cause the whole project to be delayed. Other tasks might be able to 'float' within specified periods without delaying the whole project.

In most organisations, several projects will be running simultaneously, and will make demands on the various resources. A change in one is reflected in the others.

Project information can be displayed in a number of forms. The most common charts are PERT charts (Programme Evaluation Review Technique), which look similar to flowcharts, with one task per box, and Gantt charts, which use a line system, similar to that on wallcharts.

The use of colour has greatly enhanced the use of project management software. Critical tasks can be shown in red, for example. Some reviewers advise, however, that the quality of the user interface is not a good guide to the range of features provided. Some packages are well presented but lack the more advanced features, which is fine, of course, if this is what you want.

Not all project management software, runs under a graphical environment, or supports the use of a mouse. Where sets of tasks are related as a main task with sub-tasks, it is very useful to collapse the whole into main tasks only, or to look at one set of sub-tasks only, rather like outlining in word processors or spreadsheets. Whilst some forms of printing are obviously needed, much of the work in project management is dynamic, and it is much more common to use on-screen manipulation to answer 'what if?' questions.

Other flexibility is provided by many packages to work in units of days, weeks, minutes or months. Account can also be taken of weekend work and bank holidays.

Integrated packages

An 'integrated package' is sold as a single program which carries out a number of tasks normally carried out by separate packages. A typical integrated package might provide word processor, a spreadsheet and a database, all within a single program. Retailing at around £100, integrated packages can look attractive compared with the price of buying the applications separately.

A typical integrated package will contain the three applications mentioned above, and may also incorporate a communications module, and perhaps a graphics module. Each of these separate areas will probably not have the same range of features as a specialist package in the particular application area.

In buying an integrated package, you should gain in the consistency of approach with separate applications areas looking very similar. Some would argue that, with the arrival of graphical environments, and complex linking between applications facilitated by systems such as Microsoft Windows, the integration of a single package is not important. However, for a new user particularly, a well presented single program will probably be easier to master. A single, consistent interface will mean that a new user will learn how to use the whole package much more quickly, and will find the less frequently used parts easier to remember.

Links between the applications areas within an integrated package make it possible, for example, to use a mailing list held in database form, and to mailmerge that with letters held in word processor format.

Many integrated packages work as a series of separate programs within a main program so that, for example, you can launch the word processor, but can switch to the spreadsheet when the need arises. Documents for each application are kept separately, but can be cut and pasted into each other. When original data in a spreadsheet changes after it has been exported to a word processor, it may well have to be re-exported to update the document. In some cases, however, dynamic links may be established. In other cases, a combination of uses might be applicable in a single original document. When you select spreadsheet mode for example, the document might remain on screen with a spreadsheet area reserved, and whilst the cursor remains within the spreadsheet area, the menus and icons available change around it.

Several popular integrated packages are available for both the PC and the Mac. This is a particular attraction for sites where a mix of machines is used. Core activities might be carried out in an integrated package used on both platforms to aid portability, whilst specialist work takes place on the more appropriate platform.

Many integrated packages will not have the range of specialist facilities within each separate application area provided by a specialist package. Thus features which have been recently introduced into most of the word processors in their latest versions may not be present in any of the integrated packages. Such omissions are partly to keep integrated package costs down, and more likely are to keep down the disk space needed to store the software. Once facilities become established, however, as 'standard' with a package, then they are likely to migrate down into integrated versions. This has happened in recent years with spellcheckers, for example.

Integrated packages should be chosen carefully. They are only as strong as their weakest component. It matters not a lot how powerful the word processor is if the database will not carry out the tasks you stipulate. Of course, you can buy a more powerful separate database, but this will mean losing most of the benefits of integration.

Office bundles

An alternative form of integration is provided by the 'office bundle' or 'integrated suite'. Here a number of applications packages normally sold separately are sold together, providing a major saving to the customer. Office bundles are now provided by all the main suppliers in the market and, unlike the integrated packages, the suites contain the full-blown and latest versions in each software category. Precisely what is offered within the bundle varies a little. All contain a word processor and a spreadsheet and usually a database. They generally contain at least one more application, such as presentation graphics, or an accounting package, or some other product. This is clearly an attempt by each manufacturer to make the product slightly different from the others.

Different applications within a bundle are launched separately and usually use forms of communication between them such as dynamic data exchange (DDE) or object linking and embedding (OLE), described in Chapter 13. It is interesting to see whether one firm's products have a consistent approach to menus and icons.

—— Personal information managers ——

Personal information managers (PIMs) are usually likened to a computerised Filofax. Indeed, some use an on-screen display very like a Filofax with diary pages and tabs for different sections. PIMs allow a user to hold a diary, address book, a list of jobs to be done and perhaps some other features.

The recording of time commitments within a PIM might be in the form of a scheduler, a diary, a forward planner or some combination of these. Appointments might be shown in a variety of forms. On a day-by-day basis, they might best be shown as pages of a diary, with the advantage over written records that there will be no crossings out or extra entries squeezed in to an impossibly small space. If meetings are marked for an alarm call, you will be reminded of an appointment at an appropriate time. You will have to tell the system, of course, whether a meeting is just down the corridor or is half an hour's travel away.

Regular meetings can be programmed in just as one-off meetings can. Thus you can book a regular meeting every Monday morning, or on the second Wednesday afternoon of the month. If your requirements are specific, such as blocking the Thursday after the second Monday of the month for a planning committee, then you will need to check that the software can cope with this. Diaries might also work across a network, so that if colleagues use the same system, the diaries can be accessed at the same time so that you can book a meeting when all the participants are free. Trying to make arrangements such as these can be one of the biggest time-wasters for secretaries.

Anniversaries can be entered on many of the systems, and handled as a separate list, so that entries can be added or deleted. The entries can then be automatically transferred into the diary system, either on the actual date, or with a warning a specified period before the vital date, or both.

PIMs can be used to manage 'to do' lists of outstanding tasks to help in your use of time. Tasks can usually be given some form of priority. Most systems will carry forward incomplete tasks to the next day or week. You will, of course, need to inform the system when a task has been completed. Many of the systems allow for the storage of completed tasks until you specifically request their deletion. This is very useful for reporting on work done or in analysing your use of time.

The disadvantage of the whole system is the time spent in entering and manipulating tasks up to three times at entry, completion and deletion. As with all computer applications, you have to decide on balance whether the time invested is worth the benefit, in this case mainly in time saving.

PIMs will also usually include an address book or contact list feature. Reviewers generally recommend that the system should allow for at least four telephone numbers for each person, as you may need to include a voice number, a fax number, a mobile number and perhaps a home number or temporary number (such as a hotel). A computerised address book will, of course, need just as much careful management as a conventional one. The computerised version should make searching a good deal easier, though. You may be able to search for an individual's name, or a company's, or for a town. Some systems will allow you, if a modem is fitted, to dial straight through from the computerised address book.

Some PIMs include a simple word processor for the production of memos. Such word processors are not normally fully featured, and may not be suitable for report writing or preparing presentations, but for quick memos they are probably entirely adequate, saving time in loading other software and exporting and importing text. Details of the addresses can be picked up from the address book.

The ways in which PIMs may differ relate not so much to the list of features they provide, but in their abilities to link the various sections. For example, anniversaries might be linked into the diary, 'to do' lists might be carried across. These links might be dynamic, so that no user action is necessary to copy them across.

One particular issue needs looking at if you are to use a PIM on both your notebook and a desktop computer. Ideally, you would like the two systems to be reconciled regularly, so that entries included on the laptop are transferred to the desktop and vice versa. This is a difficult task because, of course, it will mean that each transaction will have to be recorded ready for reconciliation. The system will have to know which out of two conflicting entries is newer, such as different telephone numbers for the same person.

Some PIMs will allow you to print your information. Many regular users rarely if ever use this facility. If, however, you wish to prepare a calendar of events to be shared by several people, such as a schedule of meetings, then this feature might be very useful.

In choosing a PIM, you will need to be careful to check whether your system is British. Products from the US may well include features such as states, ZIP codes and dollars. You may be able to live with and ignore some fields like ZIP codes, but calculation in dollars might create considerable work.

Security within a PIM system might be an important aspect to consider. Several systems allow for password protection of some or all the information. Particularly across networks, you might wish to allow other users access to view some of your data, but not give them rights to change it.

———— Accounting software ————

Software to handle accounts ranges from household money management to the finance of a large company. The simpler, and therefore cheaper, systems sell for around £50, and work as computerised cashbooks. Some cashbook packages are now being supplied as part of a software bundle with new hardware. It is claimed that small businesses only really need the cashbook style of accounting package. Different account types can be established, such as cash, bank accounts, credit cards, assets and liabilities. Each transaction is then entered separately, and can be given a category from a list of transaction types. The system then allows entry of details such as a cheque number and a description. A running balance is then kept on each account, as it would be in a manual cash book. With the stored data, however, the system can then produce a profit and loss statement, or other reports such as cash flow.

The larger packages normally consist of sales ledger, purchase ledger, stock control, invoicing and so on. From a single order, such a system can update the stock record, print a dispatch note, produce an invoice, and record the information for an end-of-month statement. This ability to relate several separate modules is described as 'integrated accounts', not to be confused with 'integrated packages', as described earlier. Manufacturers of the larger accounts packages ensure that their products meet the regulations of bodies like the Inland Revenue and Customs & Excise. Modules such as stock control and the various ledgers may be bought separately, so that you only pay for what you need. The modules are integrated as they are installed.

Either kind of accounts package will provide a set of tools for analysis of the data entered. Some information may be available in graphical form. Potential purchasers of accounts packages should consider whether the investment of the time needed to enter all the transactions will be reaped back in benefits. It may be quicker to keep simple accounts in a hand-written cash book. The benefits in the simpler cases will normally be seen through the analysis of the data once it is entered, rather than in the handling of the data itself. On a larger scale system, the sheer bulk of the data may well justify or necessitate the use of accounting software; analysis might simply be an added bonus. Multi-user accounting systems are complex but allow several people access to the same accounts.

Some people use a spreadsheet to make accurate forecasts of their future financial position rather than spend the time entering financial data every day.

Computer programming

You may buy a car to learn how it works. A keen parent may buy a child a cheap old car to take to bits and repair. Most of us, though, buy a car because we want to use it. We buy a working car, learn some basics about keeping it going, and for any serious work on it, we call in an expert. The analogy in computing is that most of us buy a computer to use it. We are interested in the applications. A few may wish to explore programming for their own education.

Programming languages use either a compiler or an interpreter. There is a wide range of programming languages available, each of which has its strengths. When thinking about buying a language compiler or interpreter, you will have to check that you have the correct version for the computer and its operating system. Programming language products which allow for the editing and testing of programs in a graphical environment such as Windows are becoming increasingly common.

Manuals supplied with programming languages differ considerably. Some manuals attempt to teach you the whole language from scratch. Other manuals assume you know the main language and provide simply a reference book. Some systems are supplied with sample programs, some of which are explained in the manuals. The quality and type of manual should be very important to your choice. If you need to buy a book to teach you the language as well, this could easily add a significant amount to your bill. You should also be careful to buy a book which describes the correct dialect of the language (such as Turbo Pascal rather than RM Pascal), and that it covers the correct version of that language.

If you are intending to write programs regularly, you should look very carefully at the editor provided with a programming package. Which-ever language you choose, you will be writing programs in what is called the source code, instructions which the system will then translate. You will want to move blocks of code, copy them, search for particular words and so on. Some editors within programming language packages have many features. Others are very simple. Given that the language features of the different packages can be very similar, it can be the editors that distinguish the products.

Programmers' toolkits are also included in many programming products. These help in the processes of testing, amending, and documenting programs. Some toolkit features come with a language system when you buy it, whereas others have to be bought separately.

Games

PCs, Macs and other desktop computers are widely used for games. There is a huge range of such games available and there are many magazines devoted to computer games. It would be impossible in a book like this to cover all the possibilities, so if games are one of your interests, look at magazines such as *PC Format* and *PC Review*.

Music

Some computers are very suitable for use with music programs. Computer sound output is made up of several channels. The study of computer music can become involved, covering issues such as the pitch, the tone, and the attack of various notes.

Some systems use captured sound samples, which are turned into digital form for storage. Software allows music scores to be composed on screen and the finished products to be played. Once a tune is entered and held in a digital form, it can be edited to change the tempo, pitch, and various other aspects. Most computer music systems are capable of driving other devices through a system known as the MIDI interface.

Route planning

Programs are available on a number of platforms for route planning. A typical program will hold, for example, maps of Great Britain and Ireland. You then tell the program your starting point and destination, and may opt to include places that you wish to go through on the way. With its database of information about the roads, the program is able to select a route for you. Options allow you to choose the quickest or shortest route. You can enter preferences, such as an aversion to motorways, in which case a preferred route can be worked out avoiding motorways. Each calculated route can be shown as a map, or as a list of travel instructions, stating what you should do at each junction. Intermediate timings can be shown.

Additional features on some route planning software include additional information on football and cricket grounds, theme parks and so on. As such applications develop, it is likely that a whole range of data such as specialist venues, beauty spots, and hotels will be prepared, probably for sale as add-ins.

Route planners usually show the whole route on a single screen, and allow the user then to zoom in on portions of the map. Some route planners are available with a windowing system so that maps at different scales can be shown at the same time.

─────────── Other software ───────────

A vast range of software is available, and many new packages become available each month.

Contact management software is designed for keeping track of a large number of people with whom you need to keep in touch, a task which people in jobs such as sales clearly carry out all the time. The programs allow you to keep all the snippets of information about an individual contact, ranging from 'hard' information such as sales records, to 'soft' information, such as the customer's interests outside work. A record can be kept of every contact you have had with the person. An alarm system and diary within the program enable you to make sure that enquiries are followed up, and that contacts are not allowed to go cold. This specialist software is designed for day-to-day use by people with a particular type of job. There is no opportunity for half measures; to ensure that you reap the benefits, you must use such a program for all contacts.

Another specialist form of software provides for time recording. This allows professionals such as lawyers and accountants to charge their time to a whole range of projects in which they are involved at any one time. Some of these systems are designed to work with bar code readers, with one bar code for each project.

Reference works are increasingly coming available through computers, particularly with the development of CD. Works such as dictionaries with definitions of words, encyclopaedias, dictionaries of quotations, guides to English usage and so on are now available. Most of these are accessed without leaving the current application.

Software exists to design and print forms. Such software enables you to mix typefaces, styles of lettering, shapes and shading. Once prepared, form designs can be kept for future minor amendments.

Specialist programs are available for producing labels for participants at conferences. Whilst it would be possible to use a database to do this, users who are likely to prepare for many conferences may consider the investment worthwhile.

Mailing list programs are available that are capable of sorting a set of address in postcode order according to the strict specification of the Post Office. Use of such a program can help organisations which produce substantial correspondence to save considerably on postage.

——— Some typical products ———

Project management

Microsoft Project 4.0 allows the creation of both PERT and Gantt charts, as well as presenting project information in a spreadsheet-like format. Gantt charts can have free-form text and graphics added to help interpretation. Microsoft Project allows projects to be monitored by the percentage completed by work, cost or time. It has a customisable toolbar. An outliner allows secondary information to be hidden, allowing a good overview. It requires 2 MB of memory. Balloon help is provided, so that all icons can be explained. The package also supports TrueType, and has good integration with other Microsoft products.

Computer Associates SuperProject 3.0 is the latest version of a long-standing product. This means that there is a lot of expertise in working with SuperProject amongst users. The manual is particularly comprehensive. The Assist mode provides pop-up help boxes for each field which is to be completed. The Assistant takes a user through all the steps in a similar manner to Microsoft Wizards.

Integrated packages

Microsoft Works 3.0 is a DOS integrated package which includes a word processor, a flat-file database, a spreadsheet and a communications module. Each part of the package provides adequate features, though more advanced users might find that some of the features present on individual packages within each type are not present.

Microsoft Works for Windows 3.0 also provides drawing and graphing features. It incorporates Wizards, which allow the user to carry out frequently used tasks through answering a series of questions. The Macintosh version is similar.

Lotus Works is another DOS integrated package with the same four basic applications. Though providing a different combination of features, it would again be best suited to a novice user, or one who knows that particularly advanced features will not be needed.

ClarisWorks 2.1 is the best established integrated package for the Macintosh, and is also available as version 1.0 for Windows. It has word processor, spreadsheet, database, graphing and drawing facilities. Communications features include a 'phone book and transmission of files in various protocols. The Macintosh version of ClarisWorks requires only 650 kB of memory, which could be an important consideration.

Office bundles

With office bundles, there are often two hard disk storage sizes quoted. The first is the maximum size, which includes every feature, example and help. The second figure is the minimum size, which would involve stripping away, at installation time, everything that is not necessary. In reality, most users' requirements would involve a file size somewhere between the two.

Microsoft Office 4.2 is a Windows product which contains Word, Excel, PowerPoint (presentation graphics) and Microsoft Mail. At a higher price Microsoft Office Professional 4.3 also includes the Access database. The maximum size of the package is 68 MB, with a minimum configuration of 21 MB. Within Microsoft Office is a set of icons called the Office Manager, which sits permanently on the screen to enable the user to switch quickly between applications. Its supporters would claim that it is the only suite to support full OLE 2.0 (see Chapter 13).

Lotus SmartSuite is also Windows based and contains Lotus 1-2-3 release 4, Ami Pro 3.01, Freelance Graphics, Organizer and Approach (a database). Its supporters would say that, particularly for a new user, the screen layouts are very consistent. Whereas with some other office bundles, the toolbars, for example, may differ considerably, Ami Pro, 1-2-3 and Freelance Graphics have very similar button bars. The toolbars can be customised for the current job, so, for example, you can have editing, proofing and graphics toolbars. Approach includes relational features allowing access to 10 databases. The package uses a very visual approach in an attempt to emphasise that users do not need to be programmers. Data entry includes check boxes and pull-down lists. The full version of Lotus SmartSuite takes 62 MB of disk space, with the minimum size being 27 MB.

Borland Office 2 contains WordPerfect 6.0, Quattro Pro 5.00s and the database Paradox 4.5. Presentation graphics are provided by the Presentation Advisor, an add-on to Quattro Pro. It has all the basic elements of the other presentation graphics modules in this category, has fewer templates and layouts than similar packages. The package's minimum disk space is 21 MB, with a maximum of 62 MB. Its Desktop Director is a button bar which allows access to various utilities.

Open Access IV 4.0 includes a word processor and a spreadsheet, plus a database which supports SQL. It also contains an appointment scheduler, calculator and address book functions.

Many of the integrated packages and office suites advertise several different prices. Substantial reductions are available if you trade in other products. Some users will wish to upgrade from a previous version of the same package. Other manufacturers will allow a trade in, for example, of any product in any of the application categories. This is one of the ways in which software manufacturers establish their products.

Personal information managers

DateBook Pro (bundled with TouchBase Pro at a low price) from Iona Software is a Macintosh time management and calendaring program. Schedules can be viewed by day, week, month or year, and tasks can be set with alarms and reminders. Gantt charts are also supported. To-do lists can be held, given priorities and carried forward. Print-out options include wall charts and Filofax. It is described as fully integrable with TouchBase Pro, a contact management database.

Lotus Organizer is a Windows-based package that provides an on-screen notebook which looks just like an on-screen Filofax. It has six tabbed sections providing diary, to-do lists, date planner, address book, notepad and anniversary list. Various different page formats can be selected, with appointments being entered into the diary, with reminders if required. The to-do lists can be prioritised using colour-coding. The address book will store up to 65 000 sets of details. Lotus Organizer can be purchased separately, or as part of the Lotus SmartSuite bundle.

Borland Sidekick for Windows is the Windows version of one of the earliest TSR programs, now developed into a full Personal Information Manager. It incorporates a cardfile, calendar and notepad. Several separate items are shown on screen at one time, and its ability to customise is rated highly by its fans.

Accounting

For personal or home finances, there are a several products on the market.

Quicken 3.0 from Intuit works using a spreadsheet-like screen for cashbook data entry. Its QuickFill feature suggests the nearest match for data entries as you type. These are selected if you need them, ignored if you do not. A home user would customise Quicken by setting up precisely which accounts were needed, so that payments, deposits and transfers can be handled easily. It provides a wide range of print-outs, and budget forecasts can also be made.

Sage has produced various generations of PC accounting software, aimed at different sectors of the computerised accounting market. Sage Moneywise aimed at the home accounting market, offers good asset management features, including an insurance inventory list with values. It can keep track of outstanding bills, and forecast budgets.

Other accounting software is aimed at the business market, with some products costing over £1000, clearly out of the pocket of home users, and providing many features which even small businesses are unlikely to use.

There are, however, a number of the cheaper business products which are aimed at the needs of a simple company or voluntary organisations' accounts.

QuickBooks for Windows from Intuit provides double entry book-keeping. It is said to simplify data entry, because it remembers previous transactions in order to prompt new entries. Account details, for example, can be selected from a pull-down list. A password system is incorporated to protect against unauthorised changes. All the transactions entered are available for analysis, even after the end of year close-down. All the key reports can be generated.

Computer Associates' Accpac Simply Accounting is a Windows package. It is claimed to be easy to learn, through a primer which steps the user through basic accounting principles. It has full password protection. Entries can be posted to previous periods. A wide range of outputs can be generated. Files can be exported to word processing or spreadsheet programs for customising. In common with a number of other accounting packages, it does not include payroll, but it does include stock control and job costing.

The company Pegasus has been established for many years in the DOS accounting market. It produces a range of products aimed at different sectors of the market. Pegasus Solo is described as a fully integrated accounting suite. It incorporates sales, purchase and nominal ledgers, with invoicing and stock control. It handles VAT requirements, and generates statements and aged debtors reports.

Programming

Readers hoping to explore the use of programming languages will need to consult other books to help make their selection. There may be particular languages used by organisations for which you might work. Being able to program in any language develops a level of competence, and certainly learning a second language will be a lot easier. Many firms advertise, however, that they need staff with a proven track record in particular languages.

Visual Basic is available in DOS and Windows versions. It is gaining popularity as a means of customising many of the popular packages, such as Microsoft Excel.

Other popular languages include Pascal, in versions such a Turbo Pascal, from Borland and C++, available in both Microsoft and Borland editions.

When choosing a programming package, the two main considerations may be the compatibility of the language dialect, and the editing and other utilities provided.

Games

It would not be possible or appropriate in a book such as this to give a detailed list of good games software. Prospective purchasers will usually have particular interests which will be reflected in their choice of games. Games software prices are also quite volatile. New products tend to be fairly expensive, and are snapped up by the fanatics, but then prices drop after a year or two when new versions are released or fashions change.

One successful game over the years has been Lemmings from Psygnosis, in which the user attempts to guide green-haired creatures to safety. Versions are available both for DOS and Macintosh.

Microsoft Flight Simulator has been available in various versions for the past ten years or so. At one time, the ability to run it was considered to be the test of true PC compatibility. Its latest version, 4.0, includes a choice of aircraft, such as a Cessna and a World War I fighter, and includes digitised recordings of the sounds of real 'planes.

Games tend to follow fashions, and so, for example, in an Olympic year, there will be a spate of related games on the market. If dinosaurs are in vogue, these will appear in many of the games.

Music

Specialist hardware is often needed to make use of music software. It would not be appropriate here to explore all the options. You need to know not only what software can be bought with specific music hardware, but what range of other products is currently available, and what is likely to become available in the future.

Route planning

AutoRoute Plus from NextBase has evolved through various versions, and is still the acknowledged market leader. All the versions provide the user with options to set a start point and end point. Once the first few characters of the place name have been entered, suggestions are displayed. Similarly, intermediate locations can be entered. Options can be set for route preferences. Suggested routes are then generated, and can be displayed either in table form (words) or in graphical form. The quickest, shortest and cheapest routes are generated and can be displayed. Different levels of detail within a map can be chosen by a process of zooming.

The latest version includes an additional option called MapVision Plus. This supports bit-mapped graphics, providing far more detail than the previous vector versions. The maps used are from the Ordnance Survey, proving detail as good as those from a map book, including hills and other geographical features.

AutoRoute Plus can be purchased singularly or with MapVision for an additional payment. They can also be bought together on CD.

Because it is fairly expensive the package is aimed at the business rather than domestic market, and is useful for busy sales executives.

A cut-down version called AutoRoute Express is more attractively priced for home users.

Contact management

Iona Software's TouchBase Pro for the Macintosh (bundled with DateBook Pro) is a contacts database. It allows data entry through pop-up lists and check boxes. It allows multi-level searches and sorts. Printing options include envelopes, mailing lists, address books, fax cover sheets and personalised letters. It is said to integrate completely with DateBook Pro.

12

HARDWARE: THE COMPUTER

— How do we compare equipment? —

When you read in reviews, advertising literature or talk to people who have a computer, you will inevitably come across many technical terms. Sometimes people do use technical terms to confuse, and advertisers might like to make something sound very grand, but with such a wealth of features on offer, jargon is unavoidable. If you think somebody is trying to 'blind you with science', though, just stop them and ask a few questions, such as 'what benefit is there from that feature?'.

All computer systems will have a main computer, housed in some form of casing, with backing storage, a keyboard, a monitor and a normally a printer. With a multi-user system there will be further equipment.

It is natural for advertisers to wish to show off their equipment in the best possible light, and since there are so many variations on each of the components of a system, simply describing them all can become extremely long-winded and off-putting.

Figures are bandied about for various devices, such as capacities and speeds. Many of the figures quoted can be only a rough guide. It is important to realise that whilst the figures quoted must, by law, be accurate, they may not give the whole picture. Printer speeds, for example, may depend on the proportion of a page to be covered in ink. Some printers will produce a lightly covered page more quickly than a densely covered one; for others it might make no difference at all. It is of relatively little use to have a very high specification screen display if your software is incapable of exploiting the facilities. The best advice, therefore, is certainly to look at quoted statistics, but really only to use them as a guideline rather than an infallible discriminator.

An example of confusing performance data is the clock speed of a chip, which is used to give an idea of the processing speed of the chip. However, this figure alone, does not give a full picture, as another figure, the size of the bus, also matters in processing. Some systems might send more signals per second, but they might be smaller signals (a 16 digit code rather than 32, for example).

Manufacturers will also quote access times both for memory and disk. The memory access time is the time taken to transfer a character in memory to or from the main processor within the machine (called the CPU, Central Processor Unit). These times are measured in thousand millionths of a second, or nanoseconds, and a typical memory access speed is 70 nanoseconds. A variation in this speed, even if it doubled or halved, would hardly be noticeable in most applications, such a word processing. Performance with more memory intensive software might be noticeable.

Disk access speeds depend on the layout of the disk, and where the data you want is held relative to the position of the disk head after the previous disk access. Manufacturers quote disk access times, but at best these are estimates. Different manufacturers' figures cannot be compared even if access to the same file is quoted, as file storage efficiency depends how full the disk was at the time of saving the file.

———— Central processor chips ————

All computer systems have at their heart a central processor unit, sometimes abbreviated to CPU. In a microcomputer, the main processor will be on a single silicon chip, mounted, along with chips for other purposes, on a motherboard fitted inside the computer. Board-mounted systems are easier to remove or replace, either to repair or upgrade a system.

PCs are normally categorised according to their main processing chip, with new chips coming out all the time which increase the power available.

Most advertisements and reviews discuss the speed of the CPU. The clock speed is measured in megahertz, which is millions of cycles or pulses per second, often abbreviated to MHz. The single figure of clock speed can, however, be a little deceptive on its own. The clock speed measures only the rate of data processing, not how much data is processed at any one time. As some processors process 32 bits (meaning 'binary digits', the smallest unit of storage) of information at a time, they effectively do twice as much work as a 16 bit processor with the same clock speed. Also, the speed of the fastest processors may be much greater than that of the memory chips. In these cases, the main processor is delayed, waiting for the memory chips to catch up. This problem is measured in wait states. The fastest machines have zero wait states, slower machines have an average wait state of 0.7 or 1. Again, for the purchaser, the important question is 'in the end, how do these ratings affect performance in using real software?'

The manufacturer Intel has dominated the CPU technology market for many years, largely because of the use of Intel designs in IBM computers and therefore in compatible computers. IBM has manufactured its own chips under licence to Intel. But Intel has faced increasing competition in recent years, as competitors have sought either to produce the same power for less money, or increased functionality at a similar price. As time goes by, various alliances, such as that between IBM and Intel, are made and then broken.

The 8086, 8088 and 80286 chips manufactured by Intel were used in the first few generations of IBM PCs, but are technologies that are at least ten years old. That is not to say that there is anything wrong with them; there are many machines from that era still in daily use. New software products, though, tend not be designed to work on the older technology. New machines do not include any of these chips.

The lowest specification IBM compatible machines normally available as new are based on two main types of Intel chips, called the 386DX and the 386SX, although few machines based on these chips are now manufactured. The 386DX (originally called just the 386 or 80386) was introduced in 1985. Since that time, various versions have been released, each with a successively higher clock speed. With increased miniaturisation, clock speeds have increased, so that there have been versions of the 386DX available at clock speeds of 16, 20, 25 and 33 MHz (that is millions of pulses a second). Chip specifications are normally quoted in a form such as 386DX/16, with the second number being the clock speed.

The 386SX was released three years later by Intel, as a 'cut-down' and therefore cheaper version of the 386DX. It works internally like a 386DX, having a 32 bit data bus, but communicates externally like a 286, using a 16 bit bus. The bus is the path responsible for carrying the signals along a data path. The clock speed is therefore not the only guide, as a 33 MHz 386SX is slightly slower than a 20 MHz 386DX. Some magazines, such as *Computer Buyer* have attempted to address these anomalies by rating all available processors according to a common scale. Intel has also introduced its own ICOMP ratings.

The 486DX and 486SX have a similar relationship to each other as their 386 versions, except the power of the 486SX is cut down in different ways. The 486DX2 is yet another version of the 486DX, which works twice as fast internally as the DX, using a system known as 'clock doubling'. Through its range of three different 486 chips, Intel has designed a system so that you can buy the cheapest, the 486SX, and then, when resources allow, upgrade to a 486DX2. This capacity to upgrade is known as 'OverDrive'.

 Rival manufacturers also produce 386 chips, such as the AMD 386DX and AMD 386SX, and 486 chips, like the Cyrix CX486SLC and CX486DLC. Intel has hit back at rival manufacturers both by reducing prices and through a heavy advertising campaign including the use of 'Intel Inside' stickers on products using its chips.

When Intel found it could not claim copyright on its chip numbering system, the latest range, provisionally called the 586 range, became the Pentium; again leaps forward in speed are being made.

Motorola manufactures a different range of chips, which are used in Apple computers. The original 68000 used in the Macintosh processed 32 bits internally, but uses 16 bits for external communication. Subsequent chips in the family were the 68020, 68030 and 68040. Each was a step up the evolutionary ladder, and all use full 32 bit architecture. Each has a faster maximum clock speed than its predecessor. The 68030 allows advanced memory management which can be used to implement advanced features of the System 7 operating system. The 68040 is roughly comparable with Intel's 80486DX, including its own maths co-processor.

Apple manufactures several different Macs based on the 68040 chip. These range from the LC and Performa systems to the more powerful Quadra range. The portable Macs, known as Powerbooks use the same range of chips.

The latest Apple Macintosh computers are the Power Macs, which are based around the Power PC chip. The Power PC series of micro-processors has been produced through an alliance of Motorola, Apple and IBM.

Internally, computers also differ in the way data flows within the system. So whilst two computers might use the same main process-ing chip, the way information is passed within the system can be different. The internal layout of a computer which enables internal signalling and control is referred to as the architecture.

Other chips

As well as the central processing chip, a computer will also contain one or more other chips, mounted on a single motherboard. Chips are used to control features such as the computer's internal memory, graphics, disk storage access, keyboard controller, a clock and calen-dar (which is usually maintained by a battery when the computer is switched off), and ports, which handle signalling from devices such as printers and a mouse. Not all chips used within a computer system will be mounted on the motherboard. Some will be contained within device controllers which are fitted to expansion slots (see later), and others still will be contained within devices themselves (such as in a laser printer).

Other terms are used to describe additional memory functions, and an outline understanding of them is useful when reading sales litera-ture.

There are two types of random access memory (RAM) used within PCs. Dynamic RAM (DRAM) uses one transistor and one capacitor to represent a binary digit (the smallest unit of storage). The capacitors used must be energised hundreds of times per second to maintain charges.

Static RAM (SRAM) depends on flow of current through one side or the other depending on which of two transistors is activated. This type of memeory is faster than DRAM, but needs more space, con-sumes more power and costs more. Inevitably, in most systems, a combination of dynamic and static RAM is used to give a compromise between speed and cost.

Computer memory consists of a series of chips. In most machines it is possible to increase the amount of memory by adding what is called a SIMM (single in-line memory module). This would contain, typically, eight or nine RAM memory chips mounted on a standard size of card. Many computer advertisements will quote a basic memory size, and explain that it is 'expandable to' some larger figure.

A disk cache is a reserved section of memory either from the main memory or on the hard disk controller. Each time the disk is read, a larger block of data than is needed is read. If the next request is for data held in the cache, the data can be provided much more quickly than the disk, a physical device, could provide it. When writing to disk, the cache memory can be used to store data so that it can be written in larger blocks. In MS-DOS 4 and later, main memory is used for the disk cache through the driver SMARTDRV.SYS.

Memory cache is a similar facility used between memory and the processor. This anticipates the data and instructions that may next be required to use a higher speed cache memory, such as static RAM chips.

The video RAM holds information for the image that is to be displayed on the screen. The term 'dual-ported memory' is also used, as one port is used to write to the memory whilst another reads from it for display purposes. This system ensures that the display is not delayed by the writing process.

Maths co-processor chips perform high-speed floating point arithmetic. This is useful not just for the most obvious mathematical applications, such as spreadsheets, but also for computer aided design and presentation graphics. Advertisers don't always tell you that, to be used, the maths co-processor must be activated by the program, otherwise no benefit is gained. Many programs make no use of maths co-processors.

Buses

Data travels within a computer system through a mechanism known as a bus, the electrical pathway which allows the various parts to communicate. If additional devices are to be added, these too must be compatible with the bus system, sometimes referred to as the computer's architecture. Additional devices are generally connected to the computer by slotting an extra electronic circuit board into a slot connected to the bus system. These slots are known as expansion slots and the electronic circuit boards are commonly referred to as expansion cards. When selecting a computer, it is important to consider the number and type of expansion slots available for fitting expansion cards. Most advertisements will quote the number of 'free' expansion slots, as some slots will already be used for controllers for devices within any system you buy.

Three common PC bus architectures have been around for some time.

The ISA (industry standard architecture) bus was used, in various forms, both 8 and then 16 bit versions, on PCs up to the 286 machine. IBM ensured what was called backward compatibility, so old cards designed around 8 bit architecture could still be used with later 16 bit ISA. The converse was not true: the newer 16 bit cards would not work with old 8 bit architecture.

Micro Channel Architecture (MCA) was introduced by IBM when it announced the PS/2 computer range. This was a much faster, higher performance system than IBM's earlier system, but a break was made in compatibility, so that cards for the two systems, ISA and MCA do not work together. Many of the manufacturers chose not to make the same break in continuity, so MCA architecture is less common than other architectures.

The EISA standard (Extended Industry Standard Architecture) is a development of ISA, and is compatible with the previous standard so that ISA cards can be used within the system. Again compatibility does not work the other way, and indeed, an EISA card inserted in an ISA slot will probably do great damage.

Whilst MCA cards are smaller, they cost more. MCA is designed so that the computer detects the presence of cards and operates accordingly. The EISA standard requires the setting of small switches, called DIP switches, inside the machine.

As processor speeds have increased, the gap between them and the speed of the bus has widened. These technical difficulties have meant that the three previous bus standards increasingly became a bottleneck within the system, particularly for the graphics displays used in Windows. A true colour 24-bit screen display at VGA resolution takes a megabyte of memory, and moving this amount of data regularly can slow down the rest of the processing. The system known as local bus overcomes the bottleneck by using tight coupling over a very short distance whereby data transfer can be very quick, and at the same speed as the processor clock. The VESA Local Bus (Video Electronics Standards Association) has gained rapid popularity amongst manufacturers, so that you will see most systems advertised as 'VESA' or 'VL', which mean the same thing.

The main alternative form of local bus is the PCI (Peripheral Component Interconnect) standard which has been introduced by Intel. Intel claims that PCI is compatible with ISA, MCA and EISA, and will be suitable in the future for Pentium and the planned P6 and P7 chips.

It can be argued that PCI is a better long-term prospect, as it already supports three devices compared with VESA's two. VESA, however, developed earlier and has been cheaper for manufacturers to implement, so it has gained such a hold on the market that it will be around for a long time to come.

Experts will always give differing advice on which architecture is best. All you need to remember is that all your purchases must be from within the same standard or compatible with it. In making any purchase, you must make sure you ask about compatibility, and write any conditions on order forms when you send them off.

Keyboards

Computer keyboards have alphabetic characters laid out in the traditional 'QWERTY' style. Though this layout is regularly criticised and alternatives have been proposed, 'QWERTY' is unlikely to be replaced, as so many millions of people are used to using it.

Apart from the layout of the letters, and the row of numeric keys above, there are very few other standards which everybody keeps to. On a laptop, for example, where space on the keyboard is at a real premium, keys may perform three or four different tasks when used in conjunction with other keys. Sometimes half-size keys are used.

Keys such as 'CTRL' and 'ALT' are provided solely for use with other keys. Many programs use CTRL or ALT key combinations, and these uses are explained in the manuals. Key combinations are usually based on an easily memorable code, though this is not always the case. CTRL and ALT key combinations are used within programs such as a word processor to distinguish between the entry of text (without such keys), and commands (with CTRL or ALT). Powerful commands, which the user would not wish to use accidentally, are usually accessed through a combination of keys that is difficult to press by accident. Some particularly irrevocable features, such as system reset, are called using a three key combination of CTRL, ALT and one other key.

Most keyboards also contain a numeric keypad, where the digits from 0 to 9 are accessible together, along with the decimal point, and some arithmetic symbols. The numeric keypad may double up as a cursor control pad, and so the keys have arrows showing directions of cursor movement. The four movements up, down, left, and right are usually laid out in a formation like a compass. Other keys are used for moving the cursor to 'HOME' (the start), 'END', 'PG UP' (page up) and 'PG DOWN' (page down). The numeric keypad can usually be switched between numeric use and cursor control using a key labelled 'NUM LOCK' which turns the numeric feature on and off. The numeric keypad is normally at the right hand side of the keyboard.

Cursor control is also provided on many machines through the four keys 'up', 'down', 'left' and 'right' as an inverted 'T' shape with 'up' at the top.

On most keyboards, therefore, there are dedicated numeric keys above the top alphabetical line, and dedicated cursor control keys in the inverted 'T'. The numeric keypad layout, doubling as numeric or cursor control, can then be used at the user's discretion for either role, and users can flip between the two. The most common keyboard layout has 101 keys including the inverted T cursor keys, and is known as the 'enhanced keyboard'.

Much software uses the function keys labelled 'F1', 'F2' and so on, up to either F10 or F12. Two alternative layouts are used for the function keys, either as a rectangular block at the left-hand side of the keyboard in pairs, or as a single row across the top of the keyboard, usually broken into groups of four. When you buy a package which makes use of function keys, you may be supplied with a plastic strip to place by the function keys as an aide memoire, since function keys may have several different uses when combined with SHIFT, ALT or CTRL keys.

In their attempts to keep keyboards as compact as possible, particularly on laptop machines, a number of manufacturers have altered the positioning of the keys called 'SHIFT' and 'ENTER' (sometimes called 'RETURN'). Some users feel that these positionings of frequently used keys can be quite awkward, particularly if you are using machines with different layouts regularly. If, for example, you regularly miss the 'ENTER' key, or press 'CAPS LOCK' instead of 'SHIFT', you could waste a lot of time.

Desktop machines normally have a detachable keyboard connected to the computer through a cable to enable users to use the keyboard at a distance from the computer. No such choice is normally available on a laptop, where the keyboard is fixed within the case. Detachable keyboards are generally interchangeable, and occasionally prices are quoted without the cost of the keyboard. Potential purchasers should watch for this potential extra cost when comparing prices. If the keyboard is not quoted as part of the main price, this is probably because there is a choice of different keyboards.

Some manufacturers make a major selling point of their particular keyboard. A good keyboard needs a positive feel, so that when you have pressed a key, you feel that you have struck it properly. If you press a key hesitantly, you do not want several copies of the letter displayed because the key stayed down too long. The better keyboards have a number of lights on them to indicate the mode, such as 'NUM LOCK', 'CAPS LOCK' and 'SCROLL LOCK'. These can prove very useful, and are either incorporated in the relevant keys or are placed all together at the top right corner of the keyboard.

The keys on a good keyboard are sculpted, so that are not completely flat on the top. The keys 'F' and 'J', the typist's 'home keys', and the number '5' in the centre of the numeric keypad may be sculpted differently, or may have a raised dot so that they feel slightly different in some way. These features are very useful for touch typists.

A desktop computer keyboard can usually be angled using support legs at the back. Different users find different angles, as well as different distances, more convenient and comfortable. Macintosh computers have a choice of keyboards, the most advanced of which includes wrist rests and a detachable numeric keypad.

———— Monitors and screens ————

Computers display output on a screen or monitor, occasionally still referred to as a visual display unit. The display capabilities of a monitor are governed both by the type of monitor and by the display card used within the computer (display cards are also known as video adapters). Unless the signals from the computer are sent in a form that the monitor can interpret, no picture will be shown. When choosing an initial or upgrade monitor, you must make sure that it is compatible with the display card in your system. Much software, particularly for Microsoft Windows or the Macintosh, will need particular video standards. Many of the video cards available will support some of the previous standards, which is essential if you are using older software. Your display card may need 1 MB of video RAM (discussed earlier) to display an image for higher resolution systems. The term 'true colour' is used to refer to 24 bit colour coding, which can represent 16 million different colours. It is felt that such a range is needed particularly to reflect the subtlety of flesh tones.

Monitors are capable of providing a variety of levels of fine detail, called the resolution. The higher the resolution, the finer are the dots that make up the display. Screen resolution is measured in pixels (short for picture cells) which are the small dots that go to make up a picture. The old CGA standard screen, for example, of 320 by 200 pixels (written as 320 x 200) allowed for a grid of 64 000 dots.

Regardless of the resolution of a display, monitors may or may not be capable of colour display. Displaying one colour, possibly in a variety of shades is known as monochrome (not black and white, because the screen could be green or amber). Desktop computers invariably use colour, but many laptops are monochrome because the colour screen technology for laptops is still expensive.

The computer sends out signals in a form that the monitor can interpret, through its display adapter card.

There are a number of common standard formats used for display systems. Over the last ten years, systems such as MDA, CGA, EGA and VGA have come and gone. Each generation increased the resolution and the number of colours available. The last of these allowed for 16 colours when it was first introduced, and represented a major step forward at the time. There are still many systems in use based on these previous standards, and some suppliers may have old stock using VGA. Such systems are probably acceptable for DOS applications and occasional Windows use, but later standards are more suitable for heavy use of Windows, desktop publishing and computer aided design.

The SuperVGA standard (abbreviated to SVGA) was introduced by VESA, and takes the resolution up to a minimum of 800 x 600 pixels. IBM has produced its own new standard called XGA, which supports VGA as well.

In some specialist applications, such as photographic processing, it might be necessary to use a grey-scale monitor, usually supporting up to 256 levels of grey. These are expensive, because there is a limited market for them. Some of the higher specification monitors, such as VGA are capable of displaying 64 grey-scale levels, which may suffice for such applications.

Most graphics standards incorporate separate modes for text and graphics, and advertisers will quote figures for the graphics mode, partly because these sound more impressive, but also because these are more likely to differ between different manufacturers.

Some modern monitors are now built with a system known as multiscanning. This means that they have the electronics within them to interpret a variety of standards from the computer. By electronically testing the signals that it is receiving, a multiscanning monitor will display to a number of different standards. This would be particularly important if monitors were to be swapped between various systems.

Most advertisements will quote a figure for the monitor screen size. These are consistently quoted as the diagonal distance, as with televisions, and so the measurement appears exaggerated. Because of edge effects and the casing, one inch can usually be deducted from the size given to say how much of the screen is usable. A larger monitor will not in itself improve the display for the user. If the same screen resolution is used, the dots are simply made larger. For some specialist applications, particularly those involving design, it is also worth bearing in mind that some screen resolution standards were chosen so that screen displays are exactly the same as printed output. This link can be lost if other resolutions are chosen.

Larger monitors are necessary, though, to gain the maximum benefit from higher resolution displays. There are a number of specific applications for which high resolution is particularly useful. These include Computer Aided Design (CAD), and high-end desktop publishing where, for example, you might wish to see two pages displayed side-by-side. For some such uses, monochrome is perfectly adequate but, if you are prepared to pay for them, 21 inch colour screens are available. With some specialist systems, proprietary screen adapters are used to gain maximum benefits from the high resolutions of large screens.

Many screen specifications quote a figure for the 'dot pitch' which is the measure of distance between adjacent dots on the screen. The smaller the dot pitch is, the sharper the picture. Most desktop SVGA monitors have a dot pitch of 0.28 mm. The beams sent to the screen are fired through a shadow mask, which has very small holes in it, before producing the familiar luminance when the beam hits the phosphor surface on the inside of the screen. Sony has developed an alternative technology which uses an aperture grille with long vertical slits. This patented system, called Trinitron, is said to produce a sharper, brighter image with truer colours. It is very common on Macintosh systems, and is gaining an increasing proportion of the PC market. Screens using the same type of technology as Sony's Trinitron are now being developed by other manufacturers.

The refresh rate of a monitor system is the frequency with which the image is renewed on the screen. The electronic beam sweeps across the screen very quickly, and the phosphor surface in one particular place will only glow for a brief time after the beam has hit it, and so needs to be refreshed. The refresh rate of a monitor is sometimes referred to as the frequency, and is measured in hertz (number of occurrences per second). A good SVGA monitor will work at about 70 Hz. Most users find this frequency acceptable; higher frequencies are likely to lead to the monitor burning out more rapidly. Some older monitors with lower frequencies used phosphors with longer persistence to maintain the image. This meant that graphics, particularly movement, appeared to be jerky. An effect called 'ghosting' also occured when old images lingered too long.

On an interlaced monitor, not all the lines of the screen are refreshed on each pass of the electronic gun. On one pass all the odd lines are displayed, on the second all the evens, than all the odds again and so on. The electronics for such systems is cheaper. It is preferable to buy a non-interlaced monitor to avoid possible flicker and ghosting. Though very few entirely interlaced monitors are now sold, some switch to interlacing to cope with higher resolutions.

If a similar image is displayed on a screen for many hours of a day, after several months or years, the image may become etched on the screen surface, in an effect sometimes called 'screen burn'. This could happen, for example, with the menu of a word processor which is on a screen day after day. 'Screen saver' software blanks the screen and displays moving objects if the keyboard has not been touched for a specified time, usually a few minutes. As soon as a key is pressed, the previous display is restored. Screen savers can be bought separately, or may be provided with a system such as Microsoft Windows.

The better modern monitors avoid image distortion near the edges of the screen. Many monitors also come on a stand that you can tilt (up and down) and swivel (side to side). From an ergonomic point of view this is important, so that you can work in a comfortable position and adapt the system to your environment. Some monitors come with a screen designed to reduce glare particularly from reflections. Some monitors have plastic screens to reduce glare; others simply use less shiny glass. Glare can also be reduced by using a separate anti-glare filter placed in front of the screen. Good monitors also allow the user control over the screen's brightness and contrast, allowing the display to be adapted to the environment in which it is being used. Control over horizontal and vertical hold allow you to move the image to centre it better. These controls are better situated on the front of the monitor, to save you fiddling round the back and trying at the same time to see an effect at the front.

Some concern has also been expressed about the effects on users of long exposure to the electrostatic and magnetic radiation given off by monitors. Most manufacturers now offer low-radiation monitors.

The EC Display Screen Directive, which applied in the UK to all workstations introduced into workplaces after the 1st January 1993, has helped to improve the standard of computer screens. Computer systems in use by employers before that date have until 1997 to reach the same standards which apply to the keyboard, work surface and chair, as well as to the screen and environmental issues.

One possible future development could be that of touch screen technology. This is already in widespread use where keyboard input is not possible or not desirable, such as for tourist information. Here the whole dialogue can take place on the screen with users responding to on-screen questions by pressing an area on the screen. Such systems need specialist software to exploit such a facility, and home and office use is still quite limited.

13

THE OPERATING SYSTEM

—— What is an operating system? ——

Whatever system you choose to buy, there will be two types of programs that you will run on it, applications software and systems software.

The applications programs are the programs that you use to carry out the jobs for which you bought the computer, such as accounts, word processing or playing games. There is a huge range of choice of applications, as can be seen from a quick glance at any supplier's catalogue. Underlying all applications, however, is the systems software, usually referred to as the operating system.

Many potential new users are put off by terms like 'operating system', and by the huge range of ideas involved in the way it functions. These worries almost always end up being unfounded, as the purpose of the operating system is to take the burden of day-to-day operation of the system from the user. Unless you want to become a technical expert in this field, there really is no need to know more than a few basics.

Concern about the details of an operating system is rather like worrying about how a fuel injection system works on a car. You might be really fascinated by that technology: some would argue that understanding a fuel injection system enables you to realise a better performance from it, but most users can operate a fuel injected car without having the first notion of how it works. It is a similar story with operating a computer. Some improvement in performance can be gained by 'fine tuning' the way the operating system is arranged, but once a system is set up for you, you can use it without any depth of understanding of how it functions.

The operating system handles all the communications between the computer and the disk drives, so that a simple command to copy a file, or a complex one from within a word processor, can be carried out. In similar ways the operating system handles the screen display, and communication with printers. It is the operating system which first intercepts and decides how to respond whenever a key is pressed on the keyboard. The operating system also manages the internal memory of a computer, which has become increasingly complex in recent years to make best use of the larger amounts of memory now available at affordable prices.

In addition, the use of a standard operating system also takes much of that burden away from the authors applications software. Thus the standard routines in the operating system are accessed by the applications designers. This ensures that some of the basic jobs are carried out in a standard way. Many pre-written routines, however, are cumbersome and slow, so many writers of applications software write programs that access the peripherals directly. This can cause problems on a computer using multiple applications or on a multi-user system.

From a potential purchaser's point of view, the choice of operating system is a vital one. In the early days of microcomputing, there was a bewildering array of operating systems available and many computer manufacturers developed their own proprietary operating systems. The two main reasons for this were that the licensing fees for software from other suppliers were prohibitively expensive, and that some early machines did not have enough memory or features to exploit standard operating systems fully or properly. As with any new market, after a few years, the range very much narrowed. At one time, there were two leading types of video recorders using different types of tapes, and arguments raged over which was superior. In the end, it did not matter which was technically superior. As soon as one format dominated, supplies of the other format became very short, and a standard emerged by default. Computing has not settled to a single format yet, and probably never will, because so many millions of users have invested so much time and effort into one format or another.

On an IBM-compatible computer, there are only two main operating systems: MS-DOS (at one time called PC-DOS on IBM machines, but now often called simply 'DOS'), and OS/2. In addition Microsoft Windows is used as a 'front-end' program giving a friendlier face to DOS and providing much more by managing several programs at once. Apple Macintosh computers, which use the System 7 operating system, and Commodore Amigas, which use AmigaDOS, are based around proprietary operating systems. This term was originally coined in the world of mainframe and minicomputers, where each manufacturer had a different operating system. The term is still used, and applies to those computers such as Apple, Acorn and Commodore, where an operating system is designed for a specific range of computers only and is not portable.

One significant difference is whether, as with Apple and Archimedes computers, much of the operating system is held on a chip, or whether, as with DOS machines, it is primarily loaded from disk. The first approach makes upgrading the operating system a more difficult job, as a chip has to be replaced, and is likely, because a chip will then be thrown away, to be more expensive. Replacement of a disk-based operating system is usually just a matter of using a different disk, which can, of course, be copied to the hard disk. DOS systems do, of course, use some ROM at the booting stage (see later), but this is geared to accept whichever version of DOS it finds.

When choosing a computer system, and the software to go with it, you must be careful to purchase the correct version for your machine. The first step is to discover which operating systems are available on your proposed machine. The second step is then to look at which applications packages are available in versions for those operating systems. Much of the most popular software is available in versions for different formats, but the versions may differ in the features they include, and you will not be able to run other versions on your computer.

The much larger office-based minicomputers use systems such as Unix, and mainframe computer manufacturers tend to use their own operating systems. In each sector of the market, though, there are moves to unify systems, and to increase compatibility between different systems. In the end it will benefit all the manufacturers if there is interchangeability.

Fortunately, compatibility is a major marketing benefit, so advertising literature is usually quite explicit about the interchangeability of information. PowerMacs, for example, run the proprietary System 7 operating system, but are able, through a process known as emulation, to run programs designed for DOS and Windows. You must read literature carefully, though. Files such as documents or drawings in one format may be read by different software, but the applications software itself may not be available for the target machine, and where it is, it will usually have to be purchased separately.

The operating system scene continues to change quite quickly. The two main selling points of the newer systems are portability and object orientation. 'Portability' refers to running the same program on a number of different types and models of equipment (sometimes referred to as 'platforms'). 'Object orientation' refers to the passing of items (referred to as 'objects') between applications. Part of a spreadsheet might be passed into a word processor. A graphic might be passed from a drawing program. As new systems or versions of systems emerge, the sophistication and ease with which these tasks can be carried out increases. Newer systems such as OS/2 version 2.1 from IBM and Windows NT from Microsoft continue to push back the frontiers of what can be achieved. One aspect of portability is that each operating system manufacturer is keen to ensure that a new product will read files and even run files designed for one of the other systems. Such products are then marketed on the basis that they can do all that the other products can, and much more.

Part of the operating system design includes the format used for disk storage. Nowadays, you will always be able to buy the hard disk ready formatted and floppy disks are often sold ready formatted as well. (Make sure they have the correct format.) Unlike the video analogy described earlier, although standard sizes of disks are used, the way in which information is recorded differs between operating systems. There will be times, though, when as a user you will want to format disks. If a floppy disk is accidentally corrupted, it may be possible to re-use it by formatting it again. If disaster strikes the hard disk, the whole system may become unusable until the hard disk is reformatted.

Booting

In normal working conditions, when the computer is first switched on, it will run a set of programs in a process known as 'booting'. An initial simple program may read a more complex program, which when run further reads a more complex program and so on. The term 'booting' comes from the idea of picking yourself up by your own bootstraps. The initial instructions are held in read only memory, and one of the first programs run will check that all the essential parts of the computer are present and working properly. This program will instruct the computer to search for the operating system on disk, and once it is found will pass control to it.

All boot programs are designed to search for the operating system on floppy disk first. If no disk is present, boot programs will look on the hard disk. Systems must be designed like this because when they are first used, the operating system will not be installed on hard disk. Once the operating system is on hard disk, it is not necessary to boot from floppy unless there is a major problem with the hard disk. Suppliers will tell you that it can be dangerous to boot from a floppy disk as some viruses attach themselves to the area used as the boot sector of a floppy disk.

There are times when a computer system needs to be restarted without physically switching the machine off and on. Occasionally a program will crash or the system will lock up for no obvious reason, usually when some internal settings affected by programs become inconsistent with each other, and the computer cannot resolve the conflict. The process to restart the system is termed a 'warm boot', and is achieved by pressing the 'reset' button on the machine's cabinet. If this does not work or is not available, pressing the three keys CTRL, ALT and DEL all at the same time will achieve the same thing. If all these approaches fail, then a 'cold boot' may be needed. This involves turning the power off, which will clear the memory and internal settings, before turning the machine on again in order to go through the process described earlier. The 'depth' of a reboot is a term sometimes used to describe the level to which internal settings are cleared. For example, a 'CTRL-ALT-DEL' does not necessarily clear all programs which have been loaded (such as TSRs – see later).

———— How settings are held ————

The computer is able to remember a few basic settings while power is switched off using a small amount of memory run from a recharge-able battery. This memory stores the time, the date, and systems information such as the screen type and details of the types and number of disk drives physically present. These settings are vital for the correct functioning of the system, and it is best to make a note of the settings to guard against the day when the battery fails.

Standard programs which are used all the time are usually held on a ROM chip. Such operations include handling the various requests to and from devices such as the keyboard, disk drives, the screen, and other ports (such as a mouse or scanner).

On a PC, this chip is known as the BIOS (Basic Input Output System). As new device types become available, it is possible that older versions of the BIOS are not capable of handling them. It is possible to upgrade or replace the BIOS with a more modern one. Though the process is relatively straightforward, it is worth seeking advice and following installation instructions to the letter to ensure that incorrect settings do not lose access to existing devices.

— Some common settings in MS-DOS —

Information in any computer system is held in files. Each file will hold a set of related data. A file might hold, for example, a word processed document, or a program to be run, or a drawing. A typical system will have a number of system and other files. MS-DOS uses a file naming convention that the file has a name of up to eight characters, with three further characters used for an extension to the name. Conventions have emerged so that MS-DOS users know the type of data held in a file from the extension. File names are normally written as the name followed by a dot, then the extension. 'MINUTES.DOC' would be recognised as a document file for one word processor or another. Files with the COM or EXE extension contain programs which can be run.

There are several hundred common extensions now used with particular meanings. Microsoft itself has designated about a dozen extensions for the use of MS-DOS. These conventions are explained in the MS-DOS manual. Conventions used by other applications will be explained in their manuals. Some reference books provide pages of lists of commonly used extensions. Most regular computer users will pick up the meanings of important extensions without effort from everyday use.

To keep the organisation of several hundred files in order, groups of related files are kept in a directory, which again is given a name of up to eight characters. Directories can themselves have sub-directories. For MS-DOS to search properly for a program file when it is to be run, it is important to use the PATH command, to tell the operating system which directories to search, and in what order.

In MS-DOS and OS/2, a number of files such as CONFIG.SYS (storing details of the configuration) and EMM386.EXE (memory management), are stored in the root directory. When you buy a new system, these files should be set up in the correct place on the disk and be working. The only time you will need to bother about these files is when you decide to upgrade or alter your configuration.

MS-DOS uses CONFIG.SYS to name all the device drivers to be loaded (drivers have the file extension SYS), and to set system parameters such as the number of files, the size of input-output buffers and details about drives. Amongst the files to be used will be those that manage extended or expanded memory, determining what is held in which parts of upper memory. Features such as disk caching (using a program like SMARTDRV.SYS) are also established at this stage. You can reasonably expect that when you buy a new system with a particular bundle of software, these various files are already set up to make best use of your system. A supplier will obviously use the same set up for all computers in a batch.

The values in files like CONFIG.SYS are relatively straightforward to alter using a simple or complex text editor. Care is needed, however, and users should read manuals very carefully. If, for example, extended or expanded memory is to be used for disk caching, then the relevant SYS file to run the memory driver must be installed before using SMARTDRV.SYS. Again, these issues will be taken care of in the supplier's initial set up.

— Expanded and extended memory —

You will see reference in advertisements and literature to expanded and extended memory. These terms, easily confused, actually refer to different ideas. Both are aimed at overcoming the 640 kB limitation of MS-DOS.

Expanded memory uses a system of swopping sections of memory into the usable area (called 'paging'). This system was introduced to allow full use of the 1 MB which 8088 and 8086 machines could address. Memory between 640 kB and 1 MB could be addressed by the processor but not by MS-DOS. This area is known as the upper memory area. Extended memory was designed later, and is only available on 286 and later machines. Extended memory is that memory above 1 MB which can be addressed by the microprocessor. If a DOS application has been designed according to the XMS (eXtended Memory System) standard, it can access memory above 1 MB with the aid of an extended memory manager (HIMEM.SYS). This makes sure that programs can access the extra memory and prevents different programs attempting to use the same extended memory area.

Programs such as EMM386.EXE simulate expanded memory on a system with extended memory. This then allows the use of programs designed to take advantage of expanded memory, and allows the use of the upper memory area for device drivers and programs.

Much of this detail can appear confusing to a new user, but most users need not be aware of which of these systems is in use. Once a system is set up, perhaps by the supplier, you can leave the system as it is. It is only when you wish to upgrade your system, and possibly optimise its performance, that you will need to explore the details of the different systems, explained in great detail in the MS-DOS manual.

———— MS-DOS conventions ————

A regular user of an MS-DOS system will certainly make use of, and may well wish to adapt batch files, which have a file extension BAT. These files contain a series of MS-DOS commands to be run one after the other. Many systems will be set up so that an application can be run by typing its name at the MS-DOS prompt, so that typing 'XT' followed by 'ENTER' will run the commands in a file called 'XT.BAT'. The batch file can then be used to change directories ready to run the software and to set parameters for the application that is about to be run. To change these details it may be necessary to edit a batch file. One particularly important batch file is AUTOEXEC.BAT, which, when placed in the root directory, is run automatically each time the computer is switched on. Through judicious use of this file, the everyday user can be protected from much day-to-day use of MS-DOS, as the batch file can be used to display a menu or even to run a set application automatically.

A number of other commands in MS-DOS might be of interest to a new or fairly new user. CHKDSK allows the disk to be checked for errors, and ensures that the occasional bad sector on the disk is permanently bypassed. MEM allows a user to look at memory allocation. Having gained some confidence in using MS-DOS users may like to alter environment settings through the SET command so that, for example, all directories are listed in alphabetical order. Messages can be altered by using PROMPT. Other commands like DOSKEY which allow users to create macros and MIRROR enabling the retrieval of deleted files are probably only for advanced users, who will learn details of the features by reading the comprehensive manual in detail.

DOS also uses conventions for device names. For example, PRN is used to denote the printer. Less obviously, LPT1 is used to address the parallel port. Again these conventions are explained in manuals.

Once you have made some use of an MS-DOS system, you will wish to copy, delete or move files. To carry out these tasks directly in MS-DOS will require use of the COPY, RENAME, XCOPY and DEL (for delete) commands. These, and the various options within them are explained in the MS-DOS manual, or any of the many excellent step-by-step guides to MS-DOS on the market.

——————— Compression ———————

To make the maximum use of hard disk space, it is now quite common to use some form of file compression program. Many files contain repeated characters, such as spaces in a word processed document, or background in a drawing. It is therefore possible for specialised software to hold the same information in a compressed form.

There are two main forms of compression. The first form of compression is disk compression, through products such as Stacker and SuperStor Pro. These work by creating a single file which is then treated as a disk drive. All the information is put into this file in a compressed form, and when a user wishes to retrieve the data, it is decompressed. As far as the user is concerned, then, the compression is transparent; it is as if the files were held in full form. The amount of compression that can be achieved depends on the type of file and its contents. A rough guide, though, is that compressed files will take about half their normal space. For this reason, programs of this type are referred to as 'disk doublers'.

The capacities available on disk drives are increasing year by year, so you may wonder why you would use a disk doubler at all. Laptop computers tend to have disk drives limited by the size of the casing and the weight, so disk doublers are particularly useful on laptops. In other contexts, too, buying a disk doubler might be a cheaper option than replacing a disk drive on an existing system, if indeed that is possible at all. There are, of course, other ways of saving disk space. It is argued that when users have more disk space, they acquire lazier habits and keep more copies of files longer. A well-disciplined user will copy files off a hard disk if they are not likely to be used regularly; they can always be copied back from floppy disk.

The other form of compression is file compression. This involves taking the contents of an individual file, and producing a new version with a different file extension. The original need not be kept, as it can be reproduced using a decompression program. Again, the space saving is variable, but as before averages around 50%. A number of shareware file compression and decompression products are available, such as PKZIP and PKUNZIP. File compression is a popular way to reduce the number of floppy disks that have to be mailed when issuing programs or files such as libraries of pictures. This leads to a number of products being issued in compressed form along with the decompression program. This can cause consternation for new users, but the processes are relatively straightforward (see Chapter 21).

Viruses

One increasing danger to computer files is the virus. There is a substantial amount of literature on the types of viruses and the way they work. Unless you are particularly interested in the technical aspects of the problem, you need not go into all the detail. What you will really be interested in is firstly how to reduce the chances of your computer being infected by a virus, and secondly how to rid yourself of one if it does appear.

Viruses are passed on through floppy disks being passed from one infected machine to another uninfected machine which then becomes infected (hence the name 'virus'). The virus program could be resident in the computer's memory (and may survive a warm boot) or could be on disk. Once a hard disk is infected, of course, any virus checking software held there might itself become infected. A variety of techniques have to be used therefore to protect against viruses. Some viruses infect the boot sector of the disk so that once the hard disk is infected, the virus operates every time the machine is turned on. Most virus writers use techniques such as intercepting interrupts so that everything appears normal on the disk. If a machine is booted from an infected floppy disk, the hard disk boot sector can become corrupt. This infection will happen, as often as not, through accidentally leaving a disk in the drive when switching on. Once a machine has been corrupted in this way, it will be necessary to boot the machine from a floppy with the anti-virus software on it; such a disk should be kept permanently as a read-only disk so that it cannot be infected itself. Other viruses attach themselves to program files which then run apparently normally, but have also run some other code at the same time which does the damage. Any further program files which are then run are also infected by being rewritten without the user noticing.

Anti-virus software works in a number of ways, checking for virus activity as a virus program runs, detecting changes to program files, and looking for pieces of code unique to known viruses. Some anti-virus software will check every disk as it is loaded and before use, and will refuse to use the disk if there is any infection. This process clearly slows down use, but on the faster machines this is almost imperceptible. Some virus protection systems also guide you through a process of producing an emergency rescue disk with all the essential information to reconfigure your system should disaster strike. Some also incorporate forms of protection so that access to the hard disk cannot be gained without a password, even if you boot from a floppy disk.

Because viruses are still being developed, there is a constant battle to ensure that each virus scanner detects all possible viruses. Virus writers will examine each new scanning product and attempt to find a way round it. Many companies which sell virus scanners therefore have a system whereby you can order regular updates to keep on top of the problem, usually on some sort of subscription basis.

Terminate and stay resident programs

To allow the user to have more than one program available in a computer at any one time, a system known as TSR (terminate and stay resident) programs was adopted. Once loaded these programs remain in the computer's memory and can be recalled at any time whilst other programs are running, usually by pressing of a key combination. TSR programs are a particularly useful way of providing a calculator, an alarm system or a calendar, for example, to which you might wish to refer at any time during any application. The idea of TSR programs in MS-DOS developed several years before Microsoft Windows enabled several applications to be loaded at the same time. TSR programs are also referred to as pop-up programs, as they can be asked to pop up at any time and may cover all or only part of the screen. They can just as easily be removed so that the original application can be continued with. Many TSR programs are now available as shareware utilities. You need to be aware that, because of the way that TSRs work, certain combinations of TSRs may interfere with each other.

Dynamic data exchange and object linking and embedding

Operating environments like Windows 3.0 and later and Macintosh System 7 allow users to pass information between different applications. In this way, a drawing can be copied into a spreadsheet, a word processed document or a database. The various ways in which this can be achieved are given names which have a precise technical meaning. The concepts are also described with a number of technical terms.

Dynamic data exchange (DDE) allows a document from one application (the server application) to be copied into another document (the client application). The relationship is said to be dynamic because any changes to the server document will be reflected in the client (normally a message is given to the user to verify that updating should take place). In this way, a number of different applications can access common information such as a price list or a company logo. This avoids data conflict which could occur if more than one price list were present in the system, for example. It also saves space so that multiple copies are not kept. However, because the dynamic relationship is with a named file in a named directory, the deletion or movement of the server file can cause some difficulties if the client is later accessed.

Object linking and embedding (OLE) takes the ideas further. Linking is simply the process of creating a dynamic link as described above. Embedding, however, places a fully editable copy of the server document into the client document. No link is created between the new copy and the original. The server application can be launched from the client application. This enables the user to alter the document which is coming in without affecting the original. This embedding system gives the user all the power of the client application from within a totally different application. Of course, the price to be paid is that multiple copies are kept of the server document, whether they are altered or not.

14

— STORAGE DEVICES —

Backing storage is the term used to describe all types of storage facility that hold data in a form which can be used from one session of computer use to another. The term is used to distinguish this form of long-term memory from the short-term memory within the main computer, most of which is lost when the computer is switched off. Floppy disks, hard disks, compact disks (CD) and various forms of tapes and cartridges are all forms of backing storage, and all systems will have two or three devices for handling long-term memory like this.

————————— Floppy disks ———————

The 3.5 inch disk has become the almost universal floppy disk standard. It has a rigid casing with a metal shutter covering a window through which the disk surface can be seen. The shutter is opened automatically when the disk is put into a disk drive. In this way damage to the reading and writing surface is minimised as the magnetic recording surface need not be exposed to dust, fingers and so on. The disk is spun at high speed within the drive around its metal hub. The disk itself is circular and is coated with ferric oxide on which magnetic marks can be recorded for later retrieval. The whole disk can be accessed through the window in the casing within a revolution of the disk. It is important not to damage the disk by careless handling or by opening the shutter unnecessarily.

The older 5.25 inch disks have a flexible square plastic envelope which is more liable to bending and damage and has no shutter protection, which meant that there was always some part of the surface exposed.

The smaller disks in rigid casings are still called floppy disks, because the disks themselves are floppy. Some software suppliers will issue software on either size disk, and you must specify the correct size when you order software. Returning the wrong size disks creates a frustrating delay, and can cause arguments if you opened the shrink-wrapped product before checking the disk size.

Data on disks and other magnetic systems is recorded with a read/write head which floats on a thin cushion of air just above the recording surface. It works on a similar principle to recordings on cassette tapes. Magnetic media are very sensitive to damage through bending, stray magnetism, and pollution through dust, smoke and so on.

Floppy disks have a write protect notch which consists of a small plastic square. If you slide this sideways to reveal the hole, then the disk drive will not be able to record on the disk. The disk is then said to be 'read only'. This is a very important security feature, similar in manner to write protection on domestic cassette tapes. The write protection on 5.25 inch disks was similar but worked in the reverse way – a notch was covered to protect the contents.

As technology has improved, higher recording densities on floppy disk have become possible, so that more can be packed on, giving the same sized disk a higher capacity. The lowest capacity 3.5 inch disks now in general use are described as double sided and double density. (This is for historical reasons; previous single density and single sided technology has long been superseded.) A double density disk will hold 720 kB on a PC and 800 kB on a Macintosh. Confusingly, double density is sometimes referred to as low density ('low' is a relative term). High density disks hold 1.4 MB on a Macintosh and 1.44 MB on a PC. High density disks have an extra hole at the opposite side to the write protect notch, which a computer will detect to find out the type of disk which has been inserted in the drive. Extra high density disks are also available which will hold 2.88 MB on a PC.

A variation on the floppy disk, much less commonly used, is the floptical, which records data magnetically, but uses a system of grooves on the disk surface so that the head can be lined up much more accurately over the track.

Hard disks

A hard disk has several rigid circular disks, called platters, inside a sealed case. For some years, platters have been made from aluminium, but other materials such as glass and ceramics are now sometimes used. Each disk surface is coated in a magnetisable surface made from a very robust alloy. Read/write heads move between the platters so that data can be recorded onto and read from both sides of each platter. The use of several platters not only increases the capacity without increasing the size very much, but also ensures quicker reading of data, as the main factor limiting speed is the physical movement of the head.

Data can be recorded more densely on hard disks than on floppy disks because hard disks are sealed from exposure to outside contamination. Hard disks are available in various sizes, two popular sizes being 5.25 inch and 3.5 inch. These standards allow hard disk drives to be fitted within a computer cabinet where a floppy disk drive might have been. The speed of a disk drive is normally limited by the speed with which physical movements can be made, as these take a lot longer than electronic signalling. Thus, in principle, the smaller the magnetic medium, and the closer together the data is, the quicker the disk can function. There is therefore a trade-off between capacity and speed.

An internal disk drive is one fitted within the casing of the computer. An external disk drive comes as a separate box. It is possible to upgrade a computer by having an internal disk drive fitted, but upgrades often involve the use of an external drive. An external drive has the advantage that it can be attached to different machines for access to either software or user files. Some would also argue that external drives are better for security, as they can be locked away separately and more easily than a desktop computer. Others claim the advantage of portability for external disk drives, in that they, rather than a whole system, can be transported from venue to venue. Users will have to determine for themselves whether the saving of money is worth the extra effort and wear and tear. Some users might find that there are advantages in accessing the same external disk drive sometimes from a desktop and at others from a laptop.

Disk drive capacities have continued to grow over the years. In the mid-1980s, desktop computers typically had 10 MB internal hard drives. Nowadays, desktop systems are rarely sold with less than 170 MB, and laptops rarely have less than 120 MB. Most manufacturers will allow you to select from a menu of hard disk capacities, ranging up to, say, 540 MB for a desktop, or 260 MB for a laptop. Conventional wisdom has it that many purchasers of new systems underestimate their need for hard disk capacity. Much of this extra capacity is necessary, as a typical suite of office programs, even with the minimum configuration, will take over 10 MB and perhaps as much as 60 MB. The operation systems can also occupy a great deal of hard disk space. The rest of the storage will be available for user-generated files. Word processed documents, spreadsheets and the like will take up some space, but considerable amounts of space are taken up by files for graphics and sound, either generated by the user, or copied or adapted. All users need to be disciplined in deciding which files need to be available for instant access from hard disk and which are better stored on floppy disk for retrieval as and when necessary.

Hard disks can be damaged if they are violently knocked or a sudden power surge or fall occurs, particularly when the disk head is moving, or reading or writing. Most manufacturers claim that their drives will withstand shock forces five times that of gravity ($5g$). Damage to the head or recording surface is known as a head crash, but now that there is such demand for very robust disk drives for laptop computers, the technology for all computers has developed accordingly. Manufacturers will publish results of their testing of systems to show the reliability of their products, described as the mean time between failure (MTBF). For most drives this is in excess of a quarter of a million hours of use. The main concern when a hard disk fails is not the loss of its use – it usually only takes a few days to fit a replacement – but it is the loss of the data held on the disk. Data lost can include expensive software, but also user files built up over months or years. Wise approaches to backing up can minimise the losses but, of course, failures come when they are least expected. A small number of specialist firms provide a service to recover the files that can be retrieved, in whole or in part, from a damaged disk.

During use, small areas of a disk may become unreliable, and so software is designed to bypass difficult areas, which are called 'bad sectors'. Figures quoted for hard disk capacities usually allow for a few slight imperfections to the surface which are simply bypassed from the moment the disk is formatted. For this reason, you may be able to squeeze slightly more on a disk than the advertised capacity.

If a serious problem occurs on a disk, professional help and specialist programs will be needed to retrieve as much of the data on the damaged disk as possible. For times when a hard disk is not in use, a utility program is normally provided to allow you to park the heads in a safe place. This is particularly important if the hard disk drive is about to be moved. Many recent systems now incorporate automatic disk parking.

The computer needs to be fitted with the electronics to send and receive signals to the disk devices. The devices within the computer that do this are called disk controllers, and are connected through expansion slots.

There are a number of different hard disk interface systems, each known by a set of initials. The three most common are ESDI, IDE and SCSI. Each of these supports different rates of data transfer, and they are generally not compatible with each other.

The ESDI system (enhanced small device interface) has been used for many years as a hard disk interface, and when introduced was considered to be both high speed and high quality compared with other systems.

With the IDE (intelligent drive electronics) system, the disk drive itself contains most of the controller circuitry. Many computers allow an IDE drive to be connected directly to the motherboard already containing the IDE interface, known as an IDE-ready motherboard (the connection is a 40 pin socket). Alternatively, an IDE host adapter will be fitted to an expansion slot in the motherboard. It is technically incorrect to refer to the host adapter as an IDE controller.

The SCSI (small computer system interface), pronounced 'scuzzy', allows up to eight devices to be connected, and any two can communicate through the 8-bit bus at any time. Indeed two peripherals can talk directly to each other, for backing up disk to tape for example, without tying up the machine's processor. Many commentators suggest that SCSI is the most sensible technology to choose if you are liable to expand your system, perhaps with CD-ROM or other devices in the future, though it generally costs more initially. The host adapter, used to bring in the computer's bus (which is essential) counts as one of the eight devices. Most Macintoshes are provided with built-in SCSI host adapters.

If you find yourself upgrading an existing system by adding drives, you should be careful to ask the vendor precisely what you will need to purchase to install your upgrade. The installation may require the use of a terminator to indicate to the system that this is the last device in a series, and a jumper which is pushed over two or three connector pins in order to customise a circuit board..

Access to files can be quicker if they are held on RAM disk, also known as silicon disk, or emulated disk (e-disk). This method treats part of the computer's main memory as if it were an extra disk drive. This speeds up file processing, but any files saved on RAM disk must be saved to floppy disk or hard disk before the machine is switched off. Special software is needed so that RAM disk can be set up – this is usually arranged as part of the initial configuration of the machine.

Compact disks

Compact disks (usually abbreviated to CD) are 12 cm in diameter, with data recorded in a digital form as a series of microscopic pits. This pitted surface is covered with a protective plastic layer. It is read by shining a laser on to the surface, and decoding the reflections. The system designed for use in computers, CD-ROM, uses a different track format from the music CD, and will hold about 650 MB of data. Any system using CD-ROM will require software (called CD-ROM extensions), which will include a driver for the CD player.

Whilst CD-ROM drives look and operate like audio CD players, there are three different forms of mechanisms for loading the disks. Initially, the most common was the use of a caddy, which is a rigid case into which the disk is placed before loading it into the machine. As with early audio systems, misreading could be caused by external factors. In an audio system, this can lead to part of the music being skipped, but no loss of the basic service. In a computer system, though, losing the correct place, even momentarily can lead to misloading of software or documents from which the system would find it difficult to recover. The caddy reduces the chance of dirt on or damage to the disk. This might be an important consideration if children are using the system regularly. It is now much more common for a CD to be loaded on a computer using a tray mechanism like that used for many years in audio systems. The third mechanism is the top-loading system, where part of the lid is raised for insertion of the CD in a similar way to a portable audio CD player.

There are only relatively few specialist CD drive manufacturers, and many makers of computer systems will buy in bulk from these specialists. Therefore if you read a detailed specification of a machine, or a review, you may see some relatively unfamiliar names listed under the heading of CD drive manufacturer. Computer firms are obviously looking for both price and performance from their suppliers, and whilst differences between systems will be long argued over, you must ask yourself whether this will affect the performance in your particular circumstances.

Like magnetic hard disks, CD drives are available in either internal or external form. Most early CD drives were external devices which meant they had the added advantage that one, then very expensive drive, could be used by different people (but not at the same time). As happened with audio systems in the late 1980s, CD drives became cheaper, and came to be provided almost as standard on systems. So nowadays new systems with CD can be as little as £100 more than the same system without the CD drive. Internal CD drives are now mainly tray loading and mounted on the front of the computer.

CD-ROMs are now available containing, for example, encyclopaedias which include animal sounds, pieces of music, and extracts from speeches. Dictionaries are able to include pronunciation.

Because of their high capacities, it is increasingly common for software to be issued on CD. Some major applications now run to 15 or 20 floppy disks and a single CD is much cheaper to produce.

Some disk controllers are able to read data from a variety of disk formats, including audio CDs. A single speed CD drive is able to transfer data at 150 kB per second. More recent drives can operate at double this speed but must be capable of slowing down to read other formats. Some systems are now available with triple speed, that is 450 kB per second or even quadruple speed.

Multisession CDs are those that have been generated in more than one recording session. The most common of these is the Kodak Photo CD. Only multisession drives are capable of reading these forms of CD. A single-session drive will only read the information from the first session, and will not detect data from the others. If you wish to be able to access photo CDs or to use CDs for archiving, a multisession drive is essential.

CD-I (the 'I' is for interactive) is a separate standard, developed by Philips and Sony. It allows for the interactive viewing of CDs containing audio and visual information through the use of a CD-I player which links to an ordinary television. It uses sophisticated data compression techniques to increase the capacity of the CD. It is primarily aimed at the entertainment and education market. CD-I and CD-ROM are not compatible systems. Because so much material has been developed using the CD-I format, several other systems are now available that will read CD-I format material in addition to their own native formats. A system similar in principle to CD-I has been developed by Commodore, called CDTV (Commodore Dynamic Total Vision), which also connects to a television.

Compression of video and high-resolution images is important in CD-ROM technology. The DVI (Digital Video Interface) technique developed by Intel provides 72 minutes of video on a CD-ROM, compressing video at 100 to 1 and stills at 10 to 1. Such a system requires a special DVI controller in the computer.

CD storage is attractive because of its higher capacity, but in choosing a system, it is important to think also about the transfer rate of data. In particular, systems very dependent on graphics will need to transfer large amounts of data to update moving pictures. The overall performance will depend on a number of factors, including the type of monitor, the combination of software you will have loaded, the software being used, and even its arrangement on the hard disk. Sales staff showing you a new system should be able to demonstrate the precise system which you will be using at its optimum performance. Bear in mind that this performance might deteriorate a little when the system has more on it. If you are buying by mail or 'phone, or are upgrading, the judgements can be harder to make, and it is also difficult to define a performance criterion for the system with which you would be satisfied so that this can written on the order.

Some specialist systems allow several CDs to be loaded at once, allowing access to, say, up to six disks at any one time.

Compared with magnetic media for everyday use, CD-ROM has the major disadvantage that it is a medium that can generally only be read on a personal computer system, so is not suitable for recording your own material. Equipment can be purchased which allows a user to record a CD, but this costs a few thousand pounds, so it out of the price range of most domestic or small business users. CD-ROM is a write-once medium: when a file has been written to disk it cannot be deleted. Both this factor and the high price makes CD-ROM unsuitable for general backup. However, CD-ROM is becoming an increasingly common way in which to distribute programs or files such as pictures. Several magazines are now sold with free cover CD-ROMs, rather than floppy disks.

In an organisation which needs regularly to distribute substantial quantities of information to remote sites, such as a catalogue or an information service, the production of CDs may provide a very economical solution. The medium is relatively cheap once the equipment has been purchased. The disks will withstand normal handling in the post. Where only some information has changed, the provision of a complete new disk will stimulate the disposal of out-of-date information. The updates can be made as regularly, or as irregularly, as necessary. Each remote site would only need a basic PC with CD drive to be able to access common information which, so long as it changes on, say, a weekly basis rather than an hourly basis, can be accurate enough.

A type of optical disk drive called the WORM (write once, read many) drive allows the user to save data to the disk which can then be read back as many times as is desired. Once recorded, however, the data cannot be erased. The huge capacity of WORM drives makes them suitable for some applications, but their cost limits their appeal to domestic and small business users.

Erasable optical disks use laser and reflected light to record data on a disk. This can then be read back, making it the optical equivalent of the magnetic disk. Although erasable optical disks are faster than floppy disks, they are much slower than fixed and removable hard disks. Optical drives are also much more expensive than magnetic drives, although the disks themselves are relatively cheap, given their large capacity

Software distributors also make use of the much greater capacity of CD to provide much more comprehensive sample files, tutorials and so on. They sometimes even include trial software as a 'free' bonus to those who buy disks in this form, as CDs are cheaper for them to buy and quicker to record than a whole set of floppy disks.

—— Other magnetic storage ——

Magnetic tape was used in early computer systems in a similar manner to the audio cassette. Most users breathed a sigh of relief when disk technology became cheap enough for almost all computers. There are situations, however, when tape technology is still useful. Tapes of all forms have the limitation that they can only be read sequentially, so that data can effectively only be retrieved in the order in which it was recorded. This is normally a drawback, but in some contexts this is no real limitation. Firstly tapes are very effective for making backups, and secondly they are useful for auditing purposes.

Some tapes come in cassette form, appearing to be similar to an audio tape, but made to much higher specifications. Cartridges also hold the tape in a plastic case, but are generally designed to leave less tape exposed when not in use. The case is usually not as absolutely rigid as that of a cassette. Some sizes of cartridge hold over 100 MB of data. Tapes are made of flexible plastic with one side coated with a magnetisable surface. Electromagnetism is used to record spots of polarity on the tape's surface as it passes the read/write head. This can then be read back by sensing the polarity of a recording.

Cartridges come in various sizes, such as the quarter inch cartridge (QIC), using standards compatible between different manufacturers involving over a dozen different tape capacities for two different cartridge sizes. Their system of 'serpentine recording' uses parallel tracks between which the data snakes back and forth between tracks.

Data compression onto tape has two distinct advantages. First, it saves time, as there is less data to write or subsequently read. Secondly, a greater capacity can be achieved on a given cartridge. In more advanced operating systems, such as Windows, it is possible for data to be backed up in the background without the user being interrupted from other tasks. Backing up is speeded up by a system known as incremental dumping, whereby only those files which have changed since the last backup are saved. Keeping track of which cartridges to keep is then more complicated, but the saving of computer time may justify this. One further difference between systems is the question whether the cartridge has to be formatted by the user before it can be used, as this may take some considerable time.

Digital audio tape (DAT) uses digital recording to CD quality on a tape. It uses a helical scanning system, perfected through the use of video tape, to track data diagonally in order to increase capacity. The system was introduced for the domestic audio market, but made little market penetration. Because the tapes are much smaller, they are easier to work with, and require a correspondingly smaller drive mechanism. Because the tapes are also used for domestic audio, they are likely to be more readily available in shops. DAT tapes can have capacities of 2 Gb (2000 MB) and more.

The more recent versions of tape and cartridge technology incorporate systems of error detection and correction, which use mathematical algorithms to overcome minor imperfections in the recordings, which is a useful extra safeguard when tapes or cartridges are being used as a backup when something else has already gone wrong.

The system of RAID (redundant arrays of inexpensive disks), which has been common in minicomputer systems for some time, is beginning to find its way onto the larger personal computer systems. The idea of RAID is to use several drives and to spread the data over them. First, this achieves an increase in speed, but secondly, it provides some protection against loss of data. There are six levels of RAID, ranging from 0 (the least complex) to 5 (the most complex). At the various levels, there is duplication of some data and extra data (parity information) recorded so that if one disk fails, the whole of the data can be reconstructed from the others.

15

—— MULTIMEDIA ——

—— What is 'multimedia'? ——

The term 'multimedia' has been coined to describe the use of animation, video and sound alongside text and still pictures in whatever combinations you wish. The term 'dynamic media' is used as a general term for these additions to the range of applications. All these dynamic media need hardware to produce the effects, storage to hold vast quantities of complicated information and software to control it all.

Compact disks are currently seen as essential to multimedia, as they are the main way of providing bulk exchangeable storage with fast access times to huge amounts of data. The mechanics of CD-ROM have been described in Chapter 14.

This is one application area where a wide range of manufacturers came together to define standards very early which has resulted in some compatability. The Multimedia PC Marketing Council (MMC) was founded in 1991, involving 12 major vendors. It produced the first Multimedia Personal Computer Standard (MPC). This defined a minimum configuration for MPC, and vendors can use the special logo if the system fulfils the specification. A subsequent standard (MPC 2) has also been defined, aimed at professional users. However, both standards have been launched as minimum standards, and when each standard has been announced, many of the systems on sale have exceeded this minimum in a number of ways. Unfortunately, therefore, the MPC seal of approval should only be the starting point in your search for a system.

The original MPC standard required a 386SX or compatible processor, 2 MB of memory, high density floppy drive, a 30 Megabyte hard disk, mouse, CD-ROM, 8-bit audio with analogue to digital and digital to analogue conversion, microphone input, VGA screen capability in 16 colours, ports for serial, parallel, MIDI and joystick, and sound output (speaker or headphones). Extra pieces of software, called multimedia extensions, are also needed. These support tasks such as recording and playing of audio and video, and the MCI (media control interface) for links with the CD-ROM. Routines are normally supplied with the system and are included in the file MSCDEX.EXE.

MPC 2 raises the specification to a 486 or compatible, 4 MB of memory, 160 MB disk, double speed CD-ROM, 16-bit audio, and screen support for 16-bit video.

One criticism of some CD-ROM systems is that motion pictures sometimes freeze while the system catches up with itself, as massive amounts of data have to be transferred to produce smooth motion. Buffering is used, as in most input-output systems, so that software is anticipating which parts of the CD are likely to be read next. In regular operation, for standard tasks, the user's behaviour is fairly predictable, and a good system will cope. At the limits, though, with heavy, random use, the shortcomings can become noticeable

Another concern about the MPC standard is that it does not apply to Apple computers. These have included the main features required of multimedia for longer than most PC systems. The 'AV' tag used in several Apple product names stands for 'Audio-Visual', and these systems all have graphics and sound built in, and can be specified with a monitor incorporating stereo speakers. The Apple equivalent to the Multimedia extension software is QuickTime, which adds video and sound as an extension to System 7 software.

— Aspects of multimedia hardware —

On the hardware side, the CD-ROM is connected to the computer through the interface. An internal drive would be mounted within the computer's casing. If you are buying a new system this is normally a cheaper option, and the interface would be installed as part of the system. On a PC, there is a choice between SCSI interface and proprietary buses. The only interface usually available on a Macintosh is the SCSI interface. When choosing an external drive, you will have to decide whether you will want to use the drive with more than one system

The use of video clips is an important aspect of a multimedia system. Moving film, such as that seen at the cinema and on the television uses a rapid succession of still images, or frames, to create the illusion of movement to the human eye, which can only process a limited number of images each second. The standard chosen for computer video is 25 frames per second. If full images of each frame were to be stored, this would occupy huge amounts of storage, so compression techniques are used. These enable about 74 minutes of what is termed full-motion video to be stored a CD. An international body, known as MPEG (Moving Pictures Expert Group), defined the standard.

Compression can be achieved either through hardware or software. Hardware compression cards are larger and considerably more expensive, but offer greater processing speed. Some computer manufacturers, such as Acorn, make considerable play of full motion video systems such as Replay which requires no extra hardware assistance.

The sheer amount of data to be processed when full motion video is to be shown can overwhelm the processing power of the system. To show the clip at the appropriate speed, and in particular to keep it synchronised with the sound, the software will automatically adjust the display and will miss out some frames to do this. This process is known as frame dropping, and whilst a few frames per second would not be noticed, dropping more than say 10 out of 25 frames per second will lead to a visible deterioration.

Another way of coping with the amount of processing to be handled is to show the video clips in a small window within the screen. Some software will adjust both the window size and the frame dropping rate to produce the optimum performance for the hardware provided.

The system may cope better if it has a graphics accelerator. This is an expansion card which relieves the main processor of as much of the graphics processing as possible. Graphics displays require the movement of huge amounts of data, and many complex mathematical calculations. Graphics accelerators vary in their level of power, and at the top of the range may be more sophisticated than your main processor. The card manufacturer will normally supply software drivers both to select options in the use of your card and to use software such as Windows or a CAD package.

There is a wide range of sound cards available, largely because there are so many different uses to which people might want to put sound. Sound cards come in two broad categories. Eight bit cards provide sound of approximately the quality of FM radio. Sixteen bit cards provide audio quality.

Multimedia presentations can be used either alone or with an audience. For individual use, a good set of stereo headphones is a necessity. Even when a presentation is intended eventually for an audience, it would be normal for the leader of the session to view and listen to the material in advance, whether it be pre-prepared on custom-written. If such preparation takes place in a busy office, headphones are again essential.

For good sound to be heard by an audience, it is important not to rely on the inbuilt speakers of the main computer. Some manufacturers such as Apple provide monitor options which include stereo speakers. Alternatively, you can buy external speakers to plug in to the back of your computer. There are a few key choices to be made. One is the question of how the speakers are powered. Using a separate power source is preferable, though batteries can need frequent replacement, so a mains adapter may be best. You also need to find out whether an amplifier will be needed. It is sensible to ensure there is some physical volume control rather than relying on using the software controls for this all the time.

Most sound cards have a comprehensive set of software bundled, and the nature of the bundle gives you a good idea of the jobs for which the card is best suited. Some people want a system providing stereo music, typically with 11 voices; others simply want sound effects for games. In the former case, you probably want to link up the sound to good speakers; in the latter, good speakers would not be needed. Some systems can be equipped with a microphone and software which enables you to record and handle voice messages; the Macintosh LC III is an example of such a computer. In choosing such a system, it is important to ask whether the microphone is supplied as part of the system. In-built microphones can have similar drawbacks to inbuilt microphones in domestic tape recorders.

A frequently used term for a sound system is for it to be 'Sound Blaster Compatible'. 'Sound Blaster' is the name of a range of sound cards from Creative Labs Inc. Other popular products include the Ad Lib Gold Card and Thunderboard.

If music is to be held and processed as a major part of the system, the

MIDI interface will probably be used. The MIDI standard (Musical Instrument Digital Interface) was defined to record musical information. A MIDI system uses codes to control several synthesisers at once, each playing a part of the music. The music can be edited in many more ways than conventional sound, so that, for example, the rhythm can be changed through altering timing codes, as all the data is held digitally

Other devices such as video grabbers and digital cameras can be incorporated into a multimedia system, and these are discussed in the section 'Preparing multimedia material' below. When searching for such systems, you must make sure of compatibility within a system, ensuring that all the components can be used together to best effect.

——— Using multimedia material ———

Software publishers are currently producing several new titles each month in CD format. One of the earliest, and still most popular applications is the encyclopaedia. Amongst these products are Compton's Interactive encyclopaedia, the New Grolier Multimedia Encyclopaedia and Microsoft's Encarta. Earlier versions of encyclopaedias have tended to be American versions, largely because of the size of that market compared with the British market, but it is purely a matter of time before more specifically British versions are available.

The first clear advantage of CD for encyclopaedias is how small they are compared with printed versions. The next most obvious advantage is that the elements making up the entries can be more varied than the still pictures and words of a printed book. Entries can include sounds, so that you can hear the voice of your human subject or listen to the sound of an animal, or a piece of music. Video clips can be used so that you can see an event, or a person, or a device in use. Animation can be used to show how something works or how it is constructed.

Another difference from printed material is the ability to show related items together which would not normally appear on a single printed page. Thus an entry about a famous author, for example, might include a picture of the author, biographical text, short readings from famous works, the author's voice, a map of the author's fictional area (such as Hardy's Wessex), and clips from films of the author's books.

Apart from those elements which could not be achieved without multimedia, the sheer bulk of text and pictures could not be seen at a glance on one or even two pages of a book. The user of a multimedia system can choose which of these items to have on display by opening and closing elements at will.

However, by far the most far-reaching effect of multimedia will be the impact it will have on ways of using enclopaedias. All the traditional methods of accessing entries in an encyclopaedia are retained, such as the indexing of entries (sorted alphabetically so that it is easy to find something you are looking for), and cross-referencing (elements listed under 'see also' at the end of an entry, or highlighted in a different type within the description). In addition to these, other links can be made between items. One way of accessing items is through a hierarchical system, allowing the user to explore a topic through sub-topics, which themselves have sub-topics and so on. The user can then retrace the steps taken to look down other sections of the hierarchy. Such hierarchies may be presented in a menu structure or a tree structure, with a vocabulary to match.

Another way of relating items is for the system to use on-screen windows to show the headings of related topics. Clicking on the appropriate windows then opens up further windows which themselves have further suggestions.

Another common link is provided through the timeline. Where an event is described in an entry, it is possible then to select the timeline to discover what else was happening at the same time. Other entries about events happening at the same time can then be seen alongside the existing entry.

Other encyclopaedia systems allow for searching for user-specified words. Some allow for the use of wildcards (that is characters or words with any value), and to combine searches using Boolean functions (AND, OR and NOT). These allow a user to narrow down a search for a specific topic or range of topics.

Many initial uses of multimedia were in training. A number of specialist firms have entered the business selling training packages. Materials cover a wide range of topics, with multimedia being best suited to the sort of topics that need individual tuition at a speed tailored to the user's pace. Typical examples might be Health and Safety at work, in which all new staff might need training, though aspects that need covering in depth might differ between departments. Multimedia has the advantage that the same material can be delivered as often as is necessary. The system will keep track of which areas have been covered by an individual, which is important where training has to be monitored and the fact that it has taken place needs to be recorded for company or legal reasons. Other uses of multimedia would include specialist skills training. This could include simulations which are too expensive or too dangerous to allow trainees to tackle. Multimedia is also a useful means of training in foreign languages.

Other topics include geography (such as cities of the world), history, music, literature and reference works. Such titles help to overcome the undeserved reputation that CD-ROM is primarily about entertainment, though you will, of course, find a wide selection of entertainment CD-ROMs if this is what you want. The provision of all the works of a great author on a single CD-ROM should open up many possibilities for a reader to examine links between sections of different works, providing chances to do original research.

A growing use of multimedia is also being made in retailing. Travel firms for example can allow customers to view aspects of a particular resort or hotel, sampling the sights and sounds of the venue. Other details can be covered through a simple dialogue, increasingly through an on-screen dialogue with a touch screen. The dialogue can be concluded by confirming a booking for precisely what the customer has seen.

—— Preparing multimedia material ——

As multimedia technology develops, members within organisations are beginning to see that the preparation of a multimedia presentation is within their grasp. The time spent in tailoring a presentation including video clips and sound as well as still pictures and graphics may be well spent in winning a contract or impressing a client.

Where users are attempting to create their own multimedia presentations, they will probably want to use some additional hardware, such as a scanner for still pictures, and a video grabber, which captures and digitises video sequences.

A video grabber will normally come with some software, typically a program to capture a video sequence, one to edit video sequences, and a program to allow the editing of still pictures (single frames). Most users set up their system to capture from their video recorder, but it is possible to plug in a digital camera if you have one.

All multimedia systems have substantial memory requirements, and advertisements for multimedia products such as Macromedia's Director state minimum systems requirements.

Preparing a multimedia presentation is termed 'scripting', and many of the software products use some form of analogy to help the user. A number of products, like HyperCard on the Mac, and Multimedia Toolbook , use the analogy of a stack of cards, where books of pages are assembled. Relationships between pages are created through buttons and controls. With some packages, authors will normally need some knowledge of programming to create a full script, including logic to create the various paths through the material. Other packages use analogies such as a flowchart layout or a timeline to create a presentation.

A number of the packages provide ready-written objects and routines which can be adapted by authors. Using the various tools provided, parts of video clips can be selected, filters can be applied to images, video and animation can be combined, and sound can be mixed. Transition effects, similar to those available on slide presentation packages, can be selected and combined in various ways. It is often through the skilful use of slides, zooms, dissolves, spinning cubes with several images on them and the like, that a classy presentation is distinguished from a mundane set of consecutive clips. As with all special effects created by computer, a new user is easily tempted to use too many different features in quick succession, so some background reading about the subject of transitions effects, often supplied with the package, could prove to be time well spent.

—— The next step – virtual reality ——

There has been much in the press and on television about virtual reality. This has extended the use of computer graphics into three dimensions. The computer generates responses based on input from headsets and other peripherals such as data gloves. Initial uses have been dominated by games, but virtual reality is beginning to be used for applications such as 3D design and simulation. Users are being invited to visit a virtual shopping mall, or to attend a virtual fashion show.

Whilst virtual reality is currently usually based on computer-generated images, future development may harness aspects of multimedia to enhance systems even further.

16

PRINTERS AND OTHER DEVICES

Printer features

Clearly, you will need one or more forms of printer to produce final results on paper. It is almost certainly a mistake, as when choosing a computer, to begin by looking at what is available and the various technologies rather than thinking about what it is that you want to do. Your choice of printer type will be influenced by a combination of the tasks it must perform and the price you are prepared to pay. We first focus, therefore, on those features common to several printer technologies. Once the main features have been identified, we shall look at how the different technologies work.

The quality of printing is primarily measured through the dot resolution, measured in dots per inch. Many printers achieve 300 dots per inch, with several available at 600 dots per inch. Many would claim that, to the naked eye 600 dots per inch is the most you would ever need for text; others argue that lower resolution strains the eye when reading in a manner which is not always noticed by the reader. There is a halfway position in that some 300 dot per inch printers include a system of resolution enhancement that will add an extra small dot between big dots it has been asked to print to ensure smoother edges to characters.

All printers need supplies of ink or toner, and apart from the paper, this is normally the main running cost. Some technologies use inked ribbons, others use powdered inks which come in sealed cartridges. Others still use solid inks. When choosing the technology it is always important to check the life of such supplies and also parts. With some technologies parts, such as a laser drum, may need regular replacement.

Two figures are often quoted. Firstly, you may be quoted the anticipated amount of printing between replacement, in either characters or pages. These figures are clearly only estimates, as wear and tear depend on the type of usage. Figures can only be a good rough guide. Secondly, some printers, like photocopiers, are quoted with a 'duty cycle' which is the number of pages that the printer can produce per year or per month. If your anticipated use is higher, you should purchase a heavier duty printer.

All printers require paper, and you may wish to use them with other media, such as overhead projector acetates. The choice of stationery is discussed in more detail in Chapter 19. To avoid disappointment when your system arrives, though, it is important to consider your various media options before committing yourself. Will you want to use continuous stationery (which has perforations to allow you to separate sheets), or cut single sheets, or both? Will you require paper sizes other than the ubiquitous A4? If your printer is designed for continuous stationery, can a single sheet feeder be used when you want to avoid continuous stationery? Is the capacity of the paper bins important? (If you are printing long documents, you do not wish to be held up by having to reload the feeder quite often.) Does the supplier specify the range of paper thicknesses allowed, measured in grammes per square metre? Will the printer function best when placed on a special printer stand, which adds even more to the cost?

If you have specialist printing needs, such as labels or envelopes, you will need to ask two questions. First, 'will they work at all with this particular printer technology?' Secondly 'what will it cost?'

Another major area of difference between printers often neglected by those who only concentrate on the printing technology is that the control buttons are important. Most printers contain sophisticated chips. Some of these are used under program control by the computer, others store information such as the text to be printed or details of fonts. Yet others are used to process commands from the printer user. Many modern printers, other than the really basic ones, will include a liquid display panel, similar to that on a photocopier, with which it can communicate with the user. Messages might tell the user about problems, such as where a paper jam has occurred, or which supplies are needed (such as 'PAPER OUT' or 'OUT OF TONER'). Error conditions which require an engineer are sometimes communicated in this way.

Most printers will have an array of buttons on the front for user operation, although some have little more than an on/off switch. One button allows you to switch the printer between 'ON-LINE' and 'OFF-LINE'. 'ON-LINE' means that the printer is under the control of the computer, whereas 'OFF-LINE' means that it is under user control through the other buttons. Buttons called 'LINE FEED' and 'FORM FEED' are used to line up or eject paper. Other buttons may allow a choice of font or type size. The quality of the manual is important to help explain the operation of the various buttons in clear terms.

The older technologies required you to set options on your printer by setting tiny switches on the circuit board. These options included setting the default language, saying whether you wanted your zeroes crossed, setting the paper length and so on. Thankfully, these settings are now more often controlled through a dialogue on the front panel, particularly on a laser printer. This dialogue, though comprehensive in the various topics it covers, is usually a fairly simple menu-driven system. There are circumstances, such as the use of printers in schools, where the ability to reconfigure the printer easily can be a positive disadvantage. More generally, when there are several users of a printer, a later user may not know to which settings the printer has been altered.

Other features of printers are important, and are primarily independent of the printing technology. These include automatic self-tests, so that sample printouts can be obtained without putting the system on-line to a computer. Self-test printouts can be used to check print quality, or to produce samples of various print modes, fonts and sizes. Self-test features are often activated by holding down a combination of printer buttons as the printer is switched on. Other printer features include automatic sensing of the thickness of the paper; systems where you can set the thickness manually are fine, until you forget to do this. Some printers include power saving features, so that energy is saved if the printer is switched on but not in use. If power saving mode has been entered, it is likely that the next printout will take slightly longer as the system is reactivated.

Many printers have their own internal memory, so that the computer can 'download' a document onto the printer, so that the printer can carry on under its own control ('autonomously') while you use the computer for the next task. This memory in a printer is known as a buffer, and buffers vary considerably in size. A typical buffer might be capable of holding, say, five pages of text, or one page of graphics. With modern interfaces such as Windows or the Macintosh System

7, the computer's software includes a facility called the Print Manager or Print Monitor that allows the computer to download to the printer while the computer is still being used for another task.

The method by which the computer and the printer communicate is known as the protocol. Signals are sent in both directions, as the printer normally acknowledges receipt of the data sent to it. The computer uses an interface, sometimes referred to as a 'port', into which the cable to the printer connector should be slotted. The two main types of communications protocols are serial and parallel. The serial signalling system sends one binary signal at a time, whereas the parallel signalling system sends several. These two methods cannot be used together, so if the printer can only receive serial signals, these are what must be sent by the computer. Various signalling speeds are supported within each protocol. If you are unclear, ask a supplier to confirm whether a printer will work with your particular computer.

Because a parallel port allows several digits of data to be sent at the same time by synchronising the signals on different lines, this system is quicker than the serial system. A serial system may have to be used, though, if the signal has a long way to travel, perhaps over ten metres. The term Centronics port is sometimes also used for a parallel port, as Centronics was the firm which devised one of the most popular parallel signalling protocols.

Printer technologies

There are at least eight different printer technologies. If you are thinking of buying one which is not explained here, ask the vendor for details. Vendors will usually be very pleased to describe their specific print technology, and will usually do so by comparison with the more common technologies. This will, of course, generally be a favourable comparison; your job will be to ask questions about the comparisons on which the other technology is weaker.

A dot matrix printer uses a print head consisting of a row of pins, the height of one line of print-out. The pins strike against a ribbon to make marks on the paper, so the image is formed out of dots. Some dot matrix printers use 9 pins to make up characters, while others use 24 pins, printing higher quality text by making two passes over the same line. Many 24 pin printers can switch between two modes, a quicker 'draft mode', and a slower 'near letter quality' (nlq) mode. On many printers a choice of several typefaces and sizes is available. Many dot matrix printers are described as 'Epson-compatible' in that they use the same codes for special printing effects as the Epson range of printers. Much of the software produced, particularly many of the products which have been around for some time, includes printer drivers capable of sending signals in this form. If you are considering a different type of printer, make sure you can obtain the correct printer drivers for your chosen software.

Dot matrix printers might be said to have three advantages over other printer types. They can take multi-part stationery, which makes several copies onto lower sheets as it prints. Secondly, dot matrix printers can print on a variety of widths of paper. Thirdly, they can produce a mixture of text and graphics, including many font styles on the same sheet. One main drawback is that they are noisy.

A daisywheel printer also strikes a ribbon, but uses embossed characters on a wheel, with one letter per spoke. This method is also noisy, and it cannot produce graphics output. New daisywheel printers are almost non-existent, but the technology had the advantage that the documents look typed, and different typefaces could be produced simply by changing the daisywheel.

The laser printer not only looks like a photocopier, it produces its image in a similar way, too. The heart of the printer is a polished drum. A uniform electrostatic charge is placed on the drum, and then a beam of laser light scans the drum, discharging relevant spots on the drum. A toner is attracted to the drum, where it is charged, so that a charged sheet of paper can receive toner in the correct places. The paper is then heated, to fuse the particles onto the paper.

The mechanical and optical technology around which a laser printer is built is known as its engine, and several different makes of laser printer are built around the same engine design. Because of the heat involved, only some types of paper can be used in a laser printer.

An ink-jet printer emits charged particles of ink which are deflected through an electrostatic field, so that they land on the paper in the appropriate positions to form the image. This technology is almost silent, since the image is not produced through impact on a ribbon. Many colour ink-jets use three separate reservoirs of coloured inks (cyan, magenta and yellow). Different combinations of these three colours are able to produce any colours other than white and black. White is no problem, no ink is sent. The black, which is produced by an equal mix of the other three colours, can be a muddy brown. For this reason, some printers have a separate black ink reservoir. This has the added advantage that many text outputs only need to be black on white and colour inks are a lot more expensive. Users may be required to line up the separate black gun with the colour lines to gain exact registration, as even a thousandth of an inch will make a difference. Canon has named its ink-jet technology 'Bubble jet'.

Some colour technologies, particularly dot matrix and ink-jet are prone to producing streaky output where ink has run slightly, or the timing is slightly out. This can often be reduced with special paper, but this may cost as much as 30p a sheet. Some colour technologies avoid these problems by printing in two passes with alternate dots produced on each pass, though this mean printing takes twice as long. Other means of slowing down the printing may be needed when producing overhead projector slides to avoid smudging.

Thermal wax printers are probably out of the financial reach of home users, costing about £2000. They produce excellent colour by heating wax and then shooting it at the page, which must be a special type of paper. Dye sublimation also produce images of near photographic quality, using gas jets fired at special paper, but such printers cost around £10 000.

An LED (light emitting diode) printer works on a similar electrophotographic principle to a laser printer, but uses a bank of semiconducting diodes which emit light when charged. Colour printers using lasers or LEDs are coming on the market, which user toners of different colours to form a compound picture. These cost around £8000 or more. Several of the popular electrophotographic printers which are referred to as 'colour lasers' are really based on LED technology.

Laser printers and many other page printers described here use a page description language in making up the layout of a page. These systems are described in Chapter 10, as part of desktop publishing, as this is one of the most common uses of PDLs. The printer hardware of such systems can only be exploited through the use of appropriate software.

Scanners

A scanner is a device that is able to read a drawing, photograph, piece of text or other information from a sheet of paper into a computer. This is done by digitising the image into a series of very small dots.

A flatbed scanner allows the original to be placed face down on a screen in a similar manner to a photocopier, whereas the cheaper hand-held scanner works like a hand-held supermarket scanner which is passed over the original, and reads a four or five inch strip of an image.

Scanners work on the principle of shining light over the image, and the light reflected back is detected by the reading head and converted into a digital value. Colour scanning involves triple scanning with different coloured filters. Monochrome scanners process the image in, typically, 256 shades of grey. Colour scanners working in 24 bit colour are now relatively cheap. Some scanners include a transparency scanning option, so that 35 mm photographs can be read in. It is also important to look at the lid mechanism on a scanner. If you want to scan pages of books regularly, will they fit properly?

The resolution of a scanner is measured in dots per inch. Most scanners are capable of reading at 300 dpi, and this usually produces an adequate picture. One situation in which pictures can be degraded is when a small image is scanned in and then enlarged considerably, when the picture could become quite grainy. Many vendors advise that, in these situations, it is better to enlarge the original before scanning.

Most scanners can be used with OCR (optical character recognition) software. This software interprets the image as text. OCR scanners can distinguish various common forms of typeface and pass ASCII coded text to the computer. Advanced software is able to retain the text format.

Scanners will normally be supplied with appropriate scanning software for their operation.

Mice

A mouse is a hand-held desktop device with one, two or three buttons, connected to the computer through a cable to a serial port, or a special mouse port. Programs receive and interpret signals from mouse movement or button depression. Mouse movement is reflected on the screen through an arrow or some other symbol. Special software (a mouse driver) interprets the signals.

The mouse allows for computer input while the user is looking at the screen, and in this is superior to a keyboard for many users. The mouse has been vital in the development of graphical user interfaces; users can now choose a feature, a file or a piece of text simply by pointing and clicking.

There are various mouse technologies. A mechanical mouse normally uses a rubber ball which rolls against wheels inside the casing. The movement of the wheels is then translated into a digital signal. An optical mouse, on the other hand, emits a light and detects the reflection, so that again movement can be measured.

A whole vocabulary has emerged around mouse actions. 'Double click', for example, means that the user must press the mouse button twice in quick succession. The maximum time allowed between clicks can normally be set under software control (some people are quicker than others). Cordless mice are useful where a lead would be a nuisance, though with too many in a room, they may begin to interfere with each other's radio signals. The cordless mouse itself contains a small battery for its power supply, which typically lasts a year. The receiver is plugged in to the normal mouse port.

A trackerball (or trackball) is an alternative to a mouse. It consists of a ball mounted in a stationary casing. Rotation of the ball is reflected on the screen in a similar way to the physical movement of a mouse. Some portables, such as the Apple PowerBooks and Dell Latitudes, include an in-built trackerball. The latest Apple PowerBooks use a touch-sensitive pad for a 'mouse'. Other portables use hand-held mice, where movement is made by rotating a ball, usually with the thumb, to avoid the need for mouse movement in a limited space.

Mouse design has, in recent years, been the subject of considerable ergonomic study so that you can now buy hand-held mice for left-handed users (as the thumb is on a different side), rounded mice which better match the palm of your hand, ones which encourage better wrist posture and so on. Buttons have been reshaped so that they are used with the fingers relaxed rather than arched, and buttons are more responsive whilst still retaining a positive tactile feel.

Other devices

An alternative form of output for drawings is the plotter, which uses pens to draw on a piece of paper. Most microcomputer users would use a flatbed plotter, where the drawing sheet is laid flat and secured, and the pen is moved by an arm across the paper and within the arm up and down the paper. The alternative is the drum plotter, where the paper is mounted on a roller, and the two directions of drawing are created by rotating the drum and moving the pen in one direction.

Plotters can use larger sheets than printers normally can, and can produce smooth-looking curves and shapes. It is likely that you would only consider a plotter if you were wanted to do considerable mathematical or drawing work.

A fax board is an expansion board which allows for the transmission and receipt of fax messages.

A data glove is used, particularly in virtual reality systems to detect the position of the user's hands and fingers. A data helmet is used to create a stereoscopic display, and is worn on the user's head.

17

—— PORTABLES ——

—— Types of portable computers ——

Many computer users wish to carry computer power with them everywhere they go. The last few years have therefore seen a mushrooming of smaller machines such as notebooks, laptops, palmtops and personal digital assistants. All these machines are designed for battery use. There are then trade-offs between size of battery and weight. Much of the development work is aimed at increasing the power of portable machines and reducing the weight.

The different names for categories of machines used by manufacturers are a good guide to the sort of machine you would expect, but none of the categories has a water-tight definition, so the categories are rather fluid. Price is usually a good guide to the facilities likely to be available on a machine. The term 'laptop' is generally used only for machines lighter than six pounds in weight. Smaller machines, such as those that can be kept in a coat pocket, may be referred to as 'handheld'.

A top-of-the-range notebook provides all the facilities of a desktop computer, but in a more compact form. Specifications are improving all the time, with 486 or 68040 chips, hard disks of 80 MB and above, pointing devices (mouse or trackball) and colour screen technology being available within the product ranges of nearly all suppliers. Keyboards on portable computers are necessarily compact but nevertheless provide all the features now standard on a desktop machine. Expansion slots, interfaces and other devices for linking to other computers, printers, monitors and modems are available in various combinations. Some portables are designed to be 'docked' within a desktop machine for office use.

Apple calls its range of notebooks PowerBooks. This range also includes the Duo, which consists of a fully portable notebook machine, with a docking station for desktop use. This combines the power of a portable with desktop access to full colour, printing and so on. IBM compatible portable computers with docking stations are also available from manufacturers such as Compaq.

Smaller hand-held computers (sometimes called sub-notebooks or personal digital assistants) are about the size of a Filofax. They are very suitable for a single specialist application, either individually as a personal diary and address book system, or for an organisation, such as stock taking in a supermarket, or housing benefit calculations.

In an attempt to reduce weight and cost, some of the smallest machines are made without a keyboard. Input is then via a pen which either operates an on-screen keyboard or is used to input handwriting. The handwriting system would normally recognise handwritten print rather than cursive (joined up) text. New users would need to give the machine a few samples of handwriting, but aided with this, software is now available to recognise handwritten print. As more companies write recognition software, the cost of licences for this, which contributes to the cost of such machines, is likely to fall substantially.

The pen systems used on such machines are either passive, which means that they have no electronic function, or are active and involve some form of signalling system. With passive pens, any equivalent device will suffice, as long as the tip is fine enough, though users should be careful not to cause damage to the screen. An active pen system would not allow a substitute for the standard pen to be used.

The most popular PDAs include the Apple Newton and machines from Psion.

Screens

The screen of a portable computer needs to be small enough to keep the weight down, but large enough to be easy to read. It must be sufficiently bright to be read, especially if it is to be used outside or in bright sunlight, yet must consume as little energy as possible to preserve battery life. Most users would prefer colour screens but, because of the technology, a price premium is paid for this. If you choose a monochrome portable, you will have to ensure that the software you choose is suitable for monochrome users.

Portable computers use flat screen displays. Cathode ray tube monitors are far too bulky, and so the boom in laptop and notebook sales has led to the rapid development of new screen technologies, all aiming at a clear display with low power consumption.

Most portable computers use a screen technology called 'liquid crystal display' (LCD), a simple version of which is used in digital watches. The crystals, which are less than a thousandth of an inch thick, flow when energy is passed through them. In their natural state, the crystals lie in one direction. When a charge is passed through them, they move through a right angle. By using two screens which polarise the light, the two different orientations of the crystals will produce a white or a black spot on the screen.

When a pixel is to be charged, a current is passed along the appropriate row and column such that the sum of the currents causes the crystals to move. Supertwist technology uses advanced LCD technology, and improves the contrast and viewing angle, as well as reducing power consumption.

Monochrome screens will typically display 16 shades of grey, giving 14 other shades between black and white. This range becomes essential if you are to use modern software which uses colours other than black and white for text and its background. Even if your software can be customised to work only in black and white, you will often want to use material you have prepared on a portable on a desktop machine, or you may link a colour monitor to your laptop.

The simplest LCD screens use the light from the viewer's side, and reflect that light back with a reflector behind the polarisers and crystals. A sharper screen is produced with a backlit display, which uses a form of reflector that also allows light from the rear to shine through. This type of screen naturally consumes more power.

Active matrix LCD technologies improve the screen display by use of a transistor in each position to increase the current at a pixel, which does not happen with a passive matrix LCD. The thin film transistor (TFT) technology used improves the clarity and brightness of a display, and decreases the time taken for the screen to react to changes, reducing the blurred effect.

Colour LCD depends on a technology known as birefringence which uses a crystal to spilt light into two frequencies which travel at right angles to each other and at different speeds. In this way a colour can be filtered out. Colour is produced from red, green and blue light output through three pixels in each position.

Active LCD has been the norm with colour screen technology, but this has heavy power consumption. It was argued that the people who bought the first portable colour machines were paying a substantial amount extra for colour, and were willing to pay a little bit extra for active technology. Many colour notebooks are now using passive supertwist with backlighting, which also reduces the purchase cost as well as power consumption.

An alternative, but often more expensive, screen technology uses gas plasma technology, in which an inert ionised gas contained between two transparent panels is energised, so that it glows bright orange. Clearly this form of screen does not need backlighting, and gives a good clear display in any light. It is unlikely that gas plasma technology will produce good colour displays.

In the long term, flat-screen technologies may replace the cathode ray technology currently used for desktop computers, and even televisions.

—— Batteries and power saving ——

Electrical power is an important consideration in choosing a battery-operated portable. Designers have invested considerable work in improving performance so that machines can be used longer between recharges.

Battery technology is developing so that more charge can be held for the same weight. The battery weight makes a considerable contribution to the overall weight. Some systems provide for the battery to be recharged away from the portable so that users can have a system of alternating two batteries. Many users are satisfied, however, with a system that will recharge a battery, within the portable, overnight. Typical battery life between recharging is creeping up to about six hours. With power saving techniques, which are discussed later, this is usually sufficient for normal daily use. Users who expect more use in a typical day will usually carry a mains adapter with them.

Most portables will warn you when the batteries are getting low, and give the warning while there is still time to save data to disk. Some will automatically suspend activity when batteries are particularly low, and will save all the necessary information about the current state of the machine. When the machine is next used, all the saved information is restored, and the user is reinstated in the application previously in use. Recharging can usually be carried on whilst use is made of the machine through the mains adapter. This recharging will, of course, be slower than recharging with the machine switched off. Some portables provide a simple indicator to show how much charge is left in the batteries.

There are three types of batteries in common use. Nickel cadmium batteries (NiCad) suffer from a memory effect. If they are frequently recharged before they are completely drained, the new charge will last only as long as the last charge, so users are advised to drain the charge completely before recharging. Nickel metal hydride (NiMH, or NiH_2) batteries do not have this 'memory effect', and provide more power for the same weight. They are a newer technology and are somewhat more expensive. They also cannot be recharged using a fast charge method, and a cut-out is needed to protect against overcharging. There may be cases where NiMH cannot deliver quite as much peak current as NiCad for power-intensive operations (such as a 486 machine with active screen technology). The third battery technology is lithium ion. This delivers a similar amount of power to a nickel metal hydride battery, but is only half the weight.

Whilst designers are working on providing more power through the batteries, others are working on reducing the energy requirements of systems. This is being achieved in a number of ways:

- stopping the hard disk spinning when it is not being accessed. After a set period of disk inactivity, the disk is brought to rest to conserve power. In some systems, the period of inactivity before this happens can be altered by the user.

- switching off the screen backlighting after a period of keyboard inactivity of a minute or two. Again the period may be altered by the user.

- using a disk cache to reduce unnecessary disk activity.

- reducing the CPU speed when no processing is taking place.

- using special versions of CPU chips, such as the Intel 386SL and 486SL, which have been designed to minimise power consumption. (Power consumption was not a major design issue when desktop computers were developed, but with the sharp rise in popularity of portable machines, low power chips are in great demand, so their price has fallen dramatically.)

───── Accessories and contents ─────

Portable computers contain an internal hard disk, as well as a 3.5 inch floppy disk drive. Data can then be transferred onto a desktop computer either by way of a floppy disk, or by using a file transfer package consisting of a communications program, an appropriate cable and connectors.

Developing hard disk technology has provided disks of higher capacity, with 80 MB being typical, and drives which are much more robust to the inevitable knocks caused by regular carrying and desktop use.

Many users will want to implement the same programs on portable machines as desktops, and so most would want access to a pointing device. There is a range of mice suitable for portable computers, the majority of which are adaptations, such as the hand-held mouse, which is kept stationary, with the cursor being moved by rotating a ball with the thumb. If a portable is designed for use anywhere, then a user will often not wish to use a fairly large desk space for accurate mouse operation. Many laptops use an in-built trackball system in place of a mouse. There is no standard size or position for where this might be placed within the keyboard. Other systems still use a special 'mouse key' which rocks either sideways or vertically for pointing purposes. Whichever of these systems you choose, you will need to learn a simple new technique for on-screen pointing.

On many systems, the external power is supplied through a mains adapter. If you end up carrying this around with you, it is worth remembering how heavy it might be.

A carrying case is normally essential for a portable computer and its accompanying tools. Equipment suppliers will be glad to provide one. Enquire whether the carrying case is included in any price you are quoted.

If you wish to use your system with a modem, this can be either through an in-built modem, or through an external modem, as long as an appropriate socket is provided.

A typical portable computer will have several sockets for attachments. Typically there will be sockets for:

- keyboard attachment (so that you can use a fully-featured keyboard)

- monitor output for use with a separate desktop monitor

- serial port

- parallel port

- mouse port (allowing the other serial port to be used for something else)

- ports for other external devices, such as a hard disk, modem and telephone line.

Normally input-output ports will have covers, which are either hinged or pop on and off, to protect the connections when not in use.

User control over brightness and contrast is normally provided, either through the keyboard (to save space), or through the usual dials. The settings from one session may not be remembered for the next session.

An average notebook will have a small amount of low power RAM, perhaps of 256 bytes, which retains system settings.

As space is at a premium with notebooks, very few of them have a full enhanced 101 key keyboard. Different manufacturers have found different ways of condensing the keyboard, so there is no standard, though one may emerge in the next few years. Reduction of keyboard size is achieved in a number of ways:

- keys are placed closer together

- keys are made smaller

- keys are given two or three different functions

- the separate numeric keypad is dispensed with, other keys doubling up to provide this if it is there at all

- cursor control keys are provided in a minimal form (perhaps just an inverted-T arrangement).

Potential users of portable computers are advised to try out the 'feel' of a few keyboards to see whether they like the layout, the size of the keys, the distance the keys travel and so on. When similar machines from different manufacturers are very similarly priced, personal preference about the keyboard is often one major way to narrow down the choice.

Some portable computer systems use memory cards as an alternative or supplement to disk memory. The Personal Computer Memory Card International Association (PCMCIA) has produced various standards which enable different manufacturers' products to be linked. Therefore any cards manufactured to one of the three standards will fit into the appropriate socket and will accept the signals properly. The standard does not, though, cover the format in which the data is held; you will probably find that a memory card can be plugged into another manufacturer's equipment through the standardised socket, but that equipment may not have the software to read the particular format. Memory cards come in a variety of types, including RAM, ROM and flash memory.

PCMCIA expansion is described as providing a 'plug and play' facility, as it enables a portable computer to have access to extra memory, or extra hard disk capacity, or a fax or modem. 'Plug and play' sound cards also are of great benefit, particularly when used for presentations on the move.

Programs are available to transfer files between laptops and desktops. These include Brooklyn Bridge, and LapLink, which is available in PC and Mac versions. Users who need file transfer only on an occasional basis may prefer to carry this with a floppy disk, which is a far less expensive, if slower, method.

Printers

You might want to use a portable printer with a portable computer. Many users of portable computers are quite happy with using the machine while they are on the move or at home, but can wait until they are in the office to print. It can be a fairly simple job once you arrive at work to copy files from floppy disk for printing, particularly if you have the same software at work as on the portable. This will be particularly important if you want very good quality printing.

Portable printers will prove essential, though, if you want on the spot quotations, invoices, or immediate printed records of discussions. Portable printers tend to cost about twice the amount of a similar desktop version. Portable printers are commonly ink-jets, with perhaps an hour of battery life for printing, which should prove adequate.

Other portable printers use a thermal printing technique which burns an image onto special paper; others use a thermal ribbon with ordinary paper.

Portable printers need protecting from damage in transit, and various design techniques protect the print head from damage and the ink from spillage.

___Points to ponder when buying a___ notebook

The reduced keyboard may provide fewer keys, giving each of them more functions. If some functions are not provided, or are only available through complex key combinations, this could make some packages a lot more difficult to use on a portable.

Some portables provide a facility to plug into a conventional monitor. This might prove very useful to you, but you should be careful to match the monitor to the graphics standard used by the portable.

If an external monitor connection is provided, how is it activated? Can both the notebook screen and the external screen be used at the same time? (This is particularly important for giving presentations.)

When choosing the machine, think about the weight of the mains adapter; if you are carrying it all the time, this will make a significant difference.

Does the price include the operating system?

Does the system have tools to preserve battery life provided? Are they part of the advertised price? Are they ready loaded?

Are the brightness and contrast settings, and the cursor type remembered between sessions, or are they always reset?

Do you really want a portable printer?

18

SOME SAMPLE SYSTEMS

The issues facing potential purchasers of systems are sometimes best illustrated using examples. Because computing develops so quickly, of course, such examples can date very quickly. In examining case studies, it is also tempting to concentrate on the detail of the hardware, and then possibly look at the software. The examples given in this chapter are an attempt to broaden such considerations beyond simple detail of what was purchased, but to look as well at the reasons. In the long term, it is the thinking behind particular purchases which will stand the test of time.

The six case studies that follow are based on real life situations, but elements of the detail have been changed in order to cover a wider range of purchasing issues. There are also occasions when the details of particular models have been changed to ensure that model numbers are the latest available equivalent, rather than an actual model used.

—— Case study 1 The councillor ——

Alan is an elected councillor for a large city council which provides a wide range of services such as housing, refuse collection, tourism and benefits, and which acts as the local planning authority. As an authority it has mainframe systems, local and wide area networks, and several hundred PCs.

Policy matters for the authority are taken by a whole range of committees and sub-committees. The office technology committee deals with decisions about which computer systems should be purchased, and Alan was selected to chair this sub-committee. The suggestion was made that several of the senior councillors would be able to make use of notebook computers.

Councillors undertake a wide range of duties, normally in addition to their paid employment. Local people write to them or ring up about matters which concern them, which may be housing repairs, benefit queries, matters to do with street lighting, car parking and so on. In addition to attending committee meetings which are minuted by the officers of the council, councillors also attend their own policy meetings at which officers are not present, and these meetings need careful minuting. Alan was appointed secretary to his group, which meant keeping minutes of four meetings a month.

There are also occasions when senior councillors need to prepare presentations to other councillors and officers about various proposals.

As a large public authority, the city council is obliged to invite manufacturers to bid to provide computer equipment, and in this case Dell won the contract, as the lowest bidder to supply all PCs for the forthcoming year. It was subsequently decided that notebook computers would be the right solution for some senior councillors. There were a number of reasons behind this.

First, councillors find themselves working in a variety of different places. They are keen to make best use of their time, whether it be during the lunch hour at work, on council premises or at home. There are times when a councillor might find a spare half hour between two meetings when it is not feasible to travel home, so there is chance to carry on with some work.

To take minutes of meetings, Alan needed a word processor. Meetings might take two or three hours, with minutes recording the main decisions taken, running to four or five pages. A discussion might take half an hour, but then a whole series of decisions are taken very swiftly. Experience had shown Alan that he could not write full minutes during a meeting, so he would take notes; but he could do this on a notebook computer, so that these could be turned into formal minutes later. Having his notebook with him all the time meant that he could carry out this task, sometimes working to very tight deadlines, whenever spare time arose.

The system that was chosen for Alan was a Dell Latitude 433c, a colour notebook, with Microsoft Office suite. Another specialist piece of software was also installed which enables him, by entering all a person's individual details, to give an accurate estimate of their entitlement to benefits. The Dell Latitude 433c has a 486 Intel SL Enhanced i486SX microprocessor running at 33 MHz. (The product ranges of many manufacturers use numbering systems such as this, the 4 from the 486, the 33 from the 33 MHz, and the c to indicate colour. Other manufacturers use numbers from the hard disk capacity to distinguish model numbers. Still others use codes for models which have little pattern to them.)

Microsoft Office is a suite of programs which includes Word 6.0, a powerful word processor. This proved every useful for minute taking. Excel 4 is provided as the spreadsheet, which is useful for financial analysis and statistical projections. PowerPoint is the presentation package which comes as part of the bundle. This means that when preparing presentations to other councillors, Alan can pull in information from either Excel or Word, so that financial statistics or minutes can be included. Very often a set of proposals will evolve through presentation and the discussion at several meetings, so having easy access to change minor parts was considered to be very important.

The notebook has a 170 MB IDE hard disk drive and a standard 1.44 internal floppy disk drive. There is a trackerball and two buttons on the keyboard at the right on the front which are used as an internal mouse. An external mouse can be connected instead if users prefer this. It certainly took Alan some time to become familiar with the internal mouse after using a table-top and a hand-held mouse. Alan noticed that the positioning of the inbuilt mouse would almost certainly create problems for left-handed users.

With such a computer, at first it might appear sensible to have a portable printer. However, Alan had found that he made little use of a portable printer with his previous machine, principally because of the printer's weight. He printed files by copying them onto floppy disk, and then printing documents when he was either at the council offices or at work, where there were laser printers. This, of course, depended on both places having identical software, but since this was the case, and he was at both places most weekdays, this turned out to be the best solution. Because little of his printing was very urgent (most of it could wait a day), Alan was prepared to sacrifice speed and immediacy for quality of output. Clearly it would be uneconomic to have a laser printer at home.

The NiMH batteries take under two hours to recharge fully, a huge advance on his previous system which used to take 12 hours.

By buying in bulk, the council received substantial discounts on the advertised prices of both the hardware and software.

———— Case study 2 The family ————

Ray and Joan have two young daughters, aged seven and four. Ray works for a large engineering company in research and development. Joan has not worked recently whilst bringing up a family, but trained and worked for a number of years as an accountant. Both are active members of their local Methodist church. Ray is a local preacher who leads worship about twice a month. Joan acts as treasurer to several local societies, including a voluntary home for the care of the elderly.

In selecting a system for their home, Ray and Joan decided to visit local computer shops in the City where they live, and so visited their local Escom store. The staff were very helpful, and provided some useful literature for Ray and Joan to read. After reading the brochures several times, they revisited the shop to purchase an Escom Pentium P60 PCI. It contained a 60 MHz Intel Pentium processor, and 540 MB hard drive with PCI controller. They were attracted by the tower case, the Microsoft mouse, and the 15 inch monitor, which they felt was better for the children. The intention was that the system would have to last them at least four years, so would see their older girl through to secondary school.

The software bundled with the system included MS-DOS 6.2 and Windows for Workgroups 3.11, which Ray had recently begun to use at work. Escom also offered the choice of a Microsoft application, and after some thought, Ray and Joan chose Microsoft Word, as they knew they would be doing a lot of word processing.

Included within the price was 12 months on-site warranty. This was important to Joan because with Ray working out of town, there would be difficulties for her returning a system for repair because of her child-care responsibilities.

Another option that they were offered was the installation of a CD-ROM drive at a discounted price. Though they had no immediate plans to use this, they felt that this was too good an offer to miss, and that the CD-ROM would come into its own when the girls were a little older. Ray had been particularly impressed by the reviews of Encarta which he had read, though he felt the girls were too young for this yet.

Ray and Joan also allowed themselves the luxury of a colour printer, as Escom was offering the Hewlett-Packard 550C at a reasonable price. Having read reviews of various printers, they were aware that the system uses disposable combined print head and ink supply cartridges, but they felt that colour printing would come into its own with the children, and would help promote their interest.

In order to keep her accounts on the new computer, Joan looked at a number of possible products. Amongst those offered by Escom were Intuit Quicken 3 and QuickBooks. Though Quicken 3 would have been more than adequate for her own domestic accounts, with Joan's involvement as a treasurer, she felt that QuickBooks was the best option. It is a fully fledged double-entry book keeping system, which provides key management reports as well as financial statements. Over 50 off the peg reports are ready-written, and users can also generate their own reports, which Joan felt would help her answer the wide range of enquiries which she received. Intuit, the suppliers of QuickBooks, also offered unlimited free technical support.

Ray found that he made a great deal of use of Word for his local church work. He was able to keep and catalogue all the various aspects of his preaching material, keeping careful record of which items he had used in different churches. He was able to produce orders of service and other materials for photocopying, personalised to the individual services.

Though the girls have initially used the machine relatively little, it has stimulated their interest in using computers. They are not allowed to play the aggressive 'zap the aliens' games, but as Ray and Joan take a number of monthly computer magazines, they have a reasonable collection of simple software which all the family can use.

Ray and Joan liked the convenience of a local shop, where they could become familiar with the staff, where they were not embarrassed to ask simple questions, and where they could return either to sort out problems or to buy add-ons for their system.

Case study 3 The advertising agency

Nottingham City Council both places and sells a large number of advertisements. Advertisements are placed to publicise job vacancies, events, and statutory notices. The council publishes a number of brochures offering advice and several programmes for events. Several of these contain advertisements placed by local firms. To manage this process, the council employs three staff, one of whom specialises in selling advertising space in council publications.

Because it places a large number of advertisements, the council is able to obtain substantial discounts provided that it fulfils certain conditions in administering advertisements. All departments within the council must place their advertisements through the advertising agency, and are then billed internally for them. A similar system needs to operate to provide departments with income from the sale of advertisements in their publications.

The advertising world depends on a consistent ability to meet tight deadlines. This is particularly important when publishers are aiming to sell their remaining space at reduced rates immediately before going to press, rather than leave parts of a publication blank.

The council chose to buy two computers, and decided on the Apple Macintosh LC475, each with 8 MB of memory. The council's overall policy had always been to buy PC compatible systems, so there was considerable discussion whether the advertising agency should be an exception from the normal practice. The break with policy was finally agreed because of the widespread use of Apples by so many other organisations in advertising. Initially, it was necessary to work with files that could be transferred easily to the local branch of a commercial advertising agency, Barkers, who were providing some initial services. This argument overcame the counter-argument of the need for compatibility of files and applications with other departments of the council.

Two different monitors were chosen. A 21 inch monitor was purchased for the machine that would be used intensively for graphics and layout. The more common 14 inch screen was selected for the machine used mainly for the administration; this computer is also available for quick graphics and layout jobs if the other machine is tied up in some other task. The choice of printer was a Calcomp CCL600, which is a high-specification office monochrome laser printer with a 4 MB memory, expandable to 44 MB. This was chosen for its robustness and reliability, as it would be heavily used every day. The colour scanner chosen was the UMax UC840. The scanner came bundled with Adobe Photoshop for retouching scanned pictures, so that specific areas of an image can be lightened or darkened, images can be blended, and various fills, patterns and textures can be added.

Other software packages in use include Aldus FreeHand 4.0 for drawings and Quark Xpress for desktop publishing. Aldus FreeHand provides the wide range of facilities needed by the graphic designer. Quark Xpress was seen to be particularly good in allowing up to 127 different page masters, which is important when dealing with a wide range of publication types.

To manage the large amounts of information generated in placing advertisements, cross-checking, raising and paying invoices, a database was needed, and the one chosen was 4th Dimension, published by ACI.

The systems chosen proved to be a nice balance between familiarity for those who had worked in advertising and graphic design before, yet with ease of use and learning for those staff with little experience in the particular area.

—— Case study 4 The blind student ——

Kulvinder is in his mid-twenties and has been totally blind for about half of his life. He is an experienced Braille user. He has chosen to study computing at a further education college, with specialist support from the RNIB Vocational College.

It is no exaggeration to say that the use of his notebook computer has been the key factor in enabling Kulvinder to study as part of a course with mainly sighted students whilst working on equal terms with them. He happens to be studying computing, but several of the other visually impaired students on very different vocational courses, still make use of notebook computers.

Kulvinder was issued with a Toshiba T1850/120 computer. This has an Intel 80386SX processor, 4 MB of RAM, and a 120 MB hard drive. Kulvinder is an expert touch typist, so this is his main form of input, but as he cannot see the screen, he needs to use a form of speech output. This is provided through a special hardware board which was added for him by the technicians at the RNIB College. The board, known as the Apollo, from a company called Dolphin, is fitted in the modem slot. The board consists of a motherboard for speech synthesis, with a daughterboard providing amplification. Judicious choice of add-in chips means that Kulvinder can switch the synthesiser into German, which he studies as part of his course. In addition, Kulvinder uses software, called HAL, also from Dolphin, which enables him to choose which part of the screen he wishes to have read out to him. He uses headphones to listen to the output. The power requirements of the extra board mean that the batteries do not last as long between charges, but, in addition to the notebook's own energy saving features, Kulvinder usually turns off the screen display as he does not use it. He needs to turn it on occasionally, though, to show his work to lecturers or other students with whom he is working.

The system is battery powered, using a NiCad battery with a published life of 5 hours per charge. Since he will need the computer with him throughout the day, both the weight of the system, and the battery life are important factors. The machine itself weighs just under 7 lb. Though he has an extra battery pack which he can carry with him, Kulvinder normally finds that a full recharge will last him all day. If he occasionally runs out of power, he will use the mains in a classroom for the rest of the day. The notebook in its carrying case, with an adapter, plus headphones and floppy disks make a substantial weight in additional to all the other materials which a sighted student might carry.

The RNIB Vocational College examined a number of possible manufacturers before choosing Toshiba. A key consideration was the ability of machines to operate without blemish with a range of specialist software, not just speech synthesis, but also character enlargement for those students and staff who are partially sighted.

The Toshiba has an AutoResume mode which allows the user to switch off without exiting from the applications, storing the current status in battery-backed memory. Toshiba claims that this has benefits over saving the status to disk, first because the user does not need to keep sufficient disk space free, and secondly because the application can be resumed without a long reloading process, which on some notebooks can take up to a minute. The AutoSave feature within AutoResume automatically saves data if the battery is about to fail, which is similar to features found on many modern notebooks.

The system is tuned to conserve as much power as possible by monitoring use, so that disk, screen, keyboard and processors will be switched off if they have not been used for a while. When activity starts up again, they are, of course, switched back on.

Kulvinder uses WordPerfect, SuperCalc, dBase and Turbo Pascal, all running under DOS. These are the standard items of software used by the RNIB Vocational College. They were chosen because they are primarily text-based. Kulvinder and students like him have found great difficulty in using icon driven mouse-based software. Companies like Microsoft have responded very well in the last couple of years to pressures to provide features geared to visually impaired people. Having once learnt how to use the particular products that were first installed on his machine, Kulvinder is happy to use the software which he knows and can use well. He would rather do this than attempt to learn further software for the remainder of his course.

When he requires print-outs of his work for submission, Kulvinder will visit the specialist resource room with the appropriate files on floppy disk. He can either print the material himself using a desktop system, or submit the work for printing by support staff.

— Case study 5 The retired librarian —

Brian took early retirement last summer after working for many years as a librarian and in the last few years as a lecturer in librarianship. He has seen the impact of the use of computers in recent years but he had never had all that much to do with them. He decided that he could afford to spend some of his lump sum on a computer, but was reluctant to spend too much money on something which he saw as a leisure interest for himself and his partner, who was still working.

He bought a number of computer magazines, such as Personal Computer World, in which he found a whole range of advertisements. A number of the offers caught his eye, including ones with bundled software. He found low priced systems which included a whole range of Borland packages. He was impressed that, having paid a 30% deposit, he could buy such a system at 0% interest over two years. However, having recently received a lump sum, borrowing was not his main concern. He carefully read all the small print with the advertisements. In some he noticed that though you received a software bundle already installed, you had to pay extra for the disks and the manuals. Whilst he was not confident about loading the software himself, he was loathe to attempt to use software without a manual, and no price was given for these 'extras'.

He noticed that a number of the advertisements did not state who made the processor chips in the machines. From this he assumed that it was not Intel, as that name was very prominent in advertisements for products which were Intel-based. Some advertisements did state other manufacturers of chips, and he was happy with this.

He finally settled on buying a Compaq Prolinea from P&P, who described themselves as a Compaq Authorised Reseller. From friends he found out that P&P had been in business for as many years as most people could remember. He also noticed that they sold equipment from several different suppliers.

The model that Brian chose was the Compaq Prolinea Net 1/25S. This was not the cheapest model he could find, but there were a number of aspects of the offer that appealed to him. It had a 486SX 25 MHz processor, which he felt would be adequate for his needs. Computers with lower specifications seemed all too rare in the advertisements. It had 4 MB of RAM, which again seemed to be the minimum in all but a few machines. The main machine included a 3 year warranty, with the first year being on-site. This seemed to be a fairly good service, whilst there was clearly some risk involved. The box was a slim one with an integrated monitor giving SuperVGA. The hard disk had a 100 MB capacity which he considered would be more than enough. The system was supplied with Windows 3.1 and MS-DOS 6.0 ready loaded, and whilst no manuals were supplied, his friends at the library had some good books to lend him on semi-permanent loan. Though the system was described as network-ready at no extra cost, he could not see that he was every likely to use this facility.

Having looked at the range of printers available, Brian settled for the Canon BJ-200, which was the most compact of the machines, as well as being amongst the cheapest. It printed at 360 dots per inch, and it would help that it would print on plain paper and OHP acetates.

By not opting for a system with a set bundle of software, he was able to choose his software freely. He selected Lotus SmartSuite 2.1, and as he could trade in an old version of Lotus 1-2-3 which a deceased colleague had previously given him, he could take advantage of a trade-in offer. Brian was prepared to spend a reasonable amount on software because he would have time to spend learning each package at his own pace. As well as Lotus 1-2-3 version 4.0, the bundle included Ami Pro 3.01, a word processor, and Freelance Graphics 2.01, which would help with presentations. Though he did not see any immediate need for it, he was pleased to have Lotus Approach 2.1 as a database, but the package which really clinched it for him was Lotus Organizer, a personal information manager which looked very like an on-screen Filofax. He was delighted with this and put it to use almost immediately.

Before he rang P&P, he read through lots of other advertisements to see what they were offering. He realised that he would be buying three separate items, and he should use this as a bargaining ploy. By doing his homework, he would be able to quote who else would offer the printer at £10 cheaper, and which firms offered bundles cheaper if you also bought your computer from them at the same time. After some thought about the P&P advert, he realised that there was no mouse supplied with the system as advertised. There was no harm asking about one when he rang, he thought. Perhaps other people missed this and then paid another £20 later for the mouse. He also spotted the small print in the advertisement stating that delivery would cost £15 plus VAT. Again, he scoured other advertisements for people who delivered free.

Armed with this information, he rang P&P. He gradually brought some of the other information he had found into the conversation, and he found P&P quite accommodating. They did not reduce the price on everything, but various aspects like the mouse and delivery charges were waived. They did not like his suggestion that they supply some free paper with the printer, as he realised afterwards, this would increase the cost of delivery. He was surprised that a number of prices were rounded down from the advertised figure. He finally summarised exactly what he wanted, and asked for the best price which P&P could offer. He was pleased that he had brought the price down a little. He paid for the goods by credit card.

Though he had not opted for the cheapest of all systems, Brian was pleased with his choice of a reliable system, which he could explore at his leisure and at his own pace.

——— **Case study 6 Two teachers** ———

Sue teaches in a multi-racial primary school, and has a class of 8, 9 and 10 year olds. Don teaches history in a college. Both have made a little use of computers at work, and know enough about the particular systems to set a young person up to use the software supplied. The systems which they are used to, though, are very different. Sue's school has one computer per classroom, and has standardised on Acorn Archimedes machines. Sue is fairly clear about the skills which she believes her pupils will develop when using some of her selected software. Don is very used to marking work from students written either on the college's Research Machines computers or home word processors. He has become familiar with some of the poor writing style which he associates with word processing. In particular, he is concerned about the lack of flow within essays that have been written in a peculiar order and then edited together. He also believes that some students are tempted to reuse old material when it would be better to start from scratch.

Neither Sue nor Don has made very much use of the staff computers at work. Largely because of other commitments and travelling arrangements, it is difficult to stay behind at work for a couple of hours. Both would rather do extra work at home.

Bearing this in mind, they discussed the possibility of buying a computer for home use. It was further suggested to them by a friend that they should consider a multimedia system. They were somewhat surprised at this suggestion initially, as they have no children, and most of what they had read led them to believe that multimedia was mainly for children.

Having talked to a friend who works with computers, they bought several computer magazines, and largely on their friend's recommendation, they began to look at the Viglen systems. Their friend's company had bought 20 Viglens, and they had proved extremely reliable. Don and Sue decided that they would initially be very interested in a word processor which could produce large simple print for her worksheets and possibly for wall displays. Don was more likely to use text for handouts and extracts of texts, though he felt that generating tables of information might help his students with revision.

The Viglen advertisement offered a wide range of choices. There were four different processors, and five different disk sizes with each.

There was also a choice of cases, with a slimline and more standard desktop size, plus a tower configuration. Because they were choosing a CD-ROM option, the slimline system was not considered suitable, so they chose the standard desktop model. The system price was quoted inclusive of a 15 inch Super VGA colour monitor, but they noticed a section in the advertisement which offered a reduction of £60 if they preferred a 14 inch monitor, and they were happy to accept this. The system was described as using the PCI bus.

They carefully considered the table of options for Pentium machines, and chose the middle option of a 66 MHz machine, and the second largest hard disk capacity of 500 MB. To them, it was not worth paying extra for the extra capacity of 1 GB. The main memory was 16 MB. Extending the 12 month parts and labour warranty to on-site maintenance cost a little more. As busy people, Don and Sue felt that this was worth the money. They were pleased with the way that the Viglen advertisement made the maintenance options clear.

The advertisement explained that through a scheme called the 'Software Bonus', Microsoft Works 3.0 for Windows was provided pre-installed with on-line documentation. For a small extra sum they could also have the manuals and disks. They read that Microsoft Works is an integrated spreadsheet, database, and word processor. Whilst it also contained electronic communication software, they thought they were unlikely to use that feature. They considered more advanced software systems, and could have upgraded to Microsoft Office, but felt that, in their case, this would be unnecessary. They did, however, also order Microsoft Publisher 2.0, a desktop publishing program, and Microsoft Money 3.0 for money management.

With a wide variety of outside interests in the arts, they looked carefully at the Multimedia upgrades. They were prepared to opt for the more expensive of the two offers, which included a Soundblaster 16 bit card, plus a double speed photo CD compatible multi-session CD-ROM drive, a pair of stereo amplified speakers, a microphone and three CD-ROM titles. The upgrades would be factory-fitted and installed ready for use. Though Sue was confident that she, rather than Don, would be able to fit such a system, she felt that she did not have the time to invest in learning the process, which she felt she would then be unlikely ever to use again. The three CD titles supplied were all Microsoft titles: Musical Instruments, Cinemania and Golf.

Though they did not anticipate using it, they were pleased to find that a free lifetime technical support telephone service was provided.

They completed the form, being careful to check all the costs and details, and sent off their order. Early the following week, the system was delivered, and having some spare time over the weekend, they were able to set up the system and begin to make use of it immediately.

By careful reading of various advertisements, including the small print about additional costs for delivery and insurance, Sue chose the HP Deskjet 520, which is advertised as printing 3 pages per minute. For their home use, speed would not be a particular issue. This they ordered by telephone using a credit card.

Don found the system particularly useful as he taught such varied topics, some of which he might only come back to once a year. By devising a cataloguing system for all his new material from the start, he was able to retrieve previous work for re-use much more easily than with his manual systems. He made a conscious decision not to attempt to computerise everything in a year, but chose particular areas on which to concentrate.

The bought the Microsoft Encarta encyclopaedia on CD-ROM. Don was disappointed in the range of history topics covered. The material on the Napoleonic wars gave him some new ideas for different approaches. He was frustrated that much of the material was American-dominated, when subjects like the JFK assassination and the American Civil war were not on any of his syllabuses.

Sue was able to buy a good selection of CDs over the following year to pursue her interest in particular composers, buying titles such as Multimedia Mozart. She was also pleased to find a CD-ROM to help her to learn French for their forthcoming holiday.

From a work point of view, she was pleased with Microsoft Encarta, as this enabled her to find additional material for pupils pursuing individual topics. This gave her good opportunities to develop the enthusiasm of her pupils by showing her interest in their chosen topics. She would often arrive at school armed with new print-outs of snippets of information for individuals in the class.

19

SUPPORT FOR YOUR SYSTEM

The hardest part of setting up your computer system is choosing the correct system in the first place. At the same time as making that choice, though, you must also start thinking about the practical issues of running your system. You will presumably be intending to use the system for three, four or five years, and all will not run smoothly in that time, however carefully you have chosen it. It is best to plan from the beginning how you will look after the system. It represents a major capital investment, so plan ahead.

Supplies

The consumables that you will buy most regularly will be those for your printer, both ink and paper.

As described in Chapter 16, a variety of printer technologies exist, and each technology requires a form of 'ink', or toner. For inkjet printers you need one or more inks. For dot matrix printers, you need ribbons.

Supplies for laser printers can be quite expensive, and running costs may be a major factor in your choice of system. Specialist computer suppliers stock supplies for more than a dozen main manufacturers. Laser printers consume regular supplies of toner, and from time to time you may need to replace the fuser, the developer, and even the drum. Some printer technologies also use an ozone filter which may need replacement from time to time. If your printer has a system for collecting unused or loose toner powder, this will normally be gathered in a small disposable reservoir. A replacement for this may be supplied with each new bottle of toner.

A similar large array of dot matrix or daisywheel ribbons is on offer in the various catalogues. Different types of ribbon are available, sometimes for the same printer. The catalogues often give a guide whether to buy film or fabric ribbons for particular applications.

With an inkjet printer, you will need to replace the cartridge from time to time. Supplies are available, however, which allow you to refill a cartridge from a refill bottle which is then thrown away. This can cut the price by about half, but the cartridge case itself will not last forever. With colour inkjet printers, refills are available for the three main colours and black.

In ordering your printer supplies, be careful to order the correct supplies for your make and model of printer. The catalogues are full of page after page of listings of all the common printers and the supplies needed. The onus is on you to quote the correct code number for the supplies you want. When choosing a make and model of printer try to pick one for which supplies are likely to be available for the lifetime of your equipment. There is no absolute guarantee of this: even an assurance from the manufacturer about continuity of supply does not usually commit the manufacturer to provide the printer supplies at a reasonable cost. They might be available, but very expensive. The best advice is to buy a model from a long-standing large company, or to pick a product which uses exactly the same supplies as such a model. Find out what type of supplies are needed, because you may be in the position of having to use the catalogue to look up the similar model rather than your own.

Many printer manufacturers, include a clause in the warranty which states that the warranty is no longer valid if you have used third-party consumables. This clause appears to suggest that breakdowns are not covered, even if the fault was not caused by the consumable at all. Though many manufacturers would deny that this is what the clause means, you probably don't want to be the person who attempts to test this in court. This clause genuinely worries many purchasers into buying only the manufacturer's supplies, for which they may be charged an inflated price.

A similar array of choice is available when it comes to choosing paper for your printer. Dot matrix and other impact printers are the most tolerant of a variety of paper types, including labels and envelopes, and as long as you line them up correctly, a consistently clear image will be produced.

Laser printer paper is more difficult to choose. Most papers will produce a reasonably good result, but performance is marred if the paper is not flat, as the ink transfer depends on close contact with the toner. For this reason, embossed paper is not recommended. On the other hand, paper which is too smooth or glossy will pick up every piece of stray toner, so better paper sometimes produces a worse result. Paper which is at all curled can cause difficulties with feeding, so you should avoid paper that has already been through a laser printer or a photocopier. Paper for laser printers should be dry, so think about where you store your paper. Condensation within the printer resulting from the high temperatures could cause problems.

Inkjet printers use a wet ink which needs to be absorbed. Use of ordinary copier paper can produce blurred images which are easily smudged. The ideal paper for an inkjet printer will absorb the ink without spreading, to give a clear image. Using the right paper is particularly important for colour inkjet printing. Some paper are coated with a thin layer of clay to aid ink absorption.

Recycled paper is becoming increasingly popular, as it has improved in appearance. With older printers there was sometimes a warning not to use recycled paper. There were two main reasons for this. First the surface was perhaps not as smooth which could lead to problems of toner adherence. Secondly, recycled paper was at one time notorious for the dust it created which would affect the internal working of the printer. Thankfully, much less dust is now created, and this is now less of a problem. The older the printer is, the more wary you will need to be of using recycled paper. Many recent printers have been designed with the use of recycled paper in mind, and many printer manufacturers now produce their own recycled paper.

The choices are more restricted when it comes to choosing other supplies such as labels. For a laser printer, special labels must be purchased which will withstand high temperatures inside the printer without the labels curling or the adhesive reacting. These labels also have a surface suitable for laser printing. For an inkjet printer, the paper must be absorbent enough to give a clear image which will not smudge in the post.

Envelopes need to obey the same rules as those described above for printer paper: not too heavy or thick or they will jam, not too thin or other problems will occur. There are special techniques in feeding envelopes which come in a number of sizes, usually different from that of A4 paper. A good manual will explain how to feed envelopes. Be wary if the envelopes are pre- printed; you must ensure that the ink will not be affected by the heat. The gum on the envelope too must be capable of standing the heat and pressure.

Normal acetates for overhead projection should not be used in a laser printer, as they can melt at high temperatures, so even if they are pronounced safe for photocopiers, do not use them in laser printers. Considerable, probably irreparable, damage will be done if a slide melts within the printer's mechanism. Other types of overhead films can be used in laser printers: again read the instructions and the details given in the catalogues. These withstand the heat and are capable of lying flat after printing because of a special coating.

Competition has helped floppy disk prices fall in recent years. You can save some money by buying less well-known makes, but you must judge whether it is worth the saving, as you will be entrusting some precious data to disks. Always check that you are buying disks of the right specification. Too low a specification, and the disks will probably not work, too high a specification, and you are paying over the odds for quality that you cannot exploit.

A wide range of products is available for cleaning computer equipment. Sprays can be used to clean the keyboard, casing and the screen. Systems are available to clean disk drive heads. In all cases, the message is 'clean with care'. More damage can be done to equipment through incorrect cleaning than is ever done through careful normal use. Cleaning materials are normally designed so that they avoid scratching surfaces. Screen cleaners help to reduce static electricity which attracts the dust. There is even a portable hand-held vacuum cleaner for removing dust from inaccessible places.

Ancillary equipment

A wide range of computer furniture is available. Many home users who bought early computers would use them on the dining room table and sit on a dining chair, or would sprawl in front of the television using the new-found toy. Prolonged use of the equipment in awkward positions led to many problems such as back-ache. Many chain stores now sell specific computer furniture for the home. Specialist suppliers will claim that their furniture is more suitable, and they will all use the tag 'ergonomic' to describe their product.

Good advice would generally suggest that a workstation should have adjustable heights if several different people are to use it. A chair should give good lumbar support to the lower back, and should be height adjustable. Pains in the wrist can be caused if the user has nowhere to rest them. If you are going to use a mouse, then a reasonable accessible space will have to be left for it on the desk surface. If your desktop computer is to be moved around easily, it will need to be on a desk with castors, preferably one which can be locked in position. Some people also find footrests very useful. The better footrests are normally adjustable.

The surface of a your desk should not be too reflective as this causes glare and distraction. If you are using a mouse, you should consider using a mouse mat: they increase the traction and give mouse movement a consistent feel. They also reduce the chances of scratching or marking the desk, and prevent the mouse from picking up dirt from the table. An easy-wipe surface helps keep the mouse mat itself clean.

Dust on all equipment is best controlled by dust covers whenever the system is not in use, which for home or office use is generally most of the time. Computers in bedrooms are particularly likely to be exposed to dust.

Screen glare filters help protect users from headaches and eyestrain. They cut down on reflections, particularly from overhead lights and windows. Filters also reduce the effects of static electricity. Filters are usually mounted on hangers placed on top of the monitor. Special cleaning equipment is usually needed to prevent damage to the special non-reflective surfaces used on glare filters.

Different issues apply to portable computers, as these are designed to be used on the lap or a small table. Most laptops also include inbuilt glare filters. One additional expense with a laptop, though, is a bag to carry it in. Most bags on the market are padded to reduce the effect of dropping the equipment. Most also include pockets to carry disks, pens, leads and so on. Your bag needs to be waterproof, and should have shoulder straps as well as conventional carrying handles.

——— Help and advice to users ———

Once you have bought your system, there will still be times when you need more advice. Most obviously, you will need this when your equipment malfunctions, or appears to. You may also need some help when using new software or equipment for the first time. Some of your problems you will be able easily to identify as hardware or software problems. At times, however, a problem can be a combination of the two. In an ideal world a combined problem of using a particular piece of equipment with particular software should mean that there are two places where you can ask for help. The danger, though, is that the two suppliers just blame each other.

A 'hotline' is a telephone support service for hardware, software, or both, which you can ring with your queries. Some products are now sold with hotline support as part of the price. For others you pay a small fee. A simple registration document is completed at the start of the period which then gives you a licence number to quote. Some hotlines offer 24 hour support. Others work basic office hours. It is worth enquiring about the charging system for calls. At one extreme, support is through a free telephone call (in some cases to other countries). At the other extreme, there may be no registration fee, but calls are charged at premium rates (around 40p a minute), so you pay as you use the service.

Some companies offer comprehensive advice services which take away from you any burden of deciding who to ring about the problem. Such comprehensive support is quite expensive and is geared to the commercial rather than the individual user. For a large company, the telephone support can be geared so that enquirers are led to believe that they are ringing a helpdesk within their own organisation.

——————— User groups ———————

An entirely different kind of support is available through user groups. These are useful for users to make contact with others who have similar interests. User groups tend to form either around specific software products, around hardware types, or around professions or interests (such as the *Church Computer User*).

Software user groups carry out several roles. Other users may have already experienced the problems which you have come up against. They may even have written or acquired useful utilities to use software with a particular hardware combination. Some user groups act as pressure groups on manufacturers requesting extra features. The effectiveness of this can be very variable, depending on the attitude of the company, and how representative the user group is seen as being.

Most user groups publish newsletters including tips, product reviews, letters, advice and so on. Meetings are also held by user groups, and perhaps conferences, but you may be limited by your pocket for conference fees and travel costs, unless there is a branch near you. Some advice may be offered over the telephone or electronic mail.

Some user groups have been particularly effective if the originator goes out of business or sells on the product. An independent user group might then be the only visible means of user support, and it might put pressure on the firm to provide some services.

The question of how independent a user group is can be a difficult issue. Too cosy a relationship can compromise the group; too distant a relationship might mean that the group has no real influence over the manufacturer. Some manufacturers will send speakers to user group conferences, and will circulate details of the user group with the product. Others use the core of committed users as a good testbed for future products.

Even in a large organisation, you could be one of relatively few using a particular package because of its specialist nature, so you might be forced to seek support from outside the organisation with like-minded people. For instance, it is quite common for a large organisation to be predominantly PC-based, but specialist users, such as graphic design and advertising might use Macs. Such users are likely to receive most of their support from outside the organisation.

——————— Maintenance ———————

Most manufacturers will now include some form of maintenance 'free' when supplying equipment. It is not, of course, free; you can soon see this if you negotiate with a direct seller who will give an extra discount if, for some reason, you don't want the maintenance provided. The nature of such schemes also varies considerably.

Many direct computer sellers do not provide their own engineers for maintenance, they contract the work out to firms which specialise in 'third-party maintenance' (TPM), and carry out maintenance on a variety of types of equipment. This allows the direct seller to concentrate on a core business activity of selling computers. At the end of the 'free' cover, there is usually a scheme which allows the extension of that cover. After several years' use, however, the cost, usually based on the purchase price can be very expensive compared with the value of the equipment. When a price is quoted by the original supplier, this may well include an added commission which would not be payable if you were to contact the TPM firm yourself.

Read the supplier's literature very carefully to discover exactly what form of cover is provided. Most schemes will quote a 'response time'. The problem with this is that there is no clear definition of 'response time'. It may be the time taken to return your initial call, or the time by which an engineer is on site, or the time by which the fault is fixed. In some instances for home users, an eight hour wait might not be crucial; for a business such a delay might be extremely damaging.

In the same way, it is important to examine the clauses that tell you where the equipment will be repaired. Unless it is absolutely necessary to take equipment away for repair, this can cause an awful lot of delay. If equipment is taken away, consider whether replacement equipment is supplied. Even if this clause is not invoked, it does make the engineer more likely to put every effort into repairing the equipment on site, as this may then involve less paper work and effort.

Charging also varies from scheme to scheme. Some schemes involve a flat rate plus a call-out fee. Others charge only a (higher) flat rate. Others still charge on call-out only. You will have to assess the balance of probabilities on the number of call-outs per year to determine the best form of cover for yourself, weighing cost against peace of mind. Different rates probably apply for different levels of service. A good TPM will be able to quote for a range of services, so you can pay for the level you can afford. It may also be possible to top up the standard 'free' cover to a higher level.

Considering the possibility of your supplier going out of business: the way in which it pays the TPM firm may make a difference. If the supplier has paid the TPM firm for a full year's contract, you may still be covered for some time. If it has been paying by monthly instalments, cover may cease almost immediately. On the other hand, your cover will also be affected if your TPM firm goes under.

If you are choosing a TPM company for yourself, you should check that it can actually support your equipment, and that it is approved by the manufacturer. If necessary, check these points by asking for the names of some reference sites. Visit those firms, and preferably the TPM company to see their operation. To respond quickly to you, the TPM company needs to have a local base reasonably near to you. The company should also be able to show you evidence that it is properly equipped for the job, and that it can obtain the necessary spares. It is also worth finding out what will happen if you add equipment to your system part way through the contract. Can you add the new equipment to the same contract, or must you take out a new one?

Is the TPM company prepared to give performance guarantees? What will happen if the company fails to deliver the guarantee? Possible penalties include monetary compensation, replacement equipment and reduction in future bills. Some of these may or may not be appropriate in your context.

In choosing a TPM company, all the points about financial stability and track record apply in the same way as they would to a supplier of the actual equipment. A conscientious TPM company will want to ask a number of questions of you before offering you a contract. It would want to make sure it could deliver the service you need, and could look after your particular configuration. If a TPM company is too eager to sign you up without too much attention to detail, then beware. A good TPM company will also welcome the chance to discuss terms and conditions of the contract with you.

Privacy

Security of a computer system is an important point to ponder, particularly considering recent legislation. Some of the data that you keep on a computer may be rather sensitive. Files of a confidential nature should not be left on a hard disk, where they are vulnerable to prying eyes, theft or easy copying without your knowledge. Such files are much better secured if held on floppy disk. With so many disk management tools available, it is also worth remembering that commands to delete files from a disk do not necessarily delete the whole contents of the file. In this way, a confidential file which you have deleted from the directory may still be seen by somebody with the right tools. Utilities exist which 'wash' a disk to ensure that the contents of a deleted file are thoroughly scrambled.

Access to computer files can be restricted in two ways other than protecting physical access to the computer. At the first level, access to use the computer can be restricted with various programs which prevent use without a password. The simplest form of such programs prevents the computer being booted into use without a password being entered. It is worth finding out a little about how these programs work, as it is claimed that some are bypassed fairly easily using a floppy disk containing the operating system. A second level of security is to ensure that sensitive files are encrypted so that they are always held in coded form except when in actual use. Some applications software even provides encryption as a standard feature. Such a system again depends on the use of a password or key. Users are usually recommended to vary the keys used, so they all have to be remembered, preferably without writing them down. After you have worked with unecrypted copies, these must be systematically removed from disk. As MS-DOS remembers your last few commands, there is a particular danger if your key is typed in as part of the command, so these again must be flushed out.

Insurance

Most purchasers will want to protect their valuable investment in computer equipment through insurance. The simplest policies cover the owner against fire, flood and theft. For the home user, however, computers may not be covered on the normal household insurance, or may need to be added as a named valuable item. The disruption caused by the loss of or damage to a computer can often not simply be overcome by the replacement of the equipment. The loss of valuable data such as documents, databases or dictionaries built up over many years can be devastating, and can cause considerable delays. In anticipation of such problems, a conscientious user will have made regular backup copies of files, and will store copies at a separate location.

A typical computer insurance policy will also cover breakdown of the equipment. The payment might cover the cost of replacement equipment, or demonstrable losses. Accidental damage may be covered in a policy, and deliberate damage might also be. Compensation for the loss of data can be covered, but is difficult to calculate.

Insurance of laptop computers is particularly important. By their very nature, they are designed for use on the move, and are susceptible to more damage and theft.

Some policies offer insured maintenance through which the insurer underwrites a guaranteed level of response and service. This has advantages over TPM described above because it would survive the liquidation of any individual TPM company – the contract is with the insurer. Delays might occur, though, in accessing the service, as claims will have to be made through the insurer.

Some direct computer suppliers will provide additional cover, at a price, either concurrently with or immediately after the warranty period. These additional provisions are just as varied as the policies of the main insurance companies.

Potential purchasers need to be very careful in picking a form of cover to read all the small print which covers exceptions, disclaimers and so on. The price you pay will depend on the provision which you want.

To conform with the Data Protection Act 1984, data users must register with the Data Protection Registrar the nature of the data which they will hold about living individuals, and the uses to which the data is to be put. The data must be held securely, kept up-to-date, be available to the data subjects, and must not be disclosed to unauthorised people.

Software problems

Like any other manufactured product, software can be defective. Extensive tests are carried out before software is put on general release, increasingly through beta tests with current users, but errors may occur in very complex circumstances which testing does not predict or reproduce. From time to time, software manufacturers find it necessary to issue replacement copies of software.

The terms 'version' and 'release' are used with very specific meanings in the fast-moving software world. A new version of a program will normally mark a major revision, with new features added, perhaps a changed menu, and facilities used in a completely new way. Between versions, releases may be issued to cover minor improvements or corrections to software errors. When making an enquiry for software support, you will usually be asked for the version number and the release. If the error you report has been reported already, the supplier will normally send a new release either free or for the cost of the disks. Such an arrangement will not normally take place between versions, as new versions usually have to be paid for, often at a fairly reduced fee. Suppliers rarely send out new releases unprompted; they respond when requested, and, of course, if you are the first to identify a new problem, you will have to wait for the next release.

—————— Manuals and books ——————

To achieve the best with a system it is important to have a good manual and to make good use of it. The types of software manuals available have already been described in Chapter 5. A similar analysis would apply to hardware manuals. Since virtually all components and most computers and printers are manufactured abroad, you will often find that the hardware manual is a translation, and these can be of very variable quality. Hardware manuals cannot be geared to all possible knowledge levels in readers, and this again can limit their usefulness.

Though many books are advertised by post, this method is only really suitable if you know the style and scope of a particular series, otherwise you may well purchase a book that is not geared to your ability and interests.

The type of books available include:

- 'getting started' guides, which introduce software products from scratch. These may or may not assume basic computer familiarity.

- 'getting more from' books, which covers details beyond those normally covered in the manufacturer's manual, as many manuals are limited to 500 or 600 pages, which is not sufficient to cover advanced features.

- 'applying a package' books, looking at the use of software in a particular area of interest, hobby or profession.

- hardware guides, taking the competent user into more detail about hardware features than the manuals will cover. These books may be very specific to a particular make and model, rather like the series of manuals produced independently of manufacturers for cars.

One important component to look for in a book, as with a manual, is a good index, so that you can find, from the welter of information, the particular information of interest at the time. A good contents guide is also essential so that you can achieve a quick grasp of the book as a whole.

Training

Though apparently still rather expensive for private users, computer training courses have, over the last few years, generally come down in price and improved in quality. In most big cities, there are a number of sources of training including private firms and state further education colleges. As well as the broad-based computer education which they deliver so well, many colleges now run drop-in workshops where customers can be supported in working through high-quality training materials on particular software products.

Commercial firms normally provide day courses in most popular packages and, if demand is there, will tailor courses and prepare new courses. In choosing a course, it is important to consider the target audience. A course on networking for technicians may be very different from one aimed at managers who are choosing network systems, and different again from one aimed at daily network users.

Some courses will offer detailed course notes and exercises, some of which can be completed afterwards. One advantage of this to a firm can be that staff will take materials home to study in their own time. In some cases, trainers may provide telephone support for course participants after the event. Many staff in companies would prefer training away from the normal work environment, and a good lunch is always welcomed.

An alternative form of training is the video. Priced at around £20, these are often cheaper than a good book on the subject. A professionally made, interesting video can be a very effective training tool. Again, a video can be taken home by most staff who may be embarrassed about watching the same thing several times in front of others if that is what they need. Videos can again be very specific to a product. One potential problem is that it is rarely possible to try before you buy, though if you continue to buy from the same supplier you will believe that you are likely to receive products of a consistent quality.

20

CHOOSING A SUPPLIER

───── Specifying what you want ─────

As with any major purchase, it is the person who is well prepared who is likely to negotiate the best deal, so before approaching any possible suppliers, it is important to decide exactly what you want. Many of the popular magazines include regular features which aim to guide you through this process. Several magazines produce guides which enable you to record your decisions, and to seek several quotations. Some magazines print a form on which to present your final order. Not only do these magazines offer advice and remind you to cover all the essential points, but they can also be used to claim against protection schemes should something go wrong. Readers are advised to keep carefully written records of where they saw products advertised and the exact specification given.

Typical informed advice to purchasers would be:

- Make a list before you start ringing suppliers so that you are clear in your own mind those features that are essential to you, and those that are merely desirable.

- Ensure that all prices are compared on the same basis; for example advertisements normally quote prices excluding VAT.

- Include the name and issue of the magazine in which the price was quoted (if appropriate) when ordering.

- Ask about any extra items needed to make the product usable (such as cables, connectors and plugs), as their prices can affect your comparison.

- Make sure that the price and speed of delivery are guaranteed.

- Check that everything you require is in stock.

- Probe the supplier to ensure that software offered is the latest UK version, if this is what you want.

- Question the supplier for details of after-sales support (price, hours and so on).

- Request details about possible future upgrades to the equipment or software.

- Find out about return of unsatisfactory or unsuitable goods.

- Enquire about the company's background.

- Request details of the component manufacturers used as this could affect performance and will almost certainly affect your ability to upgrade.

- Seek an assurance that new equipment will work with existing equipment if this is what you are expecting, and include details in writing.

- Obtain details of the warranty.

- Discuss extended warranties, possible training, installation of the software as extras which might be thrown in with the price.

- Confirm arrangements for payment.

- Keep a record of who you spoke to for your quotation, and the date.

- Ask for an order reference number for confirming your order in writing and for future enquiries.

- Include in your written order all relevant details of the specification which your system is supposed to fulfil, and details of any extras you have been promised.

- Cover yourself legally over delays in delivery by writing 'time is of the essence' on the written order.

- Write 'goods not yet examined' on the delivery sheet as the driver is almost certainly unwilling to wait while you check the goods thoroughly.

- Check the goods as soon as possible after they arrive and keep the packaging in case they have to be sent back.

—————— 'Green' computers ——————

An increasing number of purchasers are making environmental issues an important factor in their choice of computer. Recognising this, many suppliers are now advertising their computers and peripherals as 'green' machines.

With energy costs rising, one initial consideration is the cost of the power consumed by a computer. It is claimed that large companies can make substantial savings through the choice of the right machines. Computer screens consume much of the energy used by computers.

Laptop computing, because it has less power available, has led to the development of low voltage chips, and these are starting to be used in desktop models as well. As each new chip technology comes along, the heat generated is becoming an increasingly important problem. Systems such as those based on the PowerPC require a substantial number of heat sinks to draw away the heat generated, as well as the traditional fan. Fans tend to make considerable noise. All the techniques which reduce the power consumption prolong the life of the system as well as reducing fan noise.

Power management, such as switching off the display, disk drives and connector sockets when they are not needed, have also been common on laptops for some time. These ideas are all migrating to desktop systems as well.

Concern is also expressed by some people about the radiation given off by monitors. There is said to be a particular danger if people use computers all day every day. Pregnant women are said to be more at risk. Whatever the strength of these claims, the development of alternative screen technologies is also likely to reduce or eliminate screen radiation.

— Types of dealer and what they offer —

There are a number of types of outlets which sell computers. Amongst them are:

• direct sellers, who sell by post and telephone, and dispatch the equipment from the warehouse to your home. These firms advertise heavily in magazines, as this is almost their only way of contacting potential customers.

- computer superstores, which specialise in computer-related equipment, usually based at out-of-town shopping centres. At these you can see the different equipment available, can compare models, and can take your own equipment home. Computer superstores are, however, spread very unevenly across the country.

- high street specialist shops, some of which sell only one make of computer. These have the advantage of being easily accessible, as most large towns will have one.

- general electrical stores, which sell a wide range of electrical goods, which include a few computers. Such firms buy the models in large numbers so can offer some very good deals if the system you want is a very common one.

Everybody will advise you to buy only from a reputable firm. Very few people will be able to tell you what they mean by this, except after a firm goes bust, they will tell you they saw this coming. If you are trusting a firm with such a big purchase, you should perhaps enquire into its financial status. One possibility is to check the company's accounts. These can be obtained from Companies House, as all firms have a legal obligation to deposit annual accounts there. To the inexpert eye, though, these accounts may not make easy reading. One simple 'test' is to compare the company's assets with its liabilities. Normally you would expect assets to be double the liabilities. Be careful, though, with newer companies, who may be successful by now, but may have made returns some time ago when the company was only just building up.

As well as forming some opinion about the supplier's trading record, it is worth following up some customer references. Asking friends about their experiences with particular suppliers can be a start. Most businesses buying major amounts of kit would expect to follow up references from satisfied customers. These do not always tell the whole tale, but a supplier's reluctance to provide reference sites speaks volumes.

Potential suppliers can be expected to tell you about their returns and refunds policy, and to explain their delivery arrangements.

In terms of quality of manufacturing, several firms are now registered as fulfilling the terms of quality standards, such as BS5750 or ISO9000. These schemes involve regular and random checks by the standards bodies to ensure compliance.

Buyers should beware if a firm's address is given simply as a box number rather than a proper address. Prospective customers might ask to visit a potential supplier. Again, you might not carry out your threat, but asking to make an arrangement might tease out those who have something to hide.

In your discussion with suppliers, it is worth asking general questions about the equipment. For example, you might ask 'I have heard that some inkjet printers consume a considerable amount of ink when charging up; how does your model compare?' If a supplier can answer such a question without resorting to technical obfuscation, this will indicate the type of support you are likely to receive when things go wrong.

A good supplier will, of course, ask you a number of questions to ensure that all your requirements are taken into account. Be wary of the supplier who is too quick to quote a price, or who asks you how much you want to spend.

If the supplier is suggesting a printer that you have not heard of, ask whether printer drivers are available for common software. Ask also whether the software you are being offered will work on a named system, with a given amount of memory, a particular screen, and with your printer.

When choosing your supplier, you should use all the information available to you. If it takes a long time for the telephone to be answered when you ring the company, it could be understaffed. What will happen if you have a complaint, or need technical support? At the end of the financial year, which will differ between different suppliers, firms may be offering extra special deals in order to reach sales targets. Again, even knowing the financial year end of a supplier can be valuable information in planning your purchase.

Even if you have no intention of using a credit card, it is still worth checking whether the supplier allows purchase by credit card. Few reputable medium-sized companies would be unable to provide this service. The only firms unlikely to provide the service would be very small firms, or those who have had credit withdrawn through finan- cial problems or because they have abused the system.

When you reach the point of discussing particular products, find out how long the model has been around. Is the manufacturer still in business? Has the model been superseded? Is there a particularly special offer because this is the end of a particular range? If you have access to back copies of magazines, look at the reviews of the equipment when it first came out.

When choosing the supplier, ask about the quality testing procedures used by the manufacturer. Talk about the components used. Ask about the standards met by the monitor. Is the mouse a recognised brand (such as Logitech or Microsoft)? Is the keyboard operated by contact switches, or the cheaper membrane method?

Many suppliers belong to the PCDMA (Personal Computer Direct Marketing Association) which operates a code of conduct for its members. This covers such areas as a deliveries policy, offering written quotations, not debiting credit cards far in advance of dispatch and so on. If these guidelines are breached by a member, the PCDMA will take strong action as soon as you report the breach.

Many suppliers offer the facility of next-day delivery as soon as the payment has been cleared. With a credit card purchase, clearance can be obtained immediately over the telephone, whereas cheques take several days to clear. Delivery may be through the mail or using a courier service, and is usually charged according to the number of boxes. Special arrangements, such as Saturday delivery, can be made, but this may double the cost of the delivery charge. You might also be able to have swifter delivery than the normal service by paying a little extra.

If there are delays in the delivery process after the supplier says it has been handed over to the courier, you should ask for a reference number so that you can chase the consignment yourself. Even if you do not intend to start ringing around, this will alert the supplier that you are beginning to chase the order. This tactic will also flush out those suppliers who rely on the delaying tactic 'Oh! It's in the post'.

You will need to spend time unpacking the equipment and testing whether it works within a few hours of it arriving. Lodge any concerns over the telephone as soon as problems occur, and follow this up in writing. Try to make reasonably heavy use of the system for the first few days, when failures are most likely to occur. Ensure that all the promised software is available and installed if this was requested. Use the printer for a few basic tasks.

If the equipment does not work properly, then depending on the terms you agreed, you will either have to arrange for an on-site repair, or ship some or all of the goods back. If there are problems with the equipment, shipping it back can be a complication. First, it is a great advantage if you have saved the original packing. Secondly, you should find out exactly which parts need to be returned. There is no point returning the whole consignment for a repair to or an exchange of the monitor. Thirdly, you should be clear who will bear the cost of the return of the goods. Fourthly, you will usually be responsible for the goods while they are in transit, so it is worth insuring them. Keep records of all your costs, in case you need to pursue a compensation claim.

Before breaking the seal on software, read whatever you can see to check that it does what you want. In particular, check the version, the language, and the disk size. Software vendors are very sensitive about pirate copies of software, and once the seal or shrink-wrap is broken, they suspect the software has been used. Your supplier might have great difficulty with a third party software supplier if you do not check the goods properly, and may well take it out on you.

Finance matters

If you have one, you are advised to use a credit card for your purchase. In the UK, for any item over £100 both the supplier and the credit card company are responsible if things go wrong. The credit card company's liabilities will be covered by its insurance. There is a clear difference here between credit cards (Access, Visa and so on), and charge cards (AMEX, Diners Card and so on) and debit cards (Switch, Delta and so on). The liability according to the law is different, as only the first of these three categories is covered by the Consumer Credit Act 1974. Some credit card and charge card companies do provide specific protection as part of their standard service against non-delivery, unsatisfactory goods, and breakdown in the first few months of use. It is legal, though, for a firm to impose a surcharge when goods are paid for by credit card. The insurance position is also different for each type of card, with several of the charge cards offering automatic insurance of goods for the first 30 days. The protection offered by card companies is different if you buy from abroad.

Make it clear and in writing that the supplier is not to charge you until the goods are actually dispatched. This will avoid the frustration of having your account charged and then having an inordinate wait for the goods. It also should help cover you against the supplier going bust between taking your money and sending the goods. This is not to say that an unscrupulous supplier might not break the arrangement. It does, though, increase your financial protection if they break the agreement, as it would be breach of contract and the credit card company could claim that the card was used without your permission.

In many cases, as a result of a couple of large companies going bust after cashing customers' cheques and before supplying goods, many suppliers now guarantee not to charge the full price before dispatch.

Another form of payment is the banker's draft, which guarantees payment by your bank. For the supplier it has the benefit that it cannot bounce like a cheque. For the customer, it guarantees that payment is not received until the goods are supplied. A charge is usually made by the bank for this service.

Guarantees, warranties, consumer protection

Most suppliers will offer some form of guarantee, warranty or maintenance arrangement.

Though there is a technical difference between a guarantee and a warranty, to all intents and purposes, in common parlance, the terms are used to mean the same thing. The terms of a warranty may be written down, in which case you should ask for a copy before you buy. If there is no written agreement, the law would protect you by ensuring your right to a 'reasonable' arrangement. If a salesperson gives a verbal assurance, then this should be legally binding.

Even if you are not given a warranty in writing, as a purchaser you are protected by the Sale of Goods Act 1979, which lays down general guidelines about the goods being of merchantable quality, which should include a reasonable period of typical use. If you land up in a dispute about how long equipment should last, other similar manufacturers might be pressed to give estimates of how long their equipment is supposed to last.

In all cases, your first port of call to claim against a warranty should be the supplier who sold you the goods. If these approaches fail, you can always call on the manufacturer who also has some responsibility, but this is a card worth keeping up your sleeve.

Warranties fall into a number of different categories:

- The most comprehensive form of warranty covers, for a given time period, repairs to and replacement of any damaged parts caused in any way, and the supplier pays all the costs of either sending an engineer or of transporting the equipment. This form of unlimited warranty is only available in a few situations, and can be very expensive. For mission critical systems, it may be necessary.

- A parts and labour warranty covers you for a fixed period (generally between one and three years), and covers replacement of the parts which have gone wrong in limited circumstances. A clause in the agreement will normally explain the conditions that apply, such as the user taking reasonable care of the equipment, the use in a suitable environment, and maintenance only being carried out by recognised engineers. For most users, the conditions expressed in such a warranty would be considered reasonable.

- A parts only warranty undertakes to replace faulty parts, but you will be charged for the labour involved, which could mean paying a hefty call-out charge for a minor repair. You should not have to pay too much for such a warranty, as many of the parts will be components provided by other manufacturers which may well have longer warranty periods anyway.

A second area to consider is where the repair will take place:

- An on-site contract pays for the engineer to visit your premises to carry out the repair.

- A return-to-base contract requires you to ship the equipment to the main office or main workshops of your supplier. In these cases, it is worth checking who pays the costs of transport each way. Many schemes involve each party paying for transport one way. The supplier will normally send the goods back by the same method which you sent them.

- A return-to-local-centre contract involves you taking the equipment back to a regional base. Costs of shipping might be about the same, but you might have the wherewithal to return the equipment yourself by car.

- A parts shipment service involves you ringing the supplier's hotline. If the fault can be diagnosed, and the repair is one that you can carry out yourself, the supplier might send the part, which is a lot cheaper than sending the machine two ways, as well as being a lot quicker.

Most warranties will include clauses which explain the conditions under which they are rendered invalid. As with much electrical equipment, labels are often placed on computers suggesting that opening up the cabinet voids the warranty unless this is done by an authorised engineer. In the worst cases, this can actually mean that a qualified engineer from another firm could be responsible for invalidating the warranty. In many cases, an upgrade can cancel your warranty even if a completely unrelated part breaks down. This makes for difficulties when you are thinking of upgrading a computer by adding extra chips. An assurance from the supplier of the upgrade that this will not invalidate your warranty is not always sufficient. You may need to check this with the supplier of your original kit. Ideally, this should be done at the time of the original purchase; some suppliers may be able to provide a list of upgrades which can be made without nullifying the warranty. These are best couched in general terms, as undoubtedly new forms of upgrades will become available during the life of your machine.

The status of a maintenance contract if a supplier ceases to trade can be very difficult to unravel. If the maintenance agreement was with the supplier, then there is little chance for the small purchaser to receive any recompense, irrespective of whether the agreement was 'free' or you have parted with money. If a supplier uses a third party maintenance company, then the situation is different. In these cases, it will depend whether the supplier has paid for the TPM in advance, in which case you have a right to the service until the payments run out. On the other hand, if your supplier is paying on a month-by-month basis, particularly if this is in arrears, your service may stop almost immediately.

Insurance of your goods while in transit at the time of purchase is usually covered as part of the delivery price. You should check whether this is the case, and pay a few pounds extra for insurance if necessary.

Most magazines operate under the Mail Order Protection Scheme. This means that the magazine publishers give a written guarantee to meet a (limited) amount of financial loss to private individuals who order products advertised in the magazine from suppliers who go bankrupt or go into liquidation. This written guarantee is usually displayed prominently in every edition of the magazine, and is subject to a set of reasonable conditions, such as using the supplied form for your order, purchasing a product within the range advertised, claiming within three months and so on.

The supplier may offer a 'Free Three Year Next Day On-site Maintenance Service', but if it ceases to trade, you are left with nothing. Similarly, an offer of compensation if the repair is not carried out in a given time is also an arrangement with the supplier which would fall by the wayside in a liquidation case.

Suppliers are very much aware of the damage that has been done by the occasional well-publicised collapse of a company. Following such incidents, it is usually the smaller, less well-known suppliers which lose sales to the better-established companies. Groups like the PCDMA are looking at protection schemes for purchasers, so that customers can buy with confidence in a way similar to that run by ABTA for travel agents.

Legal redress

If you are buying a system on which you wish to run a particular version of software or with a particular peripheral, then you should ask directly whether this is possible. When buying from a business, in accordance with the Sale of Goods Act 1979, the goods should be of 'merchantable quality', fit for the purpose intended, and fit for any specific purpose which you told the vendor about. When you are buying from an individual, the law simply says that the goods must be as described but, as long as you have a witness, you have redress under the Misrepresentation Act 1967.

A supplier with whom you are dissatisfied may offer you a credit note towards goods of the same value. This should enable to replace the goods through the same supplier. The supplier may have offered the credit note rather than suffer the expense of going to law so you receive the financial equivalent without an admission of blame by the supplier. Only if you have lost all faith in the particular supplier might you be insistent on having your money back to spend elsewhere.

There may come a point when discussions with your supplier break down and you need to resort to the law to ensure your fair rights. Organisations which you can contact include the Trading Standards Department of your local council, the Advertising Standards Authority, the magazine where you saw the goods advertised, or the local Citizens' Advice Bureau (CAB). Alternatively, you could use the services of your own solicitor, and you may qualify for legal aid. Sometimes the threat of action, or an initial letter of complaint can secure the action which you wanted.

If your supplier goes out of business whilst owing you some money or a service, despite your best efforts to avoid getting into this position, you have little recourse. Suppliers and customers are classed as unsecured creditors and so are the end of the queue of creditors, behind Inland Revenue and Customs & Excise for example, when a firm goes under. Whilst you might be able to prove in court that you are owed money, if there is none, you will receive none.

If you need to seek the advice of a lawyer, it is probably useful to use the £5 Fixed Fee Scheme, under which you can have a half- hour interview with a solicitor who can determine whether your case is worth pursuing. The solicitor can also work out whether you will be entitled to Legal Aid. If you are not, you may be faced with hefty bills yourself, and this could colour your view about whether to proceed with action.

A claim for up to £25 000 can be made through the County Court, with smaller claims up to £1000 being dealt with by the Small Claims Court. The County Court process involves your completing a claim form giving the reason for your claim. At this stage a small fee is payable. The supplier then has opportunity to prepare a case; if no response is made, you have almost certainly won the case. When a case is heard the judge has a responsibility to ensure that both sides of the case are heard fairly. Even if, on a rare occasion, the supplier pays for a lawyer, the judge will ensure that the claimant is able to put the full case.

——— Buying bundled products ———

Special sales promotions can range from free pens to free cases for notebooks right up to free software. Some of the software offers can sound particularly tempting if the full list price is quoted. In some advertisements, it is made to appear as if you buy the software and are given the equipment free! Don't forget, though, that much software can be obtained at a discount of up to 50% if you shop around, and the supplier obtains bulk copies for much less than that. The software only has value to you if you really are going to use it.

Some sales promotions have ended up giving the supplier a bad name. Any proper sales promotion, according to the Advertising Standards Authority, should make clear the conditions for eligibility. Unfortunately, many people do not ask about the conditions before they buy the product, only to discover that they do not qualify.

Some particularly tempting offers and promotions take place when a product is reaching the end of the range. To the astute buyer, there are real benefits to be gained from such a deal. There are, of course, dangers in buying old stock, particularly when new models may be about to drop very quickly in price.

When buying a system with bundled software, it is worth checking exactly what is covered in the price. Unless it is explicitly stated in the advertisement, manuals may not be included, and either may be unavailable (particularly if the version has been superseded) or may cost about £30. In some cases, only an introductory guide including installation instructions may be provided with the bundle. Some suppliers will provide the full manual on disk rather than a printed version. This could be of benefit, depending on how you tend to use manuals. Any parts of the manual which you wish to study in detail can be printed, but it is impractical and costly to print it all. If you are the sort of person who reads a manual avidly, if not necessarily cover to cover, buying a bound manual may be more suitable.

Often bundled software is provided in a standard configuration already loaded onto the computer. Suppliers can carry out this task in bulk, and will often claim that this will save you a day's work. This preloading, though, will limit the number of choices you can make, either about which software to buy, or how it is initially configured. If software is provided preloaded, it is worth asking whether the original disks are supplied, as these may be necessary in an emergency. The original disks may be available at little or no cost, but the supplier may not send them unless you ask, as not sending them will again save the supplier time and money, both for the cost of the disks and postage.

21

CHECKING OUT
—— AND SETTING UP ——
YOUR SYSTEM

—— Getting the equipment just right ——

When your new system first arrives, you should check what each box contains, including the model numbers for everything you have ordered. It is worthwhile keeping the box and packaging at least for a few weeks in case equipment has to be sent back.

A patient customer would also make a note of any serial numbers on equipment at this stage. It is probably wise to wait a while before postcoding your equipment or marking it in any other way before you have had it working properly.

Your boxes should also contain the appropriate leads which you need to set up your system, and a number of hardware manuals. For the long term, you will be hoping that these are comprehensive, but at the beginning you are probably only looking for simple instructions to start you off. Read any warnings which are either attached to the equipment or come as loose-leaf additions to the manual. These last minute pieces of advice are probably the most recent, and may have been included because other people have had problems in installation. If problems can be avoided, it is in your best interest as well as that of the supplier for you to pay attention. One important example is that moving parts: for example printer heads are usually wedged firm by polystyrene or cardboard to prevent damage in transit. To switch them on in this condition could mean that the motor burns out immediately. It is particularly important to keep such packaging in case the equipment has to go back.

Most systems are now supplied with clear set-up instructions, and most equipment is clearly labelled. In the better installation instructions, you will be told how to check that the system is working properly. You might also be given a list of common problems that occur if you have not set things up correctly, and explanations of how to overcome them. The supplier wants to ensure your satisfaction with the system, and wants to avoid lots of enquiries about simple problems. In principle, then, physically setting up your computer equipment should be no more complex than, for example, setting up a new video recorder.

Once the hardware is connected up, it is possible to check that various parts of it are working. So when the main computer is switched on, something should appear on the monitor if it is connected correctly and switched on. When the printer is plugged in and switched on, there will be an indication through lights, for example, that it is receiving power. The printer self-test should be able to show you that it is in full working order.

All equipment is vulnerable to failure. Most electronic equipment will either fail in the first day or so after assembly, or if it does not will then work for perhaps three or four years without a component failing. Most manufacturers test their systems after assembly by a system called 'burning in'. The system is left running for 24 hours, and if it works for this period, then it is considered satisfactory and can be dispatched. Other factory testing may include power up testing. A system is under most stress when being switched on or off, so it is tested by being switched on and off perhaps every two minutes for a few hours. Systems which pass this sort of quality control are generally working perfectly. The most likely explanation if a system which does not work arrives on your doorstep is that there has been some damage in transit, which is thankfully quite rare.

All the equipment will have variable settings, such as brightness and contrast on the monitor. The factory testing will usually mean that these have been set to a fairly suitable setting. It is worth altering the settings first to check that the mechanisms work, and then to set the system for your own requirements.

It is not possible to check that the printer is receiving computer signals properly, however, or that the mouse is working properly without running some software, so this checking will need to be done after the software is installed.

Users will want to set up their system to suit their taste for regular use. Some users like the mouse to be more sensitive to movement and to the pressing of the buttons, while others want less sensitivity. The system might also allow you to set screen colours, keyboard options and so on. These features are controlled through a utility program in Microsoft Windows or through a control panel on a Macintosh; plain DOS users will have to run one or more DOS programs. New users may worry that, before they use the system for a while, they do not know what settings they would like, but the settings can be altered at any time. In most systems these settings, once made, will be remembered for the next time the equipment is used.

To start using a computer system fully, you will need to start storing data to and retrieving it from floppy disks. When disks are supplied they may be blank or ready-formatted. Vendors will tell you that many helpline queries from new users come about because they are trying to use unformatted disks.

Users may also have options to create logical drives as well as physical ones, so that drive letters can, for example, be given to part of a hard disk. Systems are not usually configured in the factory in this way, and users should perhaps become conversant with their systems before amending their configurations in this way. Systems are sometimes supplied with a utility which restricts access to the system unless you provide the correct access code or password. Again it might be worth waiting a few days before installing this; you will have no confidential data to hide at first anyway. If the security software is already installed, the documentation will tell you the (standard) password used at the factory, and will give advice about changing the password.

New users should resolve to look after their new machines from the start. Make sure the hard disk head is parked before switching off (in modern business systems this is usually done automatically – see the manual). Resolve to make sure every floppy disk is properly labelled. Keep a stock of printer supplies such as ink, so that you do not run out in the middle of a crucial and urgent evening's work. Make yourself rules about changing passwords regularly and decide how you will remember them without writing them down. Be firm with yourself about establishing a routine of backing up all your data from hard disk onto floppy disk.

—————— Installing software ——————

The next stage of setting up your system will very much depend on the way in which your computer has been supplied. If you are buying a complete system from scratch, the vendor will normally install a standard bundle of software on the hard disk for you. Suppliers need to test the equipment before it is sent, and to do this requires some software, so a standard configuration with bundled software is no great hardship.

If you have ordered additional software, this will need to be installed. The term 'installing' software refers to the process of copying it in a usable form onto an appropriate area of a disk or set of disks (usually the hard disk) so that it can be used. Software is usually supplied on a set of floppy disks or, of late, on CD-ROM. 'Customising' software is the process of adapting the software so that is suitable for your system or for your preferred way of working.

The processes of installing and customising normally go hand in hand in order to set up software initially. If you later decide that you wish to change some settings, then you can normally run the customising program again, so do not worry if your initial settings are not ideal, though they must, of course, work.

The amount of instruction needed to install and customise a package varies enormously between different products. One best-selling product for disk management has one page on installation, consisting of three sentences, and has nothing on customising because you can't do it. Another product, a word processor, has a separate manual just on installing and customising, running to nearly a hundred pages. This comparison is not one which says that one is better than the other, just that they are different. The disk management program assumes that all users will want access to all the features, and it moulds itself to your machine by detecting, for example, which drives are present without being told. The word processor installation manual tells you, for example, the short cuts in installation if you already have a previous version of the software, how to install a monitor or printer, how to add fonts, and how to change over 200 default settings.

There is a considerable lead-in time while manuals are printed. Minor errors creep into programs, misprints creep into manuals, and minor improvements are made to software regularly. For this reason, details of the latest news about software are normally released on disk, in a file with a name such as 'README'. You should, as normally advised by the printed literature, look at this file first for the latest news.

Because some programs are supplied on a vast number of disks, some of the files may be supplied in a compressed form to save disk space. If this is the case, instructions will be given about how to decompress the relevant files. The terms packing and unpacking are sometimes used for compression and decompression. A number of standard file extensions are used for compressed files, such as ARC.

Most installation programs work by your typing a single command which runs the install program for you. This will control the whole process of installation, and you should not abandon this program prematurely. At installation time, the program may ask you questions such as:

- What is the serial number supplied with the product, and who is the registered user, for licensing purposes?

- How would you like your disk organised, and into what area should the software be placed?

- Which printer or printers do you have?

- Will you want to use a mouse? (When the actual program is run, it will then run a utility to detect whether a mouse is present or not.)

- What form of screen do you use?

- Will you be running the software from hard disk or floppy disk?

- Do you wish to use dates in English or American format?

A good installation manual will explain the various decisions to be made. You will probably want to put all the files for a particular package in one directory, but allow access to that directory by any user. The installation program will probably alter various system files on your computer (such as CONFIG.SYS and AUTOEXEC.BAT on an MS-DOS machine). Once jobs like these have been done once, and other tasks like the entry of the serial number and the licensed user name, then they almost certainly need not be done again. Some of the other questions listed above are used for customising the initial installation but can be altered later by running the customising software again.

One feature of customising software is the ability to alter the default values used by the program. These are the values that are assumed if no other option is chosen. In a word processor the number of default values can run to a few hundred. Examples would include values such as the assumed page margins, line height, paragraph style, scroll speed and so on. Other values would be 'on' or 'off', such as text justification, automatic backup of files when saving, file directory display, and automatic page numbering.

When installing a complex package, you can specify that particular features are to be included or excluded from use. Some packages come with a number of companion programs, one example being a disk handling program supplied with a word processor program, which will search for phrases within a disk, and can be used to catalogue files. For some users this would be an extremely useful feature. For other users, who have bought more powerful disk management software, it is unlikely that this companion program would ever be used, so there is no point in installing it. Though the capacity on a new hard disk might seem greater than you will ever need, there is no point cluttering up your disk with unwanted files.

Some manuals actually explain which files you can dispose of in which circumstances, either at installation time or at a later date. Many will advise, for example, that programs like the installation and customising program need not be kept permanently on hard disk. If you really want to run them again, you can simply use the floppy disk. Other examples of files which you will not need to keep on hard disk are printer and monitor drivers for hardware you do not have. Again, if you needed them, the drivers would be available from floppy disk. Some files might be of use for a limited time. A good example of this would be a trainer or a tutorial, which often come complete with sample files. It is likely that you will use these once and not look at them again, unless they cover a sophisticated point or somebody else wants to learn the package. If they are no longer needed, both the trainer program and the sample files can be deleted from hard disk, and recovered from floppy if needed.

Some software systems incorporate sophisticated program protection, as a legitimate protection of copyright. One system involves the use of an electronic device, prosaically called a 'dongle', which is plugged into the back of a computer. The presence of this device is then detectable by the computer, and the software will not run without the dongle. Other programs use devices such as hidden files which the program will detect before running, and which prevent multiple copies being made of the software. On rare occasions, these systems conflict with disk compression or virus checking software, but software manufacturers are generally happy to sort out a problem by sending a new disk to registered users who can explain how a problem occurred legitimately.

Disk management

The management of files and their organisation on disk is a much-discussed subject. In the days before the Apple Macintosh, users had to learn a lot about a computer's operating system but the Macintosh style altered the approach to file management as much as it did to applications themselves. Experienced users of arcane operating systems commands professed not to know what all the fuss was about. They could handle the operating system, and others would just have to jolly well learn. The new interfaces now included in products such as Microsoft Windows as well as the Macintosh have undoubtedly improved understanding and productivity.

A number of file management systems are available. These are products that are able to copy, move, and delete files and so on. Some file management systems allow users to look at file contents as a series of characters mainly with an aim of identifying them by their contents rather than manipulating them.

In providing a variety of disk and file management tools, manufacturers are aware that different users have different levels of needs, and want to manipulate files in different ways. Some users prefer to use native operating systems commands for speed and convenience, particularly if they learnt the operating system when this was the only alternative. Others prefer text based systems which use pull-down menus, or a very visual approach of products like the Macintosh File System or Microsoft Windows. Others still like the variety of approaches taken by specialist file management software.

When examining the alternative methods of file management the comparative strength of one system over another is not its capacity to do something that none of the others can not, it is the convenience of carrying out tasks. All the systems, for example, can move a selection of files between disks. What is an advantage, though, is the ability to point to each file which you want and select it with a single key or button. Alternative methods might involve inventing a rule which the files required obey and others do not, or even copying some which are not wanted and then deleting them if that is quicker. Other systems still might require the files to be copied to the new destination, then the originals can be deleted.

Most disk operating systems ensure that users organise files into groups, called directories in MS-DOS, or folders on a Macintosh. File management programs allow you to view and operate on files either in the established groups or according to other criteria, such as looking at all files in alphabetical order, or in date order, or all files with a particular attribute, or a particular type of name. Users might also be able to move files between directories or folders, which can themselves be renamed, removed, joined together and so on.

File contents can be displayed, with much file management software being aware of a wide range of file formats, enabling data held in those formats to be displayed but not manipulated. Files can also be viewed in other forms, including a literal character by character representation as numbers in hexadecimal notation. Nominated files or groups of files can be searched for a particular piece of text. Simple control programs, such as BAT files, can be created in order to launch applications.

One useful safety net in file management is the feature called 'undelete', which is necessary if you make a mistake. Other features might allow you to change the date and time stamped on a file, or list all files on a disk irrespective of overall disk organisation.

Files can be archived to save storage space, and, of course, unarchived. Security features, such as washing a disk may be included. This ensures that the contents of a file are completely removed from a disk, rather than just the directory entry. This is an important privacy tool, but does mean that files can not then be undeleted. Another feature might enable you to set the computer up so that automatic backing up of files takes place, by intercepting the user when a back-up is due, asking for the correct disks and so on. Such systems are likely to work on an incremental basis, making copies only of those files that have not changed since the last back-up was made.

File management facilities are available in four styles. In effect they are not alternatives, because you can have several available in one system and choose to use the one most appropriate for the job you wish to do.

In-built operating system commands have the advantage of brevity and can carry out some jobs very quickly. Other users prefer systems such as DosShell, provided as an adjunct to MS-DOS from version 5 onwards. Such systems use pull-down menus operated through the keyboard or a mouse. This approach has the advantage that the user is immediately presented, through the menus, with a list of options. One criticism of command-driven systems is, of course, that you can only use a command if you know what it is.

More visual systems such as the Microsoft File Manager or the Macintosh File System display file details in pictorial form. Such systems allow for several windows to be displayed representing different parts of the disk. Operations such as file copying, moving and deleting are carried out by a 'drag and drop' approach, using mouse buttons, in a way which it is claimed is intuitive. Critics of such systems suggest that the meanings of various mouse button operations are not always obvious. The truth is much more likely to be that some people simply prefer a visual approach, whereas this does not suit others.

Lastly, there are management tools like XTree Gold, PC Tools Deluxe from Central Point Software, Norton Utilities and Magellan from Lotus. 'Magellan' takes its name from a famous nautical explorer as the package is a tool for navigating around the disk. This category of software provides the most comprehensive set of facilities, but involves additional expense. As this software area is such a competitive one, replacement versions of each package have shown a great mushrooming of features in order to keep ahead of rivals.

INDEX